34.50

2618

FOREIGN &

Recharting the Caribbean

Recharting the Caribbean

Land, Law, and Citizenship in the
British Virgin Islands

Bill Maurer

Ann Arbor
THE UNIVERSITY OF MICHIGAN PRESS

Copyright © by the University of Michigan 1997
All rights reserved
Published in the United States of America by
The University of Michigan Press
Manufactured in the United States of America
⊗ Printed on acid-free paper

2000   1999   1998   1997   4   3   2   1

A CIP catalog record for this book is available from the British Library

Library of Congress Cataloging-in-Publication Data

Maurer, Bill, 1968–
    Recharting the Caribbean : land, law, and citizenship in the
British Virgin Islands / Bill Maurer.
        p.   cm.
    Includes bibliographical references (p.   ) and index.
    ISBN 0-472-10811-5 (cloth : acid-free paper)
    1. British Virgin Islands—Politics and government.
2. Nationalism—British Virgin Islands.   3. Immigrants—Legal
status, laws, etc.—British Virgin Islands.   4. British Virgin
Islands—Ethnic relations.   5. Real property—British Virgin
Islands.   I. Title.
F2129.M38   1997
972.97'25—dc21   96-51247
                                                    CIP

This book is dedicated to the memory of Howard R. Penn, 1903–1994, British Virgin Islander Statesman and Scholar

"It would not be any exaggeration to say that, if the people should lose control of their lands, they may one day awaken to a situation not altogether dissimilar from the present situation in South Africa. The price of freedom is eternal vigilance and it behooves all concerned to be vigilant."

—H. R. Penn, 1953

Contents

Illustrations

Preface and Acknowledgments

The British Virgin Islands is a small place, but it is a place of incredible heterogeneity. I was fortunate during my stay to have the willing assistance of people who reflected that heterogeneity, and this book is the better for it.

Members of the immigrant communities discussed in this book graciously assisted me during the course of my fieldwork, consenting to interviews and extending their hospitality. I would also like to thank all the British Virgin Islanders who helped me during my fieldwork. I will make special mention here of some of the people to whom I owe a great debt and offer apologies to any whose names I inadvertently leave out.

The staff of the British Virgin Islands Community College (recently renamed the H. Lavity Stoutt Community College) kindly provided a base of operations and an office as well as some stimulating discussions. I would like to thank Charles Wheatley and Eileene Parsons for their generous assistance and support. Dr. Michael O'Neal was a constant source of advice and encouragement. I also owe special thanks to Janice Nibbs Blyden of the British Virgin Islands Public Library for her immeasurable assistance in finding library and archival materials and for her wit and friendship. I would also like to thank Valentine Lewis and the rest of the staff of the Public Library. Juliette Penn, Registrar of Lands, and Armina Mohammed Deonarinesingh, Registrar of the High Court, provided access to land records and court documents, and I thank them for their assistance. I thank Arthur Bruce, Government Statistician, and Wendell Potter, Department of Labour, for providing me with statistical information. I would also like to thank Marion Romney and Dennis Jennings, Department of Immigration, for their help in understanding immigration law. Several members of the bar were of great assistance, among them the late McWelling Todman, Q.C., J. S. Archibald, Q.C., and Janice George-Creque, LL.B. I extend thanks as well to Ermine Burnett, Patricia Turnbull, and Sophie Carrera for our many conversations.

Many elderly statesmen kindly agreed to be interviewed. I would like to thank Leslie Malone, J. R. O'Neal, and I. G. Fonseca, and the late Henry O. Creque. I enjoyed almost daily conversations with H. R. Penn, who unfortunately passed away before this project was completed. I dedicate this book to his memory.

Colleen Ballerino Cohen, Eugenie Todman-Smith, and Elton and Annette Scatliffe helped me get settled into the British Virgin Islands. Colleen Ballerino Cohen deserves special thanks for helping me start this project and supporting me throughout it. Abul Alam and Jammi Kumar helped me meet members of the British Virgin Islands' Muslim and Hindu communities, and Chris Ramrup and family were truly hospitable friends. I also extend a special thank you to Bee Paltoo and family and to the entire Tortola Sanatan Dharma Satsang for welcoming me into their lives and sharing so much with me.

It would be impossible to thank all of the people in the United States who have contributed to this project, and so I offer apologies to those whose names do not appear here and extend my sincere thanks for their assistance. While writing the dissertation on which this book is based, I benefited from the close readings of my advisers, Jane Collier, George Collier, and Carol Delaney, and I thank them for their support and their patience. I also benefited greatly from the comments and support of members of the Stanford Anthropology Dissertation Writers' Seminar, especially Diane Nelson and Amy Borovoy, whose friendship has been invaluable and who deserve special thanks for pushing me to rework the dissertation into this book. Genevieve Bell deserves the credit for coming up with the title for this book. I would also like to thank Beth Bashore, Shannon Brown, Natalie Carrillo, Ellen Christiansen, Jeanne Giaccia, Rowel Padilla, Renato Rosaldo, Heather Wood, and Angela Walton. Joel Streicker and Liliana Suárez-Navaz read much of this book in very rough form and helped shape its direction. A conversation with Deborah Battaglia early on redirected my thinking and helped develop the argument. Donald Moore provided critical references and constant encouragement, as did Robin Balliger, Amy Burce, Alejandro Lugo, Jackie Brown, Maria Teresa Sierra, Eve Darian-Smith, and Ruth Buchanan. Riva Berleant-Schiller, Karen Fog Olwig, Richard Price, Sally Price, David Engel, Felice Levine, and Mindie Lazarus-Black provided useful criticisms and feedback at various stages of this project. And I would like to thank Alexandra Freund, Pamela Kato, Ellen Reller, Bruce Graham, Lucia Rayas, Lisa Maurer, Marion Dennick, Jacob Micah Mason, Patty Mullally, and Peter Hegarty for putting up with me while I was writing this book.

Support for fieldwork was provided by a grant from the National Science Foundation (SES-9208273) and the MacArthur Foundation through the Center for International Security and Arms Control, Stanford University. Support for a summer of fieldwork in 1991 was provided by the Tinker Foundation through the Center for Latin American Studies, Stanford University. I am grateful for all of these sources of support. Support during the writing process came from a Mellon Foundation grant through the Department of Anthropology, Stanford University. I also owe special thanks to Christine M. Munro, Cynthia Maurer, and William J. Maurer for their financial advice and assistance. This book does not necessarily reflect the opinions of any funding agency or individual mentioned here, and I accept all responsibility for any errors and inconsistencies that remain.

I could not have completed this book without the generous encouragement of my editor at the University of Michigan Press, Susan Whitlock, who was a constant source of support and humor and who took some of the pain out of the process. I would also like to thank Kevin Rennells, copyediting coordinator, Lori Meek Schuldt, copyeditor extraordinaire, Michael Landauer, editorial assistant, and Jillian Downey, production coordinator, for all their help in turning the manuscript into this book.

Outline of the Book

This book contains eight chapters, an introduction, and a conclusion. The introduction outlines the theoretical foundation of the book, introducing the twin domains of "nature" and "choice" as productive effects of power in liberal colonial milieus. Chapters 1 and 2 chart out the creation of the "British Virgin Islands" (BVI) and "British Virgin Islanders" as a place and a people. Chapter 1 begins with an account of out-migration to the Dominican Republic in the early 1900s, the period of out-migration to the U.S. Virgin Islands in the 1940s, and the effects of these migrations on constituting classes in the BVI. Political parties arose at midcentury from class divisions marked by race. Such social divisions and parties lost their significance by the 1970s. They did so, as I argue in chapter 2, because of changes in the composition of the civil service that brought "all" BVIslanders into the fold of the state apparatus and because increasingly the state came to be conceptualized as an entity apart from "the people" who make it function. Along with this conceptualization of the state came a conceptualization of the people as homogeneous and as sharing an identity. The second chapter thus shows how BVIslanders came to constitute themselves as a group of autonomous individuals—*belongers* is the popular term—who deem themselves similar in more fundamental ways than all the ways in which they differ.

As group relationships among BVIslanders turn into personalistic ones, BVIslanders come to make themselves into a group against immigrants, or *nonbelongers*. Similarity has been achieved among BVIslanders—the very term *BVIslander* is a recent invention, as is *belonger,* both of which came into widespread use as other markers like *Portuguese* and *country* and so forth went out. *Difference* came to mean the difference between BVIslanders and all nonbelongers, not among BVIslanders. The 1991 Tourist Board slogan was "Yes, We Are Different," signifying difference from other Caribbean islands and peoples conceptualized as dirty, crime-ridden, and violent. The 1992 slogan was "Discover Nature's Little Secrets": the BVI is a place of natural beauty, where "natural"—personalistic, one-on-one—social relationships obtain in a community of equals.

The third chapter, hence, introduces BVIslander stereotypes of immigrants—in particular, the Guyanese—and suggests that these stereotypes derive from BVIslanders' articulation of a liberal civic discourse structured around the idea of voluntary contributions to the civil order. "Good" citizens, supposedly autonomous agents, make individual contributions to the nation; "bad" immigrants, supposedly bound by their clannish or ethnicist attachments, act only out of self-serving or group-serving interests because they are "needy."

The fourth chapter continues the focus on citizenship with an examination of ideas about "race" and ideas about "place" in the British Virgin Islands. Race and place, themselves central to legal citizenship, rationalize the inequalities that fall along citizen-immigrant lines. The chapter argues that liberal imaginings of a civil society produce inequalities explained in terms of "natural" differences in "racial" or "geographic" origin.

Immigrants, the subject of the fifth chapter, become "unnatural." Uprooted from their "true" place, they do not (or should not) grow in Virgin Islands soil. As several BVIslanders pointed out to me during my fieldwork, "they don't mix and [they] keep to themselves;" "they destroy the environment." And, according to some, the Guyanese "have unnatural faces." Making immigrants unnatural constitutes for BVIslanders what Nature might be. This chapter also considers how immigrants go about getting into BVI society by emphasizing their own personal characteristics and abilities and denying group allegiances.

Ideas about personal and group identities derive in large part from ideas about genealogy and inheritance. In the British Virgin Islands, as elsewhere in the Caribbean, ideas about genealogy are bound up with ideas about land. Using court documents, archival materials, and interview data, chapter 6 traces changes in landholding and inheritance patterns, demonstrating the commodification of land and attendant changes in conceptualizations of genealogy, family, and identity. The chapter highlights a discourse that sees kin and identity as derived from, on the one hand, "natural" genealogical connections ("I am related to all of my blood relatives") and, on the other, notions of paternity and ideas about socially constituted groups ("I am related only to my father's line"). Arguing that these two means help empower and enforce each other, I demonstrate implications for understandings of inequality and hierarchy in a cultural world where nature and choice are held to determine human life.

The seventh chapter explores the reasoning behind and the effects of the 1970–75 Cadastral Survey of the British Virgin Islands. The survey was meant to "rationalize" land tenure by lay-ing an objective grid over the territory and determining land titles in terms of that grid rather than in terms of deeds and contracts between people. The Cadastral Survey solidified the naturalization of genealogy discussed in the previous chapter. It also called forth a notion of land as "natural" and "real" and entailed a shift in land law away from the idea that people own *estates,* or temporal abstractions of rights to land, and toward the idea that people own the land itself.

The subject of the eighth chapter is BVI national identity and its relationship to the outside world, particularly the United Kingdom and the transnational space of financial services. It considers the actual writing of laws and the distinction created through legal authorship between the British Virgin Islands and the United Kingdom. This distinction is paradoxically articulated through an identification with Britain, and an imagined British "tradition" of "law and order." The writing of law became a powerful symbol of national uniqueness. Struggles for self-determination involved disclaiming the ability of "other" selves to write BVI laws while holding forth a unique BVI self capable of self-regulation. Writing their "own" laws, BVIslanders demonstrate their essential difference from others and their ability to rule themselves. They also facilitate the offshore financial services sector, the large-scale movement of capital across legal regimes, and the exclusion of immigrants from participation in the BVI state. In the conclusion, I discuss the paradox of the BVI's newfound national identity and its continued colonial subordination, arguing that the production of national difference is not in conflict with globalizing tendencies and, indeed, is called forth by such tendencies.

Finally, a note to readers in the British Virgin Islands. The views expressed here are my own and do not reflect those of any person, business, or government agency in the British Virgin Islands. The legal practices and principles discussed in this book reflect my best understanding but should not be taken as a reference to the law or a statement of official policy. This book is also not intended to be a guide to future policy or a proclamation by an outside "expert" of how things ought to be done in the BVI. I make no pretense to being an expert on the BVI. As Charles Wheatley told me, "If you go to the BVI, you go to University!" I will always be a student and never a graduate of that university.

I was fortunate to speak with many people during my time in the British Virgin Islands, and I am grateful for being allowed the opportunity to conduct research there. If anything written on these pages offends anyone, the best I can do is to offer my sincere apologies and to stress that no affront was intended. It is sometimes difficult to write about people in ways they find flattering when one writes about legal disputes, political processes, and immigration issues. I hope that by my presenting my thoughts here, others will engage with this text, pull it apart, and point out its shortcomings.

British Virgin Islander readers will find chapters 1 and 2 especially interesting. They contain historical materials never presented before and discuss documents buried in the Government Archives until recently. I think that BVIslanders will also find the chapters on land and the Cadastral Survey (chaps. 6 and 7) of interest, given the ubiquity of land disputes and the general interest in legal issues surrounding land. There are a number of good "inside jokes" in chapter 6 involving certain long-standing land disputes that some BVIslander readers may recognize despite my alteration of person and place names to protect their identities. I hope that my comments on immigrants and their treatment by BVIslanders in chapters 3, 4, and 5 do not offend, but rather offer an occasion to reflect on what will continue to be a pressing social issue in the territory.

Above all, I thank my readers in the Caribbean for their indulgence.

Introduction

While the image of the ethnographer as the lone traveler heading out into the unknown may little occupy the time of contemporary anthropologists, it still informs tourists and many other travelers who depart from the United States or Europe for a voyage to places like the British Virgin Islands. Even the most skeptical sometimes reach their destination with that image in their minds, if not with the expectation that their entry into a land they feel is alien and exotic will have all the magic of a moment of first contact or a visit back into the past—a past of friendly natives and colonial charm (and no colonial terror). Malinowski's description of this moment of arrival stood as the paradigm for a certain twentieth-century genre of ethnographic writing, and while this genre has for the most part been abandoned by contemporary anthropology, it is big business and good marketing strategy in the tourist industry. "Imagine yourself suddenly set down surrounded by all your gear, alone on a tropical beach close to a native village, while the launch or dinghy which has brought you sails away out of sight . . ." (Malinowski 1922:4).

My sister came to visit me during my fieldwork with the attitude of the skeptical traveler who looks behind the facade of the colonial storefront and the charming West Indian house for the computer hookup and the satellite television dish. Before she could even begin her deconstruction of the British Virgin Islands as they are presented to tourists, however, she was hit with what may be the new paradigmatic scene of arrival for modern-day travelers (and ethnographers), for my sister found herself standing in the wrong line.

Tourists (and anthropologists) arrive in the British Virgin

Islands by way of a direct flight from Puerto Rico to the Beef Island Airport on Beef Island, just off of Tortola, the main island of the British Virgin Islands. There, they walk across the tarmac of the runway to the terminal building, where they are greeted with placards advertising beach resorts and sailing opportunities, as well as two painted signs: big black capital letters on a white background instruct the arriving passengers to form two lines, one for BELONGERS AND RESIDENTS and the other for NON-BELONGERS. As my sister tells it, she was perplexed, and understandably so, by these signs. She certainly "belonged" in the British Virgin Islands, for she had come all the way from Newark to visit me there, and she was pretty sure that my plans had not changed and taken me elsewhere since we had last spoken. She was not a resident, she knew, but she thought that I might have been, and she did not think she was a "nonbelonger" since she had intended to come to the British Virgin Islands and thus had in fact arrived where she "belonged." So, she decided that the nonbelonger line must be for people just passing through on their way to somewhere else, or perhaps people picking up parcels for transport.

My sister stood in the wrong line, the belongers line. Someone told her before she reached the head of it, and she moved sheepishly into the nonbelongers line and waited for her passport to be stamped with all the other nonbelongers like herself. She noticed, too, that the nonbelonger line was not made up solely of white people from Europe or the United States, but also nonwhite West Indians and Spanish-speaking people from the Dominican Republic. She noticed that it is not just tourists and anthropologists who come to the British Virgin Islands and stand in the nonbelonger line, but also immigrants (and some tourists) from other Caribbean islands who, like her, are informed immediately upon their entry into the country that they do not "belong."

The modern-day anthropological arrival scene is enacted at the customs and immigration checkpoint, surrounded by barbed wire and the border guard. The players in this scene are supposed to have come with their legally created identities guaranteed by their legal documents and if they have not, they are quickly assigned one not of their choosing. Yet anthropological literature has been surprisingly silent about the legal underpinnings of both fieldwork and the field. This book is about the ways law creates conditions of possibility for the structuring and restructuring of reality. Legal categories like "belonger" and "nonbelonger" are part of this process, for they create the types of personhood that shape the ways people live their lives. The British Virgin Islands has always existed as an entity carved out by the legal structures of colonialism. This book attends to the ways various groups of people, at various times, have dealt with such legal structures and the worlds they create and re-create.

The British Virgin Islands, a "dependent territory" of the United Kingdom, is located about thirty-five miles east of Puerto Rico and consists of about forty small islands and cays. Its citizens call themselves *British Virgin Islanders, BVIslanders* (pronounced "bee-vee-islanders"), or *belongers*. There are four major inhabited islands: Tortola, on which the capital city of Road Town is situated, Anegada, Jost Van Dyke, and Virgin Gorda. Tortola is the largest island and is eight miles long by three miles wide. Other islands include Salt Island, Peter Island, Norman Island, Cooper Island, Ginger Island, Guana Island, and Great and Little Camanoe (fig. 1). The "territory," as its residents call it, is home to 16,108 persons. Slightly more than 50 percent of these people were born elsewhere. Noncitizen immigrants, from a total of eighty-two countries and territories, make up about 60 percent of the workforce, and more than half of these do not have the right to work without a permit.[1] "Belonger" and "nonbelonger" are legal categories that regulate rights to work and to own land, but often these terms come to stand in for "citizen" and "noncitizen."

I conducted my fieldwork on Tortola, with short trips to Virgin Gorda and Jost Van Dyke, and to St. Thomas in the United States Virgin Islands. I lived in Road Town, at the end of a road called Horse Path that wended its way up a steep hillside from the town below, in a two-story pink-and-white house divided into three apartments. My BVIslander landlord and landlady lived upstairs, and a Trinidadian consultant lived in the downstairs apartment next door to mine. Every day I walked down into town, past the Police Station, BVI High School, and Legislative Council chambers. Often my first stop would be the BVI Community College or the Public Library. Road Town is a small, haphazardly planned, often dusty place of about eight thousand residents, with an old

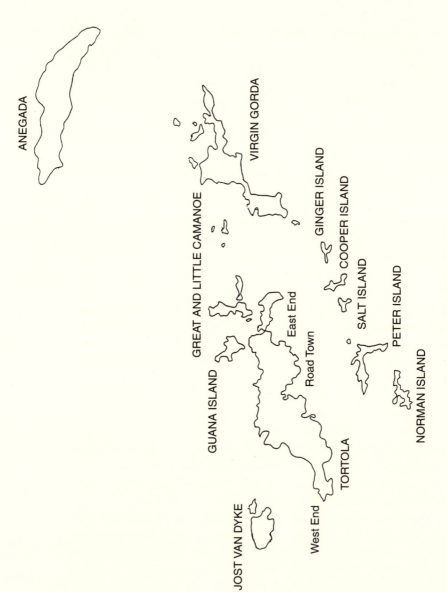

Fig. 1. The British Virgin Islands

"downtown" strip fronting Road Harbor, its many plaster and wood buildings giving a quaint "West Indian" appearance, and centered around the Post Office and the old Administration Building (which, when I was there, housed government offices). The "new" downtown, probably more important to the life of this city, is a wide stretch of flat land jutting out into the harbor to the east of Main Street. This is Wickam's Cay, a piece of land reclaimed from the sea in the 1960s and on which the college, the recently completed new Administration Building, and a number of retail stores, supermarkets, financial offices, and parking lots now stand.

Road Town is small, but it is not without a certain hustle and bustle. Many people drive from the country into town for work (fortunately for the visiting anthropologist with weary feet, who can catch a lift up the hill to his house), and as a result, there are brief moments of rush-hour traffic. Cruise ships dock in the late summer, bringing small numbers of white tourists who traipse around town, looking for T-shirts. But most tourism is distant from Road Town, in consciousness and in space, occurring on the north side of the island, the sleepy "country" side, characterized by beautiful sandy beaches and cool breezes.

While in the BVI, I taught an introductory course in anthropology at the community college to a group of high school teachers interested in enriching their knowledge and having an opportunity to reflect on the emerging "multicultural BVI" and their own multicultural classrooms. I also ran a seminar series on multiculturalism and education for high school students enrolled in the college's teacher training program. Both experiences gave me fresh insights into BVIslanders' assessments of immigration and development in the territory.[2]

There is a popular image of the British Virgin Islands familiar to many North Americans as a place to get away from the hassles of life in the northern metropolis, to relax in the sun, to sail and surf and dive. One BVI Tourist Board advertisement claims, "Our beaches have more shells than people" (fig. 2). As Jamaica Kincaid eloquently argues in her attack on tourism in the Caribbean, *A Small Place* (1988), there is a world of difference between the islands the tourist sees and the islands Caribbean people inhabit. Having lived on Tortola for a little more than a year (in the summer of 1991 and from June 1992 to July 1993) and having spent a good deal of time with belongers and nonbelongers alike, I would write a different version of the tourist advertisement. My BVI is not a depopulated one, but one of incredible human diversity. There is more to the BVI than empty beaches.

On any Friday night on the island of Tortola in the British Virgin Islands, this is what you can do: you can go to the Old Recreation Grounds and see a game of Dominican softball, played by the descendants of British Caribbean men who emigrated to the Dominican Republic in the early 1900s to work in American-owned sugarcane fields. You can go to the New Recreation Grounds and watch Guyanese immigrants of South Asian descent play cricket with some of the resident Englishmen. The Guyanese are third- and fourth-generation descendants of Indian indentured laborers brought to Caribbean shores in the mid-nineteenth century. If you wander out of Road Town, the capital city, down into Huntums Ghut, a small community that borders a small rivulet (or *ghut*), you might come across a vigorous game of dominoes played by a group of "down-islanders"—immigrants from the eastern Caribbean islands to the south of Tortola—slamming the pieces down on their makeshift table.

Farther along, more down-islanders will have congregated at the Church of God of Prophesy and will be testifying and shaking with the Holy Spirit. If you go even higher upstream, you could encounter a group of French-creole–speaking people from Dominica or Haiti. You could go back into town, maybe to see an American movie. Or wander into one of the shops on the waterfront owned by Palestinians; you can enjoy a hot cup of Turkish coffee and have a long discussion with them about local affairs in the West Indies and the West Bank. Or venture into the Botanical Gardens, where the middle-class Toastmasters Club is holding a poetry reading. You might try to insinuate yourself into the round of cocktail parties that follow the event.

You could go west to Slaney, where, in a house on a hilltop, a group of Guyanese immigrants are holding a Hindu *pooja* (ceremony for paying of devotions) at a shrine modeled after an Indian greeting card. You may just want to get away from it all and travel to the north side of the island where the tourists congregate: at Long Bay Beach Resort enjoy an elegant, five-star buffet in your best formal wear. Stop in at Quito's, a casual nightclub. Are you a

Fig. 2. "Our Virgin Islands Are Still Virgin"

hippie? If you look like one, you will have had trouble getting into the country at Customs and Immigration, because of a statutory order barring entry to "the class of persons commonly known as hippies" (SRO No. 39 of 1980). But if you've made it this far, then go hang out at Bomba's Shack with the surfers. You could also venture to Brewer's Bay and find some Rastas—they are all BVIslanders, since, like "hippies," people with "dreadlocks" (another legal term) are barred entry into the country (see Minutes 2/6/70, 3/14/86).

You would not read about this diversity in a tourist brochure. Nor would you read about these kinds of exclusions. One magazine advertisement for a cruise line begins, "There is no law that says you can't . . ." and then lists the activities one might engage in while anchored in the British Virgin Islands (fig. 3). To the tourist, the BVI is a territory apart from the law, a virgin land of sun, sand, the sea, and servants. This book is intended in part to repopulate that territory for a North American and European audience, to show the struggles of the people, both citizen and immigrant, who make it their home.

The Caribbean and the Creole Condition

> Democracy loosens social ties, but tightens natural ones; it brings kindred more closely together, whilst it throws citizens more apart. (Tocqueville [1835–40] 1984:233)

Tocqueville's *Democracy in America* was completed between the years 1835 and 1840, the same period during which slavery was abolished in the British Caribbean islands. Founded in the sixteenth century when hierarchical models of political and social life dominated European societies, Caribbean colonies rehearsed variations on patriarchal aristocratic themes and, with the emancipation of the slaves, egalitarian ones. How did the "natural" ties Tocqueville saw becoming increasingly important in liberal societies instantiate themselves in the transformations of a colonial society under liberal principles? What were the effects of the creation of "natural" and "objectively real" entities like kinship, nationality, race, place, and land, and how are these entities the effects of power? The main contention of this book is that the lib-

Fig. 3. "There Is No Law That Says You Can't . . ."

eral state was central in the creation of a determining nature, both through its direct legislative and administrative actions, such as citizenship laws, and through its tool kit of techniques and technologies.

The Caribbean has become a trope in recent anthropological writing on the globalization of culture and capital and the increasingly important movements of people and commodities across international borders.[3] Anthropologists and those we study express doubt about previously held beliefs on the nature of culture and identity as boundaries and borders are challenged by these modern movements. Words like *hybridity, heteroglossia, mimicry, deterritorialization,* and *diaspora* appear with increasing frequency in journal articles and conference discussions, and often the Caribbean is invoked to illustrate and to explain these concepts (Miller 1994). These terms point to a rethinking of culture, a concept no longer held to signify a fixed and unchanging whole with discernible roots and definable branches, but rather a process of continual revision and articulation. And social theorists have seen these processes of revisioning and rearticulation as paradigmatic especially of the current "postmodern" condition.

James Clifford captured a certain mood in anthropological circles when he contrasted the monolithic view of culture to what he called the "Caribbean experience." Clifford's mission was to challenge the popular sentiment conveyed in Levi-Strauss's *Tristes Tropiques* that cast the post–World War II era of globalization as one in which local cultural differences gave way to an invincible consumer monoculture embracing the entire world.

> Alongside this narrative of progressive monoculture a more ambiguous "Caribbean" experience may be glimpsed. In my account Aimé Césaire, a practitioner of "neologistic" cultural politics, represents such a possibility—organic culture reconceived as inventive process or creolized "interculture." The roots of tradition are cut and retied, collective symbols appropriated from external influences. For Césaire culture and identity are inventive and mobile. They need not take root in ancestral plots; they live by pollination, by (historical) transplanting. (Clifford 1988:15, references omitted)

Other authors have followed suit, using the "Caribbean experience" to redefine notions of culture and likening the emerging world condition to their visions of "the Caribbean" or, alternately, holding up "the Caribbean" as paradigmatic for the current world order (e.g., Hannerz 1990, 1992; Clifford 1988; Appadurai 1990; Gilroy 1993; Hebdige 1987; Benítez-Rojo 1992).

While I am sympathetic to the project that motivates them, I am skeptical of such claims for the basic reason that they depend upon the assumptions of another very powerful discourse that seems to justify new forms of inequality and exclusion. This other discourse concerns "nature" and seems more and more to hold sway in spite of (or because of) the disjunctures and creolizations the world is witnessing. It is relatively unexamined in the literature on the "Caribbeanization" of the world and also wends its way through the literature on postmodernism without any of the self-critical scrutiny that postmodernist approaches in anthropology have made their trademark. Writing of Clifford's invocation of the Caribbean, Marilyn Strathern asks us to "listen . . . to how images of recombination and cutting work. Listen to what happens when one imagines Clifford's vision of the postmodern world as though he were thinking of kinship of the English kind" (Strathern 1992b:110). What we hear are stories about hybridity that embody "the old reproductive idiom of biological kinship," an idiom animating Tocqueville's "natural ties" and tying us to particular notions of identity:

> Persons are natural hybrids: the creative recombination of already differentiated genetic material makes everyone a new entity. The past might have been collected into ancestral traditions, but the future lies in perpetual hybridisation. (Strathern 1992b:111)

When scholars invoke models of hybridity and creolization, they rely on the metaphors of biological reproduction and genetic recombination. Their language ultimately rests on ideas about "natural" substances from which new variations are called forth by cuttings, mixings, and rerootings (Young 1995, Thomas 1996). There need not be anything transcendent or eternal about these natural substances, for they themselves can be conceptualized as the outcome of other hybridizing processes. But this, too, makes perfect sense in the idiom of biogenetic relatedness through which many modern Western peoples "think kinship" (Schneider 1984; Strathern 1992a).

If the Caribbean is a microcosm of the world, and if the world is becoming more and more like the Caribbean, then the task of charting what we mean by "the Caribbean experience" becomes an urgent one. If the Caribbean experience is one of the progressive hybridization of thought and practices where such hybridization is imagined in terms of a biogenetic idiom of kinship, for example, then it becomes increasingly important to analyze and understand the hold biogenetic explanations have on contemporary culture.

This study of law, land, and citizenship in the British Virgin Islands highlights the ways in which ideas about nature and a natural order come to justify a social order where half of the population is deemed "not to belong" and is denied the rights of citizenship. An ordering of the world under purportedly natural dictates has resulted in the exclusion of people from political participation, the exploitation of labor, and the movement of capital across international borders and legal regimes. Here is where I see the Caribbean reflected in the world, as states rely on exclusionary politics, as "free trade" initiatives foster the movement of money at the expense of people, and as nationalist and anti-immigrant sentiments justify the exploitation and criminalization of migrants whose labor is nonetheless necessary for the regimes that exclude them. This is the nature of "the Caribbean experience" and its global reinscriptions.

The title of this book, *Recharting the Caribbean*, is intended to shift the debate in anthropological circles about the Caribbeanization of the world, and to rechart debate in four respects. There is merit to the intellectual project of mapping the Caribbean outward onto the globe, of citing West Indian immigrant communities in London, Toronto, Miami, and New York and the reformulation of identity these communities engage in as indicative of postmodern processes more generally (Basch, Glick Schiller, and Szanton Blanc 1994). Yet I am disturbed by the quick romanticization of the Caribbean experience in other quarters, and the writing of this experience as one of mixing and hybridization, when such concepts rely on notions of nature that serve to exclude as well as include, to unidentify as well as identify, to dissociate as well as incorporate. One historical recharting of the Caribbean, for instance, the dissolution of the British Leeward Islands Colony and the subsequent delineation of the islands into separate national states and dependent territories, had the effect of differentiating and dividing, not recombining or hybridizing. It created whole new types of nationals (and foreigners) out of a collection of people who before had all been British subjects (figs. 4, 5).

While challenging the romanticization of the Caribbean, this book aims to challenge traditional Caribbeanist scholarship. The anthropology of the Caribbean has been, on the one hand, the anthropology of social structure, household, and family and, on the other hand, the study of syncretisms, "Africanisms," and cultural change within a capitalist world system.[4] Rarely have Caribbeanists looked to the role of the state and law in shaping family or in changing cultures (with a few exceptions, such as Lazarus-Black 1994, Olwig 1993, Mahabir 1985). Many ethnographies of the Caribbean fall into the rhythms of peasant life and subsistence agriculture, seldom noting the integral connection between Caribbean agriculture and global relations (as Baber [1982] and Trouillot [1988] point out). The rich literature on colonialism and the creation of national consciousness that has been developed for other colonial situations (e.g., Guha 1983; Chatterjee 1988, 1993; N. Dirks 1992; Cooper and Stoler 1989; Thomas 1994) has no counterpart in the scholarship on the Caribbean. My focus on the colonial process and the state is intended in part as a corrective to Caribbeanist research, a recharting of the territory of Caribbean studies to include more centrally the problematics of colonialism, colonial discourse, and national identity in state contexts.

Ethnographers of the Caribbean have been particularly attentive to class, race, and gender dynamics in the region.[5] The BVI case is interesting in that race and class distinctions among British Virgin Islanders have been diminishing at the same time that BVIslanders increasingly draw sharp distinctions between themselves and immigrants, distinctions that are marked in race, class, and gender terms. The BVI leads to an examination of the liberal

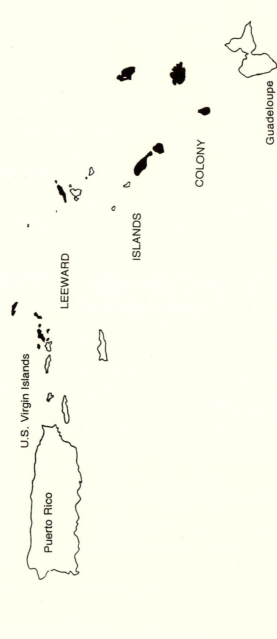

Fig. 4. The Leeward Islands Colony, 1949

Puerto Rico

U.S. Virgin Islands

LEEWARD

ISLANDS

COLONY

Guadeloupe

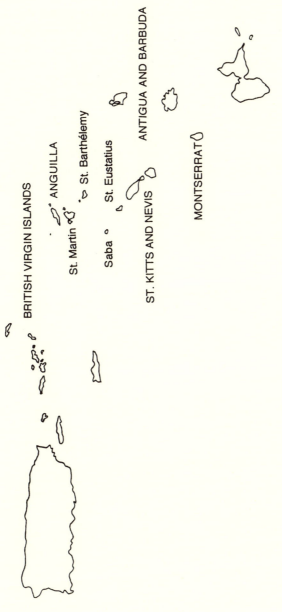

BRITISH VIRGIN ISLANDS

ANGUILLA

St. Martin   St. Barthélemy

Saba   St. Eustatius

ANTIGUA AND BARBUDA

ST. KITTS AND NEVIS

MONTSERRAT

Fig. 5.   The Contemporary Leeward Islands

legal foundations of much race, class, and gender hierarchy in the Caribbean and may have implications for other New World societies structured by hierarchy under a liberal framework of equality.

Finally, the title plays on the word *chart* and the qualities charts have when they are taken to be objective representations of a measurable, observable reality. The imagining of a world where "charting" is a sensible activity is crucial in understanding how land, kin, race, place, and nation became conceptualized as objectively real and natural entities, representable on survey maps, kinship diagrams, human faces, and legal documents. Recharting the "natures" that are held to determine human life opens up the productive power of liberal legalities to constitute new kinds of persons and new identities.

Democracy, Law, and National/Natural Difference

As the Caribbean comes to stand in for the "new world order," notions of law and order, nature and culture, and "objective reality" become increasingly important in liberal democracies engaged in sorting out inequalities among their participants. Why would liberal democracy foster the construction of a determining and determinate nature, when under democratic principles it is people themselves and not forces outside of human control that are called upon to make a polity? As Stolcke (1993, 1995) argues, the construction of a particular kind of nature resolves contradictions born of the liberal legal dictum that all persons are equal and the empirical observation that some people seem to be more equal than others. Liberal law constructs persons as equal in an abstract formal sense but depends also upon the notion that equal individuals are different from each other and have different interests. These differences are called up by the demand that liberal law mediate the conflicting interests of different individuals and are then relegated to a domain of the essential, the natural, and the given (Collier, Maurer, and Suárez-Navaz 1995; Pashukanis 1929). People under liberalism are formal, legal equals, but liberalism does not deny—and in fact demands—that people are substantively, "naturally" different.

But substantive differences pose another problem for democratic society, as political philosopher C. B. Macpherson (1962) argued in his classic study of the theories of liberalism. Macpherson wanted to understand how, without reference to the will of God or a hierarchical Great Chain of Being, people could form a theory of political obligation that would work to maintain the state and keep order in society. He posited two conditions that had to be met for the invention of liberal democracies founded not on God's will but on the "people's" will. First, the people in a liberal society must view themselves as equal "in some respect more fundamental than all the respects in which they are unequal" (272). Second, individuals must be sufficiently similar to each other for there to be a "cohesion of self-interests, among all those who have a voice in choosing the government," otherwise the pursuit of self-interest by each member of the policy would result in political fragmentation and degenerate into a Hobbesian war of each against all (273). Macpherson argued that the first condition was met during the inception and heyday of liberalism, from the seventeenth to the nineteenth centuries, by the consensus that all persons were subject to the inevitability of market forces and that this subordination to the market was morally rightful. The second condition was met by the restriction of the franchise to men of property.

By the middle of the nineteenth century, however, neither condition was being met any longer. In the capitalist core, industrialization had helped an industrial working class form and envision alternatives to the current order; it no longer seemed fair or just or inevitable that the market should determine life chances. In the periphery, like the Caribbean, revolts and unrest challenged the foundations of liberalism and the contradictions at its heart. Meanwhile the privileged classes increasingly extended the franchise to other members of society, thereby providing the possibility that the cohesion of self-interests among those choosing the government would gradually erode.

Macpherson left his analysis here, wondering whether the days of liberal democracy were numbered and proposing that perhaps international class solidarity and war fulfilled his two conditions on a global level. What Macpherson did not consider, however, is the role that nationalism increasingly played in the nineteenth and twentieth centuries and the possibility that nationalism might satisfy his two conditions. First, nationalism can construct as equals the citizens of the nation, who as possessors of a national identity are rendered fundamentally similar to each other. Second, nationalism limits the franchise and provides coherence of interest through nationality and citizenship laws, which deny voting and other rights to persons deemed to be noncitizens or nonnationals and unify citizens as voters.[6]

The first half of this century witnessed a flurry of legal activity on citizenship and nationality law, as nation-states sought to consolidate themselves and relieve internal fractures by controlling and limiting the voting population, extending the franchise to some and denying it to others (Baty 1918–19; Randall 1924; International Union for Child Welfare 1947; Salmond 1901, 1902; Sandifer 1935; Koessler 1946). In the late twentieth century, increased immigration brought about by global economic restructuring has brought citizenship and nationality back into public debate. Race discourses have also gained in prominence, as have biological renderings of gender difference. During the writing of this book (1993–95), California Governor Pete Wilson called for amendments to citizenship policies that would deny citizenship to children born on U.S. soil to Mexican undocumented workers, and National Guard troops were sent to the United States–Mexico border to "control" immigration. Meanwhile, three conflicts erupted, capturing the attention of the world media—in Bosnia, in Rwanda, and in Chiapas, Mexico. All three, in different ways, involved relatively recent articulations and imaginings of "natural" differences, whether ethnic, racial, or national, and all in other ways involved gender (as in the rape of Bosnian women and ideas about inheritable Serbian identity, and the role of women rebels in Chiapas; see Delaney 1995 and Hernández Castillo 1994, respectively). The Chiapas case is interesting in that the U.S. media at first were incapable of interpreting the rebellion as anything other than essentially "Indian" or ethnic in character, while the rebels themselves articulated their concerns first and foremost as members of the Mexican state, invoking in their claim on the state their (natural) Mexican "nationality" (EZLN 1994). Both accounts fall back onto notions of identity as naturally derived and given— though contestable. These kinds of exclusions and conflicts may become more common as crises in liberal states and capitalist markets bring the contradictions underlying them to the fore and as an invigorated Nature comes to the rescue to justify inequalities old and new.

The British Virgin Islands: Tourism and Immigration

The British Virgin Islands was a *presidency,* or subunit, of the Leeward Islands Colony until that colony was dissolved in the 1950s. Since then, it has existed under nominal Crown rule but with its own, locally elected legislature. Most of its immigrants came to work in construction and service jobs created by a boom in luxury tourism during the 1960s and 1970s and in the offshore financial services sector in the 1980s. They are from the other islands of the eastern Caribbean, the Dominican Republic, and Guyana. A governor appointed by the Crown oversees ceremonial duties, sits with elected ministers of government as part of the executive, and is responsible for external affairs and defense. Since 1969, by an act of the local legislature, the official currency has been the U.S. dollar, facilitating commerce with the neighboring United States Virgin Islands and the United States itself. The fact that the territory is British and the currency is U.S. has the added effect of making the BVI one of the only places in the Western Hemisphere where a person can trade pounds sterling for U.S. dollars without restriction or fee, which has contributed to the recent phenomenal success of the territory as a tax haven.

When, in 1960, Laurence Rockefeller put up the capital to construct Little Dix, the British Virgin Islands' first luxury resort, a lack of skilled labor led to the mass importation of workers from other Caribbean islands. The resort was completed in 1964, but the pattern of immigration continued into the next three decades. There is an apparent contradiction in BVIslanders' assessments of the impact of the tourism industry and the labor movements to which it gave rise. On the one hand, they sometimes describe the islands as a land of plenty. Tourism, they say, has brought the islands away from poverty and peasantlike subsistence farming and into the twentieth century. It is no surprise, they say, that immigrant laborers from other, not so well-off, Caribbean islands should set their sights on the BVI; and there is more than enough prosperity to go around. As one elderly man stated, "Wherever there are berries, there will be birds. Wherever there's flies, there's fish. It comes down to this: wherever there's food, people want to be there." The BVI is a promised land for the dispossessed of the Caribbean; BVIslanders are willing to share with the less fortunate.

When they are asked specifically about particular groups of immigrants, however, and not the general conditions they attribute to the tourism industry, BVIslanders are often somewhat less sanguine. One shopkeeper stated, "We're so small we can't bear too many people," adding that "we need workers, but then they don't stay workers—they get into business and become proprietors and our competitors." This same man continued, "The cream is being skimmed by other people, and you know that whoever skims the cream gets the best part of the whole milk; the natives are left with the nonfat milk!" BVIslanders worry that immigrants are taking over. The BVI is a small place, with limited resources. A perceived overall condition of scarcity is creating competition between "locals" and "outsiders." Tourism has cast the locals out of Eden; they must fight tooth and nail to hold on to what is rightfully theirs.

The language BVIslanders use to talk about the dilemmas of their present situation only occasionally attains such biblical dimensions. More often, BVIslanders will make use of images and language that seem to resonate with the promotional materials and marketing campaigns for the islands' tourist industry. Tourism promotional themes, secularized translations of the popular Christian ones, depend on a twofold construction of this British dependent territory as infused with both the true spirit of "England"—civility, gentility, and law and order—and the mystery, fertility, and beauty of Nature (see Cohen and Mascia-Lees 1993). The BVI Tourist Board's most recent slogan for the islands is "Discover Nature's Little Secrets." When they discuss the changes brought about by tourism and immigration, BVIslanders blame immigrants for eroding law and order and for destroying nature. Their perceptions of immigrants' levels of wealth, work habits, and consumption behavior "prove" to them that immigrants have a lack of regard for law and order and a lack of respect for nature. In making such claims, they construct a story about their own history and heritage as a nation and culture, about who "belongs" and who does not, about who is truly "local" and who is not.

Meanwhile, BVIslanders are far from unified on the issue of

tourism's benefit or harm to the territory. Many do not feel that tourism has had much of a direct impact on their economic well-being and wonder who "really" reaps the rewards of the industry. Seeing profits go to foreign investors and wages go to "outside" labor, they look for fellow BVIslanders who are "selling out the territory" for their own personal advancement without considering the consequences. People who have directly benefited from the tourism industry—mostly the owners of bars, restaurants, laundries, and other service-related enterprises—claim that outside labor is a necessity because local workers are not only unskilled, but lazy. These differences of opinion are reflected in people's descriptions of the class structure of the territory. According to one elite man actively involved in the production of national culture and in tourism, "There is only upper middle class . . . ; everybody is about the same; there are no poor people." But according to a member of the civil service, "We didn't used to have classes, but we getting some now." Neither of these BVIslanders, however, counted the laboring class of immigrants in their assessments of the BVI class structure. And neither commented on the increasingly important offshore financial services sector of the BVI economy, which, during the time of my fieldwork, outstripped tourism in its contribution to the territory (see Maurer 1995b; Meyers 1993b). The implications of this sector for class and immigration in the BVI are only beginning to take shape.

Transition Narratives

BVIslander discussions about immigrants are discussions about change and transformation. They constitute transition narratives that figure prominently in BVIslanders' assessments of the past century. As such, these stories invoke a stable natural ground in the past that has deviated from its "original" and "true" course. Transition narratives portray the British Virgin Islands' past as a time of bounty, and, at the same time, they portray that past as a time of hardship. They invoke both continuity and change. For many, the changes are frightening and represent a threat to what is today perceived as a cherished, old-time way of life. One elderly BVIslander told me with alarm—and citing the Trumpets of the Apocalypse (Revelations 8–9)—that he no longer recognized people on the streets like in the old days, since so many immigrants had come.

> We have a phrase, the people of the British Virgin Island have a phrase, call them "Garot" [an old slang term for non-BVIslanders; see R. Dirks 1975]. That's a phrase. And if you blow a trumpet, my wife and you blow a trumpet you can sound from East End and all around, villages around, and said "All the Garots come out, we want to see them," boy, you would be one to know where them heap of people come from [laughs]. And then blow a next trumpet and say "Born Tortolians come out"—ain't much!
>
> When you go to a graduation, we just had graduation from the high school . . . and I have a list here, man you look at that list—very few Tortolian on that list. And primary school you have the primary graduation too and hear the names—expatriate children. And—too many things. We Tortolians in Tortola . . . Tortolians in Tortola are not the people that original, now, [as] when I were five years old and going up. Things change that you can't distinguish.[7]

These transition narratives deploy conceptions of both continuity and change held in constant tension. Continuity and change imply continuity with a source and change from a source. Linton, an old man from East End, had the following conversation with me early in my fieldwork.

> *Linton:* The land is very important, or *was, is* or *was* very important to British Virgin Islanders, because I would not refrain from telling you that [there were] plenty people who owned those lands that was very skillful until they die out. And left it for their, as inheritance, for their children. And let me tell you a lot of those children 'come rascal. You know what I'm talkin' about?
>
> *BM:* Rascals?
>
> *Linton:* Yeah. That's it. And they neither here no' there. They don't work [. . .]. But looking at them I can't see where they're going, nor where they will lead. Only God knows. So, to the other people who sit holding their ground, land

is of very great importance to us here in the British Virgin Islands because my grandfather bought two estates and we cherish it, we honor it, and God bless them, if they weren't there, I don't know [. . .]. It had once we were cultivating the land and everybody were living out of the land, but today the role, the general role in the British Virgin Islands have changed. Agriculture is only, in the British Virgin Islands today, a thing of the past. The real role in the British Virgin Islands today is tourism.

Transition narratives portray the past of the British Virgin Islands as a time of hardship. But they also portray the past as Edenic. Nature is the enemy and nature is the blessing. Images of nature are deployed when BVIslanders talk about "how much" things have "changed" in their homeland. Transition narratives thus seem to depend upon as they construct an ontology of "nature" where nature is the very stuff of continuity and change.

Let us listen to two snippets of conversation. These occurred within a few minutes of each other and involved the same married couple, Wilbur and Gilda, and yet they express quite different sentiments. The first is a story of a past when people had to battle to make a living because the BVI was without resources; the second is a story of the Eden that the BVI once was, before tourism and immigration. These two contradictory images can be maintained because in each, "nature" is the stable ground, a nature that is held to determine livelihood.

> *Wilbur:* We had one hundred bag of charcoal—I ain't talking about no rice bag, I talking about those big—
> *Gilda:* Sugar bag.
> *Wilbur:* Two hundred and fifty pound bag. And when we sell that we get one twenty dollars [bill].
> *Gilda:* Twenty-two.
> *Wilbur:* And it was, you couldn't imagine, there was nothing else to do!
> *Gilda:* That's right.
> *Wilbur:* You had to still go tomorrow and chop wood again. To burn more coal. To save your life. We had to go to school—
> *Gilda:* No shoes.

Wilbur: No shoes, partly naked. When you left school, three
o'clock you come home, you have to go all the way out near
by Sage Mountain [. . .] to find a calf, see who get a calf to
get a cow hide, to get a drop of milk for small children, the
morning before they could go to school. Only World War II
changed the condition of the Virgin Islands. I can tell you!
Tortola!! I thank and I praise God for how I find myself
today.

Wilbur: [to Gilda and me] Things in the British Virgin Islands . . . . Where we sit here you look up the valley there:
when I was I child I used to go up there for the water; there
was a spring of water up there. Today, it's a parched desert.
We have on the estate in the country, me and she go out
there and we work, and the water going there flowing down,
and we work out there up to the time when all this tourism
business come up, were were still working up there. And
since we stopped this, I went out there some time ago, and
looked around, and the places where you used to have
fishes in the ghut, running water, the stream, man if you go
out there you don't carry water from home, you die the
death of a dog. There, all over this place, the whole island
change—*change!* So it's no comparison; It ain't no good that
I telling the children what happened, how it was—they say it
could never be. You see? All say is I'm glad I living; see,
those who live the longest see the most. Yeah.

Some BVIslanders tell stories about their past that find good
in every evil. Another old man describes a scandal involving an
unscrupulous development company that attempted to lay claim
to Wickam's Cay:

Still, every evil work out for a good. It was a lucky thing that
that company did come *here,* with good intention or bad intentions, and happened to *be,* and it happened because now we
have some body as you come doing research to Road Town,
because if you look at it [before], we only had the one street,
you had to go up Main Street and we couldn't, couldn't manage. But *today* we can show something, Wickams Cay One,

Wickams Cay Two, and the Deep Water Harbour and all this arise as a result of this Wickams Cay condition. So out of every evil, what I'm saying about *that* subject, I will be quite honest in saying it's a good thing it happened in that way.

Transition narratives tell teleological stories. If it is a tale of change, we need to know how much and to what ends (see Strathern 1992a). If it is a tale of continuity, we need to know what has kept things the same, and what *constitutes* the same. Transition narratives are founded on inevitabilities, on real objects that have real and predictable effects. It is the task of this book to chart the making of those real objects.

From Nature to Choice: The Example of Marriage

Each chapter of the book attends to a different technique through which real objects and natural qualities are created together with liberal, rational human individuals who make choices and who find their choices constrained by "objective facts" of "nature." Here, however, in order to make my theoretical discussion more concrete, let me briefly illustrate the argument with reference to changes in marriage practices in the British Virgin Islands.

Speaking of the early twentieth century, one elderly man related to me the following: "The practice was—if you're going to marry my daughter, then you have to have somewhere for her to live. You have to ask permission in an endorsed letter, in writing, to come and visit her, and I have to endorse it if I give you permission." This practice of making a written request of a bride's father died out around the time of World War II. After the war, engagement rings became popular. "Then, [there was] engagement with a ring you give her signifying that this is your sweetheart, and then you start building the house. Pregnancy sometimes happened, so that even though you were still building the house you'd get married. If you own land, then you build on your own land; if not, perhaps the other side has it, sometimes a good friend or relative would give it without charge—not like today!"

Before the 1960s and hotel construction, the mother of the bride would hold a reception in her "yard," the area behind her house, and would construct a tent made of coconut palms. Family and friends would cook food; everyone would bring something to eat or drink at the bridal reception. The bride's mother was responsible for the cakes, tarts, and fruit. The groom's family was responsible for the drinks—the men of the groom's family would bring quantities of cane rum for the occasion, and the groom's father would bring a bull for the feast, or sometimes a pig or a couple of sheep.

Nowadays, in contrast, people host catered receptions in a banquet hall of one of the resorts or hotels, such as the Prospect Reef Hotel, the Admiralty Inn, or Maria's. These establishments generally do not allow people to bring in their own food, since the silverware, kitchen facilities, and so forth are the hotel's own and they want only their "professionals" to handle them. Wedding costs, as a result, have skyrocketed, since not only does one need to rent the hall but also to hire caterers. The catering can cost from fifteen to twenty dollars a head, and so people have to put a lot of forethought into their invitation list. One woman described to me four "circles" of who would be considered, in order of decreasing priority, for the invitation list: the "immediate family, just the parents of the bride and groom, and the brothers and sisters," "the next circle, with the grandparents, aunts, and uncles," then "all the cousins and a few friends," and finally, "the whole community." A guest list of two hundred could cost nearly four thousand dollars. Even people who wish to hold a "big traditional BVI wedding" find they have to pare down their plans due to the expense and limit their guest list.

According to one elderly man from the north side of Tortola, past practices were superior, mainly because the lower costs allowed for unrestricted relations of sociability. The limits placed on weddings today lead to quarrels, since people need to limit the numbers of friends and relatives and thus to make decisions about the relative importance of different people to their social world. This man linked changes in marriage practices to changes in the valuation of land.

> The way it [marriage] was before was better, there was not so much confusion, contention, family disagreement. Part of what caused it—there are others who know better than I, I suppose—but, when I was coming up, land had value in a

sense, in that you work on it, grow things, vegetables, fresh fruits, livestock, and so on, but no one was craving for it because it didn't have value as such. It used to be five or six dollars an acre. And sometimes, you'd have an old, needy person, you'd help them out and they might give you land as compensation. That was how land had value. After a while, with development increasing, people started to send money back to build on their land, and then tourists come who want land for retirement or development, so land starts to take on value, and people come back to get their claim even though they don't know anything about it, and this led to confusion and arguments. Before land take on its value, what you got was to raise food—vegetables, keep your lifestock, make bone charcoal to sell to St. Thomas, raise fruits and everything fresh; that was your livelihood, it keep you alive. Now it's different. The change started from 1940 on, people went to St. Thomas and that's when the change came. They made money, sent it home to build a house, and today if you want land in the BVI you have to pay a high price for that—after the war was the change.

Younger people, in contrast, seem to prefer the new arrangements to the old. To many young people, small weddings with "close people" are more fun than big "family affairs" where guests are compelled to interact with people whom they might prefer "unintentionally" to forget to invite. One woman in her forties who has attended both types of weddings commented that the change to "simpler" weddings—as she described the current practices—was a good one, since now the people hosting the reception do not have to bother with so many arrangements and can instead "enjoy themselves." Sociability, enacting ties of obligation to others, has given way to having a good time.

The transition narrative constructed here is that there used to be "sharing," sociability and community-wide involvement; now there are smaller, "family" affairs and with them a new conception of "family" as the "immediate family," defined exclusively by bio-genetic "closeness" to the people being wedded. It is of note that "economic" constraints are perceived as having helped construct "biology" in this manner, a manner that permits for the "rational" allocation of resources for weddings. New weddings elevate personal preference and choice over the extended family and the demands of social obligations. Weddings are no longer necessarily about such obligations, but about having a good time with one's friends (that is, the people one chooses to associate with). However, one must include the "inner circle" of "family" (that is, the immediate "biological" relatives whom one simply cannot ignore). In this new milieu, one can "choose" one's family, but only up to a point and within certain "natural" limits. Hierarchy and equality, inclusiveness and exclusiveness, come together in the nexus of "nature" and "choice" to create both the immutable, natural facts that constrain choices and the freedom—or the necessity—to "choose" itself.

Materializing Nature in a Liberal Order

Transition narratives are technologies that presuppose as they produce the stable, real objects that are their subjects, in this case, nature and choice. They are reiterative, in the sense Judith Butler (1993) discusses, where their reiterations produce the force and materiality, the "reality," these narratives are supposedly about. This approach to the determining natures BVIslanders construct that are held to determine their social life owes much to recent attempts to retheorize the essentialism-versus-constructivism debate in various areas of social inquiry. Butler's innovation is to emphasize the practices of reiteration, a continuous or repetitive calling forth that materializes a reality as stable and nonconstructed and from which cultural constructions supposedly follow. Butler asks (1993:xi), "What are we to make of constructions without which we would not be able to think, to live, to make sense at all, those which have acquired for us a kind of necessity?" She turns to the processes that constitute such necessities, to the "reiterative and citational practices by which discourse produces the effects that it names," much as reiterations of transition narratives continually re-cite/re-site "nature" and "choice" as powerful, meaningful entities with an import seemingly all their own. In this, Butler's perspective-shifting inquiry is similar to Foucault's:

Rather than seeing [the modern soul] as the reactivated remnants of an ideology, one would see it as the present correlative of a certain technology of power over the body. It would be wrong to say that the soul is an illusion, or an ideological effect. On the contrary it exists, it has a reality, it is produced permanently around, on, within the body by the functioning of power that is exercised. (Foucault 1979:29, quoted in Gilroy 1993:102)[8]

Bruno Latour (1993) proposes similar ideas. Rather than discussing the limits of nature and culture, Latour looks to the work of what he calls "hybrids" between these domains and traces how they constitute nature and culture as separate, solid, and meaningful. His notion of hybrids is quite different from the old notion of creoles, in which creole-hybrids refer to novel recombinative products of old and stable sources and which seem to recapitulate the "natures" whose materiality should be our point of analysis. For Latour, hybrids are not products of divergent domains but rather mediating technologies; specifically, mediators between "nature" and "culture." At the same time that hybrids connect nature and culture, nature and culture rely on technologies of mediation and purification to keep the appearance of their separateness. The work of mediation and purification becomes the center of Latour's new anthropology, not arguments about the limits of nature or of culture. "Natures-cultures" become the objects of this new inquiry. In my thinking, this shifts the "creolozation" debate entirely, away from the discussions of the putatively stable cultures that meld or combine into creoles and toward creoles themselves as the technologies that conjure up the "pure" cultures they are supposedly made from.

Marilyn Strathern has pushed the limits of this kind of thinking in anthropology by calling attention to problems with Western notions of nature and culture, construction and essence, and continuity and change, and their insinuation into cultural analysis (and without which cultural analysis would not be possible; Strathern 1992a). Strathern historicizes social constructionist thinking, noting that it only makes sense in a context where humans are envisioned as productive individuals who make things separate from themselves and who also are their own subjects of self-improvement without having to defer their creative abilities to a transcendent God or Nature. Not coincidentally, this (Western) historical context corresponds to Macpherson's period of crisis of liberal democracy, from the middle of the nineteenth century to the present (or at least very recent past). What humans make, they make from "pure" natural substances or else from substances that have already been worked upon by other people. At the same time that people construct society and things social from nature, society works back on individuals to "socialize" them, to work the raw nature out of them and to produce social persons. Yet the practices that engage nature are the ones that constitute nature itself and that deny nature's construction. Social relations "map onto" natural ones and reinvigorate nature at a deep and determining level. Differences among people are cast not as the product of socialization but as the product of the internalized nature that socialization attempts to work on and sometimes work out. This conflict between social pressures and individual aspirations motivates Western social thinking about "society."

In her discussion of the new reproductive technologies, relevant here for its illumination of the themes of nature and choice that animate BVI transition narratives, Strathern argues that the late twentieth century has witnessed a further elaboration of this logic, or a collapsing of that logic inward onto itself. Social construction reifies nature by positing social life and individual character in the last instance as constructions after natural facts. To Strathern, this invigorates and collapses "choice." A biogenetic theory of the reproduction of individuals would hold that the number of unique individuals is always increasing, since new combinations of biogenetic substance are continually coming into being. Strathern argues that new reproductive technologies seem to usurp the production of diversity from this explosion of individuality and the production of individuality from the explosion of diversity. For instance: cloning, at least in the imagination, provides the possibility of unique individuality without diversity (since cloning makes possible repetitions of unique individuals), while "cyborg" technologies that would join human, animal, and machine provide the possibility of diversity without unique individuality (since cyborg creations meld the individualities of their component elements). To Strathern, reflecting on the implications of new reproductive technologies highlights the models of choice available to late-twentieth-century human subjects:

> Individuality without diversity: the customer is pressured into the exercise of choice, an emphatic promotion of preference, as a mandate impressed on all consumers alike. Diversity without individuality: the riot of consumer preference collapses all other possibilities, choice becomes consumer choice, not just rearranging the same variants but converting social relations into market forces. (Strathern 1992a:193)

"Choice" itself changes. Previously a marker of distinction, good breeding and rationality, choice now takes on the character of gut-level preferences, opinions, or intangible predilections (Strathern 1992a:216). As in the construction of a wedding invitation list, nature itself becomes the object of choice and whim, even as nature provides the options available from which to choose and the choice-making ability of modern individuals.

Two caveats are necessary here. While I am interested in the equality constituted by liberal theory and its links to nature and choice, I do not wish to recapitulate a "transition to modernity" narrative, which critics have rightly argued is teleological and Eurocentric (e.g., Chakrabarty 1992). Like other transition narratives, the "transition to modernity" story posits real objects and orderings without explaining them and smacks of essentialism. In the story of the transition from feudal hierarchy to liberal equality, for instance, such objects would include the social types of persons vertically arranged in a hierarchy of ranked statuses, say, versus autonomous individuals freely associating in horizontal relations with each other and not bound by vertical ties.

Second, and just as important, I wish to avoid a reading of individualism, nature, and choice in the British Virgin Islands that appears to be a performance of a European script with Caribbean actors. To produce such a play would be to transcendentalize the objects that ought to be historicized. This book rather presents a local story with global themes.

Karen Fog Olwig's (1993) recent book on the interplay of ideas about hierarchy and equality in the cultural history of Nevis nicely captures the movement between the local and the global and the Caribbean and the European in a way that resists a Eurocentric construction of transition. She notes that the early colonial society in the Caribbean drew from late medieval and early modern notions of a hierarchical patriarchal sociolegal order. Seventeenth-century English landholders in the Caribbean incorporated their African slaves into a model of patriarchal farm and home life. Under hierarchical principles, slaves, like servants, occupied an established social position. By the beginning of the eighteenth century, however, as colonial agricultural production shifted from yeoman farming to industrial-model plantations, this hierarchical and inclusive ordering gave way to a social order founded on notions of equality. This horizontal, "egalitarian" ordering was only open to those free men who observed the bounds of respectability, moral family living and propriety. Those who could not—women, children, slaves, the insane—fell out of the egalitarian system, becoming less than human (see Foucault 1980).

Slaves responded to these hierarchical and egalitarian orderings by developing norms of sociability, on the one hand, and respectability, on the other. The inclusion of slaves into a hierarchical social order demanded the extension of "sociable" relations with others. Sociability (Wilson's [1969, 1973] "reputation") refers to mutual ties of obligation and support inherent in a hierarchical system. Olwig argues that, just as the hierarchical order was giving way because of new forms of plantation organization, Caribbean slaves forged solidarities and cultures to counter the situation of social death they experienced as unfree persons that resembled earlier English hierarchical modes of obligation and hierarchical social interaction (Olwig 1993:61). They were thus able to express new cultures through a hierarchical "English" form. Later, freepeople of color adopted the English emphasis on respectability, where persons were free and equal only in so far as they could clearly demonstrate their rational and godly living—through legal marriages, the work ethic, and "'decent and correct' manners and morals" (Mosse 1985:1, quoted in Olwig 1993:69). They did so in order to differentiate themselves from the mass of the unfree. After emancipation the culture of respectability "came to underwrite the new colonial order which emerged as the plantation regime declined" when the ranks of the respectable middle classes of color swelled and colonial infrastructure depended on local lackeys (Olwig 1993:13; Lazarus-Black 1994). Respectability relied on educational and religious institutions, which taught upright and independent living, not such sociable activities as rum drinking and the incurring of debts and obligations.

Olwig argues that the twin values of sociability and respectability have played off one another, at least since the end of slavery, and have been crucial in the process of Caribbean decolonization, state formation and late-twentieth-century migrations. Political self-determination brings the conflict between sociability and respectability to a head, as it demands ties of obligation (to the nation-state and its agents) and denies them, casting them as interfering in the political process (as graft, patronage, and corruption). It demands respectability and equality of persons, but economic conditions make respectability difficult to achieve and maintain.[9]

Olwig's discussion of the principles of hierarchy and equality, sociability and respectability, is helpful shorthand for configurations of inequality in the British Virgin Islands. In its egalitarian order, the maintenance and justification of inequalities almost goes without saying, since such a (horizontal) conception of society allows the possibility for people simply to "fall out" because they are not quite up to par with being "equals" to their peers. Notions of a hierarchical, inclusive (vertical) conception of society enter the picture, however, through the grand compass of "kinship" conceptualized as a biogenetic and deeply natural thing that expresses "natural" and always already-given connectedness: everyone has a "place" on the kin diagram, so no one "falls out" the way they do in egalitarian orderings. This fact—that modern Caribbean peoples (and Western anthropologists and others) think of kinship in this fashion—itself points up the fallacy of the "transition to modernity" narrative, for there is no real transition from hierarchy to equality as such if kinship continues to be defined in biogenetic—that is, "natural"—terms.

But the irony here, an irony that makes Strathern's discussion of choice so relevant and that makes the modern Caribbean quite different from the world of divine kings (but not Euroamericans), is that the flexibility and compass of biogenetic relatedness has become the effect of rational choice-making individuals deciding who in the "objectively real" network of biogenetic kinship to "recognize" as kin. As humans, we are all "related." Yet we pick and choose from the "natural ground" of the grand kin diagram to create distinctions and differences. Race, nationality, ethnicity, family, and other identities deemed inheritable thus can in certain circumstances appear to become matters of choice and preference, at the same time that their bases appear deeply embedded in "nature."

What is uniquely "Caribbean" here is that the discourses and practices of hierarchy and equality, while seeming to derive from European ones, in fact call forth in their reiterations "Europe" and the "Caribbean." As eighteenth-century Caribbean slaves acted out European norms of sociability, and as nineteenth-century Caribbean freepeople acted out European respectability, they reiterated norms of sex and morality and in so doing constituted and empowered the referents of these norms. In a sense, then, the "Other" wrote "Europe," and not the other way around. Rather than some blending of European and African cultures, *this* creolization is a mediating technology between Europe and its colonial others that constitutes them and participates in the same logic of transition narratives that mediate continuity and change, nature and choice, and thereby stabilize them.

It should be clear from this discussion that I do not read the "nature" materialized in liberal social orders as a truly determining or stable ground. "Nature" as an effect of technologies of power, such as liberal law and transition narratives, produces the effects it names. Nor do I see liberal law as determining "nature" in the last instance. Law and nature are held together in a complex of overdeterminations and are mutually constitutive. They condense each other, the meanings they generate, and the effects they produce (see Hall 1980). Their most powerful effect is perhaps the illusion of their separateness and internal coherence. The task of this book is to chart out the processes by which they mark themselves out and preserve the fiction of their stability and determinative power.

Chapter 1

The Rise of Class, Race, and Party: Making Differences, 1890–1949

A popular version of the story of Virgin Islander men who emigrated to the Dominican Republic at the beginning of this century
has it that only the truly poor would have risked the journey and
embarked on the rickety sloops headed across the Mona Passage to
the sugarcane fields. People who tell this story associate the poverty
of the emigrants with their "country" origin, the fact that they were
"from the hills," and usually assume as a matter of course that these
men were "dark," not "light." The first people who told me this
story, on separate occasions, were a wealthy, light-skinned former
civil servant and a middle-class, dark-skinned secretary. I heard it
often. British Virgin Islanders familiar with my work, most of whom
expressed a keen interest in my research into the period of out-
migration to the Dominican Republic, were rather surprised when
a librarian and I, poking in the Government Archives, turned up a
passenger list of one of the sloops that took workers to the Dominican Republic, for this list showed that greater numbers of Anegadians made the voyage than Tortolians. Historically, Anegadians
have been anything but country bumpkins and are today among
the more successful inhabitants of the British Virgin Islands. Furthermore, census data from the early part of the twentieth century
indicate that Anegadians may have been lighter in skin tone than
Tortolians, since the census records 73 percent of Anegadians as
"colored" and 27 percent as "black," but only 19 percent of Tortolians as "colored" compared to 80 percent "black."[1]

A curious reversal, then, has occurred in the stories people tell about the period of migration to Santo Domingo, for it was actually lighter-skinned folk who went in greater numbers than the dark, and in many instances it was through their experiences abroad that these people laid the foundations for their later fortunes. This finding is counterintuitive to British Virgin Islanders today since they assume it would have been poor farmers who went to work in the cane fields, while in fact it was often fishermen who did so. Except for some exceptional cases, the distinction BVIslanders sometimes make today between "big money people" and everyone else did not predate the Santo Domingo migration, but rather grew from it. The association of light skin with money also gained credence through this migration. The cane fields of the Dominican Republic took what was a basic division in the pre–twentieth-century Virgin Islands—between fishermen and farmers—elaborated upon it, and transformed it, as fishermen increasingly emigrated and farmers stayed behind.

The out-migration to the Dominican Republic was not solely responsible for the creation of divisions among British Virgin Islanders. Throughout the early part of the twentieth century, people had been emigrating to the Panama Canal, to Puerto Rico, to Cuba, and to St. Thomas. But different groups of people took these different voyages at different times. While Anegadians and people from East End and Virgin Gorda were moving around the former Spanish possessions under U.S. control at the beginning of the century, "country" people from throughout Tortola and Jost Van Dyke did not start going to St. Thomas en masse until World War II. Migration to the former Danish West Indies—the U.S. Virgin Islands since 1917—had been a constant feature of life at least since the 1850s (O'Neal 1983:74), but this migration became truly significant for the invention of a sense of British Virgin Islander identity only with the spurt during World War II to work in U.S. munitions and defense projects on St. Thomas. For it was here that the mass of people living in the British Virgin Islands had their first experience of wage work in a cash economy and with it their first taste of labor politics and political organizing.

This chapter must be read with three other histories kept in mind—the history of U.S. imperialism and dominance in the northeastern Caribbean at the beginning of the twentieth century, the history of sugar, and the history of the Eighteenth Amendment to the United States Constitution. The former begins, for our purposes, with the U.S.-supported revolt of Cuba against Spain in 1895 and the subsequent Spanish-American War, which led to the U.S. occupation of Cuba, Puerto Rico, Guam, and the Philippines. It continues with Theodore Roosevelt's interest in Panama and the 1903 revolution that separated Panama from Colombia, facilitating completion of the Panama Canal in 1914. The story takes on a fast pace with the Wilson presidency, with the 1915 U.S. occupation of Haiti, the 1916 occupation of the Dominican Republic, and the 1917 purchase of the Danish West Indies for $7.2 million, their subsequent renaming as the United States Virgin Islands and their administration directly under the U.S. Department of the Navy. By 1917, the United States had achieved a near-total military occupation of the northeast Caribbean. U.S. shipping interests in the Canal Zone and St. Thomas, along with sugar interests in Haiti, Cuba, Puerto Rico, and the Dominican Republic, guided American policy in the region, and the perceived threat posed to "America's Mediterranean" by German submarines helped justify the continued military presence.

By the early eighteenth century, sugar, as Sidney Mintz (1985) notes, had become a staple of European and American diets (as had other "high energy food substitutes," such as tea, coffee, and chocolate, especially for working classes). Cane had been the primary source of sugar, but the rise of the central European sugar beet industry in the nineteenth century derailed somewhat the successes of plantations in the Americas. For the U.S. market, however, new possessions in the Caribbean and Pacific made continued production of cane sugar profitable. As World War I devastated the sugar beet industry in Europe, the U.S. presence in the Caribbean, and particularly in the Dominican Republic, led to a sugarcane boom there. With the end of war and the onset of the Great Depression in 1929, boom turned to bust.

Meanwhile, in the United States itself, the Eighteenth Amendment to the Constitution, prohibiting the manufacture and sale of alcoholic spirits, sparked a complicated network of bootleggers and smugglers that extended down the Caribbean. The U.S. Caribbean possessions became major production and transshipment points for this underground economy, and the British Virgin Islands were uniquely placed to take advantage of it. Situated conveniently close to St. Thomas and St. John, British Virgin Islanders found thirsty black markets for their cane juice and rum, and British Virgin Islanders with boats made profitable use of them by smuggling liquor to their neighbors. British Virgin Islander subsistence farmers, too, found a niche for their labor during Prohibition: one elderly farmer remembers seeing "the hillsides disappear to the top of the ridge" as Tortola's mountains were deforested to make charcoal so that smugglers could hide their stash in the holds of their boats under big bags of coal. As one octogenarian remembers, "it took 1,000 bags of charcoal to cover 100 bottles of scotch!"

The story about migration to the Dominican Republic is instructive because it lends insight into both the former and the present divisions British Virgin Islanders have made among themselves in terms of skin color, wealth, occupation, and life circumstances. Today, the story is more likely to be told in the context of explaining why people coming from the Dominican Republic in the 1980s and 1990s to settle in the British Virgin Islands should not be believed when they claim BVI ancestry. As one woman told me, "These people coming back are light, Spanish-looking; and our boys who went over there were dark."

People who hold these views often have them corroborated by those Dominicans who *have* successfully obtained BVI citizenship by proving their BVI "blood," for such immigrants tell tales of a Dominican Republic brimming with racism against "dark" people. One woman, born and raised in the Dominican Republic but now at "home" in the BVI, relates that "with my dark color and funny last name, both together, make it very difficult for me. When I come here, I feel very comfortable, very relaxed. There, I'm a nigger with a funny last name and both together make it difficult; here I'm a nigger with a last name people know and love!" The woman's use of the term *nigger*, rarely heard in the BVI and then only from the mouths of BVIslanders who have spent time abroad, points up the difference between the racial discourse of the Dominican Republic, where the mere fact of one's "African" or "black" ancestry is the root of one's "problems," and that of the BVI: someone considered "light" in the BVI would be deemed "dark" or "black" or

"African" in Santo Domingo. That BVIslanders and Dominicans
have distinct ways of talking about race never enters these conversations, and hence Dominicans with BVI citizenship who talk about
"Spanish" racism directed against them reinforce BVIslanders' perception that only the "dark" went over to work in the cane fields in
the first place and provide justification for those BVIslanders who
would deny rights to Dominican immigrants who "look too Spanish." The remembered history of emigration to the Dominican
Republic thus becomes one of a number of stories BVIslanders use
to distinguish themselves from other Caribbean peoples. It has
become particularly powerful now that increasing numbers of
Dominicans are coming to BVI shores. It also reveals BVIslander
beliefs about past distinctions among BVIslanders themselves: the
light-skinned were well off and did not have to emigrate; the dark-
skinned were poor and saw few other options. Yet the pattern of
emigration was exactly the opposite.

This chapter chronicles the emergence of class, race, and
political party distinctions among residents of the British Virgin
Islands during the first half of the twentieth century who would, by
the second half of the century, come to define themselves as
"British Virgin Islanders." It traces early-twentieth-century migrations to the Dominican Republic and Cuba and later migrations to
the U.S. Virgin Islands. Men who emigrated to the Hispanic
islands before World War II returned to the British Virgin Islands
to become an important merchant class. Men and women who
emigrated to St. Thomas during World War II gained cash but
remained a working class. Upon their return, they were mobilized
by members of the merchant elite in large-scale demonstrations
for local autonomy. Early conflicts among segments of the elite
and working populations, especially conflicts having to do with
relationships with the colonial apparatus, translated themselves
into political factions. Local legislative autonomy was won in 1950.
As the next chapter shows, it contributed to the decline of the
social distinctions that had emerged in the BVI before 1940 and
led to new ones.

A caveat is necessary when discussing difference in the British
Virgin Islands. I do not want to overdraw distinctions or split hairs.
After all, very few people are involved, and most today would deny
the importance of whatever past distinctions may have existed

among them. Nevertheless, certain people's trajectories bear out the following claims regarding the emergence of difference: first, the people who participated in the Santo Domingo migration of the 1910s–30s—many of whom had been fishermen and boat-builders in the BVI before migrating—"made it" economically, early on, and were in a wonderful position to become (nationalist) leaders; and second, the people who went to St. Thomas in the 1940s—many of whom had been farmers before migrating—gained from the experience a new political awareness as well as cash but could not outdistance their compatriots who had gotten a head start. In any case, the end of World War II saw most people earning a wage and thus set up the conditions for popular ideals of equality among BVIslanders. A liberal revolution could begin, and it did. The teleology of that revolution was that all people with claim to the name *BVIslander* did become equals of a sort, an equality consolidated by and demonstrated in state practices. It is no surprise, then, that for many older BVIslanders, World War II and the years immediately following it take pride of place in people's stories about their personal and the islands' political histories.

The Emergence of Distinction: Sugar, Smuggling, and Subsistence, 1900–1937

People from the British Virgin Islands engaged in frequent commerce with the sister islands of St. John, St. Thomas, and St. Croix in the Danish West Indies at least from the time of emancipation, and probably before. St. Thomas had become a nexus of trade in the Caribbean owing to its possession by the Kingdom of Denmark-Norway which, throughout the seventeenth, eighteenth, and part of the nineteenth centuries, maintained policies of neutrality during wars between other European powers. As Sheridan notes, "St. Thomas was able to conduct a lucrative neutral trade with the colonies of belligerent nations. Here was found a money market for sale of captured ships and cargoes and courts to dispose of prizes brought in by the privateers of different nations" (quoted by O'Neal [1983:75]). Harrigan and Varlack quote the president of the British Virgin Islands in 1854, who noted that frequent commerce with St. Thomas was resulting in a failure of local businesses to develop, as people living in the Presidency of the Virgin Islands had "learnt to regard St. Thomas as the market town for the sale of their produce and for the purchase of all the supplies they require[d]" (quoted in Harrigan and Varlack 1975:68; and O'Neal 1983:76). But in the latter half of the century, St. Thomas entered into a decline. A brief period of free trade among former enemy nations in Europe, as well as the German-Danish wars of 1848–50 and 1864, spelled the end for St. Thomas as the only free port in the Caribbean; a cholera epidemic in 1853–54 did not help matters; and increasing U.S. interest in its Caribbean neighbors—particularly, at first, Cuba and Panama, and later Puerto Rico and the Dominican Republic—took the wind from the sails of the St. Thomian labor and produce market. Virgin Islanders continued their steady back-and-forth trickle into and out of the Danish West Indies but also were increasingly looking farther afield for cash, work, and markets (see O'Neal 1983:76). Much of this migration was seasonal; but as O'Neal indicates, many migrants never returned: between 1850 and 1899, the population of the British Virgin Islands had declined from 5,892 to 4,607 (O'Neal 1983:78).

By the first quarter of the twentieth century, one colonial representative wrote, "the majority, I may almost say all the able bodied men, emigrate during the months of October and November to Santo Domingo where they find ready and lucrative employment at from 3£ to 6£ per day at the sugar factories, returning in July to spend the interval in recuperative ease" (quoted in O'Neal 1983:78; Harrigan and Varlack 1975:119). One elderly man remembers his father's migration in 1899 to Puerto Rico. From there, his father moved on to Cuba. In 1911, he returned to Virgin Gorda and bought some property with the cash he had earned on the sugar estates driving the centrifuge. In 1920, he went on to the Dominican Republic where, his son remembers, "things were humming." This was a pattern for many people from the Virgin Islands who emigrated to the Dominican Republic. Usually they had had some experience working in the other former Spanish colonies on sugar estates owned by American companies. There, they learned a trade. Few of the early migrants to the former Spanish possessions ended up cutting cane when they went on to the Dominican Republic. That task fell to other migrants, from St. Kitts, St. Martin, and elsewhere.

The migration experience of Virgin Islanders at the beginning of this century was not merely an occasion to earn cash and learn a trade. Emigrants from the Virgin Islands often faced difficulties. All the early documents pertaining to out-migration located in the Government Archives by Janice Nibbs Blyden, the librarian in charge of the archives during my time in the BVI, indicate great hardship and challenge. The earliest piece of evidence for migration from the Virgin Islands to the Spanish possessions comes in the form of a memo dated the thirteenth of December 1872 from the colonial secretary of the Leeward Islands, based in Antigua, to the president of the Virgin Islands. The memo informs the president of "alleged ill-treatment of certain British subjects at Culebra," an island to the east of Puerto Rico and, at the time, a Spanish colony, and indicates that "an enquiry instituted by the Spanish government into these charges" was being made (VICO 22 of 1872). Records of this inquiry, and further details of the ill treatment, do not survive. But this early document is corroborated with more recent and more complete ones, which relate continued abuses committed by Spanish colonial officials and American estate owners against their Virgin Islander workers.

In 1908, a woman from Road Town named Catherine Dawson[2] wrote the commissioner of the Virgin Islands asking for compensation in the shooting death of her relative, Henry Alfred Stephens, in the Dominican Republic. The documents that survive do not indicate whether Henry was a son, brother, or husband of Catherine. The commissioner sent her petition to the office of the colonial secretary in Antigua, who in turn contacted the British consul in Santo Domingo. The British consul contacted the Dominican minister for foreign affairs, who received a report of the shooting from the procurator fiscal of the District of San Pedro de Macoris. The consul recommended to the colonial secretary that this report of the shooting be conveyed to Catherine; the colonial secretary agreed and furthermore wrote to the commissioner that "in the circumstances, it does not appear possible to obtain compensation" (LICSO 106/1764 of 1909; in VICO 615 of 1909). The story Catherine would have heard, written by the procurator fiscal to the procurator general of the Court of Appeal of the Ministry of Foreign Affairs in Santo Domingo, was as follows (translated by the British consul):[3]

In pursuance of an order of this Department, by despatch
No.475 under date of the 4th instant, I transmit to you
extracted from the papers bearing on the case, the date relative to the death of the British subject Henry.

On the 7th day of October four of the guards serving here
were detailed to proceed to a place known as 'Ortiz', a plantation in this jurisdiction, in order that they might, together
with the Justice of the Peace, and the guide Julio Guzman,
carry out the capture of a criminal named Ubaldo Canar who
was hiding somewhere about that locality.

During the first night, while passing along a path which
skirts a cattle ranch belonging to Senor Gregorio Velasques,
the patrol entered and knocked at a small hut standing there,
in order to ascertain if there was any one who could give them
information; without obtaining any reply they noted that
there was a light within, and thereupon the Magistrate
ordered that those within should answer, but without obtaining any notice the light was extinguished, and the patrol sus-
pecting that there must be some criminal sheltering there,
guarded the doors and intimated in the name of the law that
they should open—those within however maintained perfect
silence and tried to open a door which they thought was not
guarded, and, simultaneously two shots resounded close to
the guard, and a man came out followed by another; the
guard returned fire but the men passed, and after a few paces
the foremost man turned round and faced them exclaiming "I
am Ubaldo," and firing his revolver, shots which were
returned by the guards, which took effect on his companion,
who fell dead.

Up to the moment of the firing, the neighbors, among
whom were British subjects, Portoriquenos, and Dominicnans
[*sic*] distinctly heard the intimation of the guards to open the
door, and there are those who recognized that the first two
shots were fired from a revolver.

The patrol believed that they had killed a criminal and companion of Ubaldo, until, summoned by the Magistrate, the
arrival of the neighbors, labourers and foremen of the estate,
who identified Henry, and explained that certainly silence
must have been imposed on him when the patrol ordered

them to open and that intimated at the resistance to open, and by the shots fired by his guest he fled with him.

These are the more salient facts which I can furnish to you relative to the death of Henry.

Another case was brought before the commissioner in 1909. No records survive except for the initial petition, made by two Anegadians, Benjamin White and Joseph Potter (VICO 286 of 1909), and a letter dated 1910 from the commissioner to the parents informing them of his intention to send their petition on to the secretary of state for the colonies for assistance (VICO 583 of 1910). White and Potter's letter was written on September 30, 1909.

Sir,

We the undersigned Parents of the foregoing persons, (Viz), Joseph Nathan Potter . Age 25 . and, Hetty-Linda White . Age 28 . natives of the British Virgin Island of Anegada, do hereby request your Honour to place this our Joint Petition before His Excellency the Acting Governor in chief of the Leeward Islands that he may Exercise those functions in him vested with the proper authorities in this our grievance, in the protection of our Son and Daughter, His Majesty Loyal British Subjects, who is held at present, unlawfully, in the prison, in San Predo [*sic*] de Macoris—Santo Domingo, under false Suspicion, a charge of attempting to shoot, or wound, (one) William Gowry, Administrator, Cristobal Colon Estate, San Pedro de Macoris, as parents we have made all necessary enquiries in this matter and both persons are entirely innocent, as they were many miles away from the Estate where the out-rage was committed. We further state for your Excellency information that the said William Gowry is a tyrant manager, and all the semi-savage natives are against him (Hence the out-rage) and the Virgin Islands people who are compelled to immigrate are invited by the American Estate owners on this Island as they find them to by hard-working, honest, and quiet people, the natives being lazy, rebellious, and of savage nature. And it is very unfair, for the Dominican Government, to take an advantage of His Majesty's civilise people, for the barbarous acts, and deeds of their own savage tribe, on the slightest imaginary suspicion without any grounds whatever. The people of the Virgin Islands are known by their own Government to be entirely free from such cruel deeds. We therefore request your Excellency, to investigate this our grievance and have these poor innocent British subjects release and demand an indemnity, for their false imprisonment and cruel treatment for over three months. We know that His Majesty's Government will not allow the meanest of his subjects, to suffer innocently without just reward.

> We have the honour
> To be Sir Your Obedient
> Servants,
>
> Benjamin White
> Joseph Potter

It is difficult to know for certain the author of this letter, but people I showed it to had little problem accepting it as written by its signatories with only a little help from a clerk, and probably a native Virgin Islander one at that. Hence, it is fair to assume that the sentiments expressed in the letter about the peaceableness of Virgin Islanders and savagery of Dominicans captures something of popular opinion in the British Virgin Islands at the time. Today, vox populi attributes the "laziness" of the Dominicans for the "need" to emigrate and "help out" at the cane fields. British Virgin Islanders who employ Dominican immigrants today complain that they always want to "dance and party," and not to work. One employer told me it reminded him of the "old days," when "our boys" had to make the journey to Santo Domingo in order to "get the job done."

Other sources relate that Virgin Islander and other British West Indian immigrants to the Dominican Republic made much of their status as British subjects, "leaving on record," according to one historian, "a supposed arrogance, aggressiveness, and some conceit as a member of the British Empire" (Bryan 1985:245). A commentator during the 1930s wrote that in Central America, "the big problem is the Jamaican Negro, proud of being a British subject. When the latter, with his 'cocky' attitude, is placed under the eye of a white boss from the south of the Mason and Dixon line, trouble is bound to ensue" (quoted by Bryan [1985:245]). One British colonial representative was concerned about the effect of this situation on the reputation of the motherland and complained in 1914 that "in the minds of the great mass of Dominicans an Englishman is a native of the British West Indies, while British subjects [*sic*, meaning British whites] are popularly classed as Americans, and British prestige suffers as a result" (quoted by Bryan [1985:240]). A memo in the Virgin Islands Government Archives dated 1912 comments on the "problems which will arise in connection with the return to the West Indian colonies of the labourers now employed in the Panama Canal Zone" (VICO 345 of 1912); we can speculate that these problems not only involved a mass return of migrants, but the uneasiness on the part of British colonial officials with a return of people for whom status as British subjects would have taken on an enormous importance to self-identity during their time abroad. What rights as British subjects might they now demand?

In spite of hardship, Virgin Islanders continued to embark for Santo Domingo. In his letter to the colonial secretary in Antigua on the subject of the 1911 Census of the Virgin Islands, T. L. H. Jarvis, the commissioner, explained an overall increase in the population since 1901 attributable solely to a rise on Tortola. He felt it necessary to point out that "it is roughly estimated that at least 200 men were absent from Anegada, and another 200 from Tortola and the other islands on the date of the census, owing to the annual migration of labourers to Santo Domingo and Cuba for employment in the sugar factories." Sex ratios from the census figures suggest that a greater proportion of men from Anegada ($m/f = .59$) emigrated than from any other island, followed by Virgin Gorda (.79), Tortola (.92), and Jost Van Dyke (1.1). Recall that people on Anegada were not being regarded as "black" but as "colored": the census reported 2.7 "colored" persons for every 1 "black" on Anegada, compared to .23 "coloreds" to 1 "black" for Tortola, .41 to 1 for Jost Van Dyke, and .74 to 1 for Virgin Gorda.

In the 1910s, the colonial regime began to express concern about the large number of emigrants, their treatment, the problems they faced in moving across international boundaries—usually without any kind of papers and only their skin color to mark them as subjects of the British Empire—and the cost to colonial coffers in the event emigrants had to be repatriated, not to mention the cost to local agriculture as it "languished" in the hands of women (who, of course, were not farmers to colonial officials, but "wives of farmers"). In 1915, the colonial secretary of the Leeward Islands issued an order to establish a system of passports for people leaving the Colony of the Leeward Islands. Passports were specifically intended to give Leeward Islanders on visits to England easy passage back into the colony, for the Colonial Office was concerned that non-British subjects might slip into England by way of the British Caribbean and wanted a means of sorting out "their blacks" from "other blacks." Few emigrants to the Dominican Republic bothered to obtain them, but the passports were deemed important by the colonial government and were a first step toward maintaining the "integrity" of the colony (see VICO 421 of 1915).

In 1916, the Commissioner's Office of the Virgin Islands made its first official statement on the out-migration to the Dominican Republic. The colonial secretary in Antigua had received a letter from the British chargé d'affairs in Santo Domingo, asking for information on how to obtain laborers from the colony for an English manager of an American-owned sugar estate. The colonial secretary forwarded this request to the acting commissioner, whose response was frigid: "I beg to state that I am personally not in favour of encouraging labourers to go to Santo-Domingo from this Presidency. A number go to work on the sugar estates there every year who would be as well employed on their own lands at home." He added, "It would be well to let people know of the conditions of labour in towns in S. Domingo and to advise emigrants to carry passports" (VICO 362 of 1916).

The Commissioner's Office also heard concerns about the safety of vessels bound for Santo Domingo and Cuba. The administrator on Dominica on one occasion had written the colonial secretary in Antigua asking whether ships bound for Cuba departed from Tortola and, if so, whether the colonial secretary would convey to the commissioner of the Virgin Islands his worry that these ships were taking on too many passengers. The commissioner responded that, in fact, all such ships left from St. Thomas. He did suggest instituting safety regulations for ships carrying laborers. At first, the regulations permitted only one passenger for every ton of ship. These rules were changed in 1924 so that one passenger would be allowed for every eighteen feet of ship (VICO 198 of 1924).[4]

Tales of easy money and good work in Cuba and Santo Domingo must have spread rapidly throughout the Leewards in spite of the colonial administration's efforts to discourage migration. A boatload of people from Dominica going to Cuba stopped in the Virgin Islands in 1925. Twenty of the laborers on board, six carpenters and fourteen unskilled workers, had been promised to the Public Works Department on Tortola to assist in construction of new government buildings. Upon arrival, however, all twenty laborers signed a written request that they be allowed to continue on to Cuba instead. The commissioner contacted the officer in charge of the Northern District (Portsmouth) on Dominica, whence the workers had come, asking his advice, while the workers remained on their sloop, the *Roma*. The reply came: the officer gave his consent to the commissioner to "compel them to remain in Tortola." But the commissioner did not take the officer's suggestion. Instead, as he explained in a letter to the officer, "other suitable men were found in the 'Roma' and landed here to work under the Public Works Department" (VICO 215 of 1924).

Disaster hit the BVI in 1926, when the schooner *The Fancy Me*, en route to the Dominican Republic, went down during a storm. Forty-nine men were lost at sea. The mourning of the *Fancy Me* tragedy represented the first time since emancipation that the various communities of the British Virgin Islands shared a common experience. One elderly man recalls that it took quite some time for the news to reach the BVI, and even when it did, people weren't sure who had died and who had survived. He remembers, "everybody crying, it was a cry *all* around; most of the people from around here [Cane Garden Bay] were drowned; all you heard was the crying, crying, crying." In addition to bringing together British Virgin Islanders as a group unto themselves, the loss of the *Fancy Me* served to discourage others from making the journey and further dampened emigration during the late 1920s. The same man remembered how, as a boy of eleven years, he had dreamt of going to Santo Domingo. But, "from the time [the *Fancy Me* disaster] happened, I forget my desire—canceled that! Didn't think of that again."

Official discouragement of emigration continued. In 1928,

Edelberto Rodriguez, a representative of the Cuban Chappara Sugar Company, came to Antigua looking for laborers—and not "semi-clandestinely," as he admitted to having done in the past. Rather, he asked permission to visit the various presidencies. The colonial secretary in Antigua informed each presidency that "Rodriguez should be discouraged from visiting the Leeward Islands as there is a shortage of labour for local industries due to hurricane conditions" (VICO 259 of 1928).[5]

The difficulties for Virgin Islanders abroad come out vividly in another document surviving this period. Samuel James Parsons related his suffering to the commissioner in a 1929 letter:

Sir,

I Samuel James Parsons of New Bush Tortola born 11th June 1904, myself and James Hills of the same Tortola V.I. on the 26 Feb. 1929 as pardeners working on a small lanch [launch] so call a Litta taking sugar from Estate Consuelo to a steamer in Santo Domingo Harbour; After delivering the sugar to the steamer was trying to defend her from been smash against the steamer the waves been high was brought up to the steamer stern catch my left arm between the steamer and Litta and was awfully damage there. I taking to the Hospital where it was taken off, remaining 13 days in the Hospital which was 10th March 1929 was dispatch to same Consuela Estate on 11th March 1929. I went to the Managers Mr. Warmoth and Mr. Kilbourn asking my support after been damage on the company job. Their reply was they will give me work as to do with my one arm. I would not agree to their offer as I told them I would like to come home. . . . I went to the English Council Mr. Beer on 12th March 1929 telling him my accident and asking his aid to my trouble [;] his reply was he will see the managers that they will give me some aid; I await for eight days after receiving no foreward reply I return to him a second time which was 20th March 1929 [;] his reply was of the same as first. Therefore I troube [*sic*] him nor them no more, remaining there with the help of my brother and what I had before I got damage until the 17th of June 1929 I leave Santo Domingo.

Sir here I forward my application to your services this 2nd day July 1929 as to my honour,

Samuel James Parsons

The commissioner consulted with the Reverend A. H. Beer, the vice consul in the Dominican Republic stationed in San Pedro de Macoris. Beer informed him that Parsons's hospital expenses had been paid by the company. He had been offered a "light" job as a watchman at a railroad crossing for one dollar a day, which he refused, and so he was returned home at the company's expense. The commissioner could offer Parsons nothing more in compensation.

But because of cases such as Parsons's, colonial officials became more and more concerned with the status of their subjects in the Dominican Republic. Working conditions had not been good during the period of United States occupation (1916–24), but with the U.S. withdrawal and the rise to power of Rafael Trujillo, they got worse for British West Indian laborers. Throughout the 1910s, Dominican officials had attempted to limit the numbers of *cocolos*,[6] or dark-skinned West Indians, entering their "Spanish" country (see Bryan 1985). But the Dominican government was unable to prevent American estate owners from making their own arrangements to acquire labor, especially given their backing by the U.S. occupation force. Still, British officials became more and more concerned for the safety of their West Indian subjects in the Dominican Republic. Meanwhile, the end of World War I meant the end of the sugarcane boom worldwide, as beet production in the temperate regions of the world came back to prewar levels.

In 1929, the colonial secretary put into place the "Emigrants Protection Act (Leeward Islands)." It provided for an account to be set up on the federal level that would be used in case British subjects of the colony needed to be repatriated.[7] The act was extended to emigrants to Cuba, Curaçao, and the Dominican Republic. As a result of the act, the Virgin Islands Commissioner's Office drew up a list of emigrants for whom a deposit of one pound five shillings was to be made. This list was the first serious attempt to keep track of the movement of people into and out of the Presidency of the Virgin Islands and the Leeward Islands Colony to destinations other than the metropolis. It is notable that movements *within* the colony, from presidency to presidency, went for the most part unremarked until the late 1940s and early 1950s (as discussed in the next chapter). At this point in its history, the

Leeward Islands Colony began acting almost as if it were a "modern" state with its "own" population of subjects.

But for those subjects, the changes in policy were hardly felt. No one I spoke with remembers ever benefiting from the Emigrants Protection Act. Several people joked about claiming their "one pound five" and all the interest that should have accrued. As for passports, a document from 1939 shows that only 171 of them had been issued out and paid for (the charge was one pound) between 1936 and 1939 for *all* of the British Caribbean: the Leeward Islands, the Windward Islands, Jamaica, Barbados, Guyana, and Trinidad and Tobago (VICO 3133 of 1939).

By the mid-1930s, however, emigration to the Dominican Republic had become less of an issue for islanders and the colonial regime alike. Fewer and fewer made the journey; those who did found that they were increasingly unwelcome. The sugarcane boom had ended, the depression of 1929–33 hurt international trade generally, and in the Dominican Republic, Trujillo's campaigns to "Dominicanize" the workforce made dark skin a liability. In 1932, Trujillo called for a halt to all immigration from the West Indies. In 1934, the United States withdrew from Haiti. Also in 1934, the last ship of British Virgin Islanders to go to the Dominican Republic returned home.[8] And in 1937, Trujillo ordered the massacre of ten thousand to twenty thousand Haitian men, women, and children living and working in the Dominican Republic in his effort to "Dominicanize" the country and make it less "black" (Ferguson 1992:83). Meanwhile, oil was discovered in the Dutch West Indian colonies of Curaçao and Aruba, and the oil fields drew West Indians away from the cane fields. Few Virgin Islanders, however, made the trek so far south.[9]

Another boom had ended for Virgin Islanders as well, this time for the farmers who had remained behind when their fishing and boating compatriots had labored in the Dominican cane fields. In 1933, the Eighteenth Amendment to the U.S. Constitution was repealed and Prohibition in the United States came to an end. The years of Prohibition brought prosperity to some Virgin Islanders—particularly those fishermen with boats from Jost Van Dyke, Anegada, Virgin Gorda, and East End, Tortola. Smuggling had a long history in the Virgin Islands, and both documents and memories suggest that these communities were at the center of it. Names that turn up in records relating to smuggling cases include O'Neal (Virgin Gorda), Penn (East End), Faulkner (Anegada), Callwood (Jost Van Dyke), and Flax (Virgin Gorda). A contemporary Virgin Islander will note that these names are those of some of today's more successful families. Indeed, H. R. Penn, who served as a member of the first Legislative Council and who had had a long political career, begins his memoirs by relating how his first big break came when he worked in David Fonseca's liquor shop and helped run a small smuggling operation. They packed bottles in crocus rice bags and covered them with charcoal before loading them on small boats. These small boats would meet up with larger vessels from St. Thomas or Puerto Rico (Penn 1990:14).

Prohibition did not benefit just boat owners and the few merchants who had established themselves in the British Virgin Islands. J. R. O'Neal, a local statesman and historian, remarked to me that while "Prohibition made a few here fairly well-off compared to their fellow citizens," it also provided a huge market for charcoal and thus was a boon to subsistence farmers. "Smugglers came," O'Neal remembers, "*ostensibly,* to buy charcoal." At first, the boats used in this trade were open canoelike vessels, called *cobles.* They had to be filled to the top with coal in order to cover the liquor, and the loading work was slow, tedious, and unhealthy. When shipwrights started to put decks on their boats in the mid-1920s, O'Neal recalls, "it went like wildfire." The only problem was that the decks trapped the charcoal dust inside the sloop, so "you'd get dust in your lungs when you'd unload." O'Neal cites the end of Prohibition as the end of the first period of real stability for the islands. After the Dominican migrations and Prohibition, "there was no employment anymore." But this environmentalist and founder of the BVI National Parks Trust added to me, with a grin, that the end of Prohibition and of the mad rush for charcoal "saved what was left of the forest!"

Men's memories of their time in the Dominican Republic speak to the divisions that were emerging among people from the Virgin Islands at the time. One from Virgin Gorda remembers that the foremen on the sugar plantations were always Anegadians, as were the shop stewards. They were in charge of the centrifuge, they often took sugar down to the docks, and they even recruited new laborers for the estate managers. This same man remembers that these Anegadians were "lighter men, and strong, well-built fellows." "Men from North Sound [Virgin Gorda] were big, strapping fellows, so they always got a place" when scouts went out recruiting. Furthermore, he claims, "no Anegadian or Virgin Gordian ever cut cane." This was a job left to the Anguillians, Kittitians and others "who had a tradition of cane cutting." Some of these were Tortolians, especially from Cane Garden Bay and Ballast Bay, where elderly people today remember that "all the hillsides were nothing but cane—sugarcane, sugarcane, sugarcane, sugarcane!"

Another elderly man from Anegada recalls, "Anegadians . . . were not the cutters of cane but worked in the factories." He remembers that, during the *Fancy Me* disaster, the heaviest losses were of Tortolians and that this was a real blow to Tortola's migrating population; some were lost, and many thenceforth refused to go. He recalls living just off the Romana estate in the Dominican Republic in the 1920s when he was ten years old. He lived with his father's sister in a "town abutting and adjoining" the estate—he repeatedly noted that he lived in "town," and not "on the estate" itself. He continued, "I never even saw the area where the canes were 'til I was a big boy; it was around 1930, so four years I had been there before I saw canes!" He remarked that "the smart people" who went to the Dominican Republic were "the people who returned at the end of the crop with cash and did something useful with it—they built houses, and boats of their own, and would start trading between here and St. Thomas," purchasing agricultural goods from farmers and carrying them across the channel to the St. Thomas market. Others, however, were not so smart, he recalled: "Those who remained [in the Dominican Republic during the off-season] in the great majority did not do well. Everything was tied to the site of production. In the crop season, there was work and money. In the dull season—no work, no money. Estates gave credit: those people who were regular employees of the estate could obtain credit to help them through the dull season, and it would be deducted from their wages. There was a six-month cycle of production, a six-month work season." In other words, for half of the year or more, people who stayed on the estates lived off credit and were effectively bound to the estate during the next season working off their debts. He remembers, further, that factory workers who remained during the off-season had a worse time of it than field workers, for the sugar factories were idle during the off-season for the full six months, while "there would always be some little thing to do in the fields."

There was less of an incentive, or an option, to leave during the off-season if one were a cane cutter than if one were a factory worker. Since Anegadians were factory workers, they would have tended to leave while the Kittitians, Anguillians, and Tortolians cutting cane might stay. Anegadian factory workers and foremen therefore would not have accumulated as much debt as other West Indians. On the contrary: the late Henry O. Creque, an important BVI statesman with roots in Anegada, told me in a 1993 interview that "those who came home brought what they saved—the family kept up the subsistence crop and cattle while they were away—so many didn't even have to spend what they saved! So they could with small sums invest it in something and increase their capital, providing for themselves an economic base whereby they could live without working for anybody else. If they could buy a couple of boats, and a good seine, they could go to St. Thomas and sell their fish, for instance."

The Trujillo regime brought an end to Virgin Island migration. Those last years in the Dominican Republic, Creque related, were difficult times: "He had the army behind him. During the depression years the American sugar estates' administrators—the managers were called 'administrators'—were each of them a power in Santo Domingo and also had the favor of the authorities. American inspectors were at customs in La Romana and San Pedro de Macoris. It was commonly said, too, that customs duties were securities to loans. Trujillo was a dictator; civil liberties were denied. But in spite of this Trujillo did a good deal of good for his country as a whole—he built schools, roads, bridges, and so on, and there was a minimum of crime. You could walk any time without fear. But don't call his name! Almost certainly that would get you put in jail! Armed soldiers performed police duties; if there was a group of people in the street and one of them say 'Trujillo,' they'd lock them all up!"

The years between World War I and Prohibition had been lean ones for Virgin Islander farmers. The war had increased the demand for food in the U.S. possessions, and the BVI had more than adequate surpluses of yams, other produce, and especially cows. Off and on during the first quarter of the century, however, colonial officials bemoaned the sorry state of agriculture in the islands. Various agricultural experiments with onions and tobacco failed; cotton failed; coconuts failed with the hurricanes of 1916 and 1924. Only the war and Prohibition provided good returns on agricultural labor. The people who benefited the most were the traders of produce to St. Thomas: men with boats who took advantage of women's agricultural labor and the labor of "country" men without boats. J. R. O'Neal remembers a sea captain named Pickering who used to boast during those years that he'd never needed to go all the way to Santo Domingo to make his fortune—he'd done just fine shuttling produce to St. Thomas.

Those men who did go to Santo Domingo left their wives and siblings to tend the land and livestock. People who stayed did not starve, and those who emigrated brought cash back and kept living standards higher than they otherwise might have been. People also found clever ways to avoid paying customs duties on the cattle and produce they took to sell in St. Thomas and the manufactured wares they brought back. Virgin Gordians coming back from St. Thomas might stop off at Cooper Island or Salt Island and unload their goods there. O'Neal recalls that "people would say bulls were bullocks to avoid a higher export tax" and that "it took an honest man from Jost Van Dyke to stop at West End, passing by his home, to pay duties, and go back."[10]

Those who remained on the Dominican estates became bound to their creditors, and those who never left the Virgin Islands in the first place were subject to more colonial administration than those who were able to escape, if only for a time, the disciplining processes of the state. As already noted, the history of colonial administration for this time period (1900–1937) is a drawn-out tale of attempts and failures at spurring on agricultural production through various experimental programs (see Harrigan and Varlack 1975:115–25). Most of these stemmed from the patronizing spirit of the administrators, who grew frustrated with the failure of "the natives" to accept "innovations" and modern techniques. According to one, "there are no white planters here for the negroes to imitate; the negro agriculturist lives a secluded, isolated life in a place almost out of this world . . . and is loathe to abandon black sugar and rum" (117). The mission of the colonial administration became, therefore, to "educate" (117). Failures were continually attributed to the almost natural propensities and attitudes of the islanders; and, for colonial administrators, every island had its own "type." The Agriculture Department attempted to introduce sisal to Anegada but concluded that "local conditions, the habit of emigration and the character of the Anegadians" would result in failure. Similarly, "the Jost Van Dykes people are renowned smugglers and breakers of the Revenue Laws, and it is no use mincing matters when they are caught" (119).

A pattern of differentiation among island communities was becoming well established by the beginning of World War II. Emigration helped solidify a group of wage earners who were better off and better connected to the outside world than the group of farmers who remained home, who tended to be women and Tortolians of both sexes. Members of the nonmigrating population, essentially subsistence farmers with occasional ties to St. Thomas markets, were subject to the state's efforts to "educate" them. And the state, for its part, began to take note of, even as it wrote into existence, differences between island communities. The only real effort to bring emigrants into the purview of colonial administration was the introduction of passports (which emigrants ignored) and the Emigrants Protection Act (which little served them).

World War II: The Making of a Nationalist "Bourgeoisie" and a Politically Conscious "Proletariat"

The last group of Virgin Islanders to emigrate to the Dominican Republic had returned home in 1934. Prohibition had ended. The United States had withdrawn from the Dominican Republic in 1924, leaving Trujillo in power, and had left Haiti in 1934. The United States Virgin Islands were placed under the authority of the U.S. Department of the Interior. It seemed that U.S. interest in the region was dwindling and, with it, opportunities for Virgin Islanders seeking wage work.

World War II brought a tremendous and lightning-quick change. The United States abandoned its position of neutrality in 1941; German U-boats had early successes off the American coast during 1942. In that same year, in an effort to strengthen its position in the U-boat war, the United States began the construction and operation of several military facilities in St. Thomas: an airfield, a submarine base, and a munitions factory. These had to be speedily built and brought on-line, and St. Thomas alone did not have the labor resources. People from the British Virgin Islands, mostly Tortola, left for the U.S. Virgin Islands (USVI) en masse. As Harrigan and Varlack report (1975:127), "upwards of 50 percent of the working population entered St. Thomas," both legally and illegally. Demand for produce also increased in the USVI. Mass emigration to St. Thomas left few to work the land. One woman remembers that "the land was abandoned." Another recalls that "*all* between sixteen and sixty—men, women, children—went to St. Thomas." But for those who did remain in the BVI to grow produce, the high demand in St. Thomas made the fruits of their labor all the more profitable: "The value of exports was higher than in any preceding year since 1820" (Harrigan and Varlack 1975:127).

People who had done well during the preceding years in trading and fishing handsomely increased their returns because of the increase in food prices. This situation led to no small degree of resentment among those who had remained on the land during the 1910s and 1920s instead of migrating to the Dominican Republic and who had not prospered. The military operations in St. Thomas meant wage work for the first time for many of these people. It also meant a new consciousness of class. One woman from the "country" remembers her mother thinking that "some people during the war had it easy while everyone else suffered." "We had to go to St. Thomas to work; them others sat here and made money."

Norwell Harrigan argues (Harrigan and Varlack 1975:153–58; Harrigan 1990, part 3) that the military factory experience of great numbers of previously subsistence-oriented British Virgin Islanders helped bring about the beginnings of a British Virgin Islander political awakening. In the factories and the construction sites, British Virgin Islander workers came into contact with their American cousins who, since 1936, had had a civil government with limited self-representation. There, the first elections with full suffrage had occurred in 1938, while no such event had as yet taken place in the neighboring BVI. The 1938 elections, meanwhile, reflected a change in USVI leadership, from old landed officials to new "heroes of the people"—"the union leader, the newspaper editor, the college-educated youth, the smaller businessman" (G. Lewis 1972:112). The USVI Progressive Guide, the first political group, was formed in 1937, and later transformed into the United Party, an organization with strong labor roots and commitments, which managed to push through labor legislation (Workmen Compensation and Wages and Hours Acts) during the War (G. Lewis 1972:112).

The late 1930s and the decade of the 1940s were times of labor and political organizing throughout the Caribbean. Sir Arthur Lewis's pamphlet, "Labour in the West Indies," was published by the Fabian Society in 1939. Nationalist movements in Puerto Rico, Trinidad, and Jamaica during this time had a strong trade unionist component. General strikes and demonstrations occurred throughout the region. In the British Virgin Islands, civic-minded BVIslanders who had achieved rather impressive economic stature in the territory after the Santo Domingo migrations and Prohibition put together the Civic League, devoted to furthering the political and economic development of the territory. The founding members were David Fonseca, H. R. Penn (who had worked under Fonseca during Prohibition and moved from East End to Road Town), C. W. Georges, and J. R. O'Neal (both businessmen and importers who came to be based in Road Town), and Hope Stevens. The latter was a Tortolian who had emigrated to the United States and become a lawyer. Upon his return in 1938, he and his friends put together a petition calling for the reinstatement of a representative Legislative Council. They gained support from the Pro-Legislative Committee, a group that had formed in New York City under the auspices of a Virgin Islander immigrant organization called the British Virgin Islands Benevolent Society.

The Virgin Islanders living in New York were an important force in helping Virgin Islanders back home organize themselves for political ends. New York during the 1920s had been the fulcrum of the Harlem Renaissance, and many Caribbean nationalist leaders who were exiled in the 1920s gained followings among New York City's new African-American and Caribbean immigrants (see Marable 1987:17–18; Wintz 1988). The BVIslanders in New

York were mostly from Anegada, and many of them had made their way to the city via the United States's Caribbean outposts, especially Puerto Rico, Cuba, and Culebra. In New York, they developed political sophistication and gained experience in political organizing.

World War II saw another attempt to build a mass movement, on the heels of an agreement between the United States and the United Kingdom to form the Anglo-American Caribbean Commission to coordinate military activities in the region. H. R. Penn, David Fonseca, H. A. Abbott, and R. L. de Castro formed a group called the Virgin Islands Welfare Committee and drafted a petition listing their grievances against the colonial government, which they presented to the commission when it met in St. Thomas in 1942. They collected eight hundred signatures—at public meetings watched over by the police—and proposed political unification of the U.S. and British Virgin Islands under U.S. sovereignty "if other ways and means of effecting a satisfactory solution of the interrelated economic, social and political problems of the Virgin Group be found impracticable or impossible" (quoted in Harrigan and Varlack 1975:155).

A political movement was beginning to take shape. A series of small incidents demonstrated public dissatisfaction with the colonial regime, and especially the British Virgin Islands commissioner, D. P. "Papa" Wailling.[11] Wailling today is remembered as a despot. An elderly man from Fat Hog's Bay related the following story:

> The British Virgin Islands in my day were governed by one man called the Commissioner. That man were the Chief Medical Officer, he were the Attorney General, and he were *everything—and* he were Magistrate! When he tell you you're dead, you're dead, whether you're living. You just have to accept that you're dead! You ain't nobody to say anything.
>
> I can remember right down the street here, had a old man had a big cow. And that cow was lawless and she would run right over the man on the beach, and that day he was successful in getting her catch down by a big almond tree down there, and he haul up that cow, and he was beating the cow and talking to the cow as if he talking to human.

And there the Police, the Commissioner, the Doctor, and Everything was riding around at the same time, on his horse, on horseback. And he stopped his horse and he said, "YOU KNOW WHAT YOU DOING? COME HERE!!" And he called that man to him and he stand up in his stirrup and he said "DON'T DO THAT!!!" and he had him well-flogged and he said, "Go and loose the cow," and he couldn't move [he was so bruised]! Then he took loose the cow and carry it right back. Things like those, there, you do that beating, you'd be before the High Court in the British Virgin Islands today.

Wailling truly inspired fear. Civil servants who signed the Welfare Committee petition lost their jobs; police surveillance of public meetings became routine (Harrigan and Varlack 1975:158). Partly for this reason, action on the future political status of the British Virgin Islands took the form of debate in the USVI press, mainly the St. Thomas *Daily News,* founded in 1936 by USVI college graduates who had returned from the U.S. mainland. W. S. G. Barnes was appointed acting commissioner of the BVI from 1943 to 1945 and was succeeded by J. A. C. Cruikshank, a man who developed a reputation for incompetence rather than violence but who, like Wailling, could not hold the respect of the people.

In 1945, labor leaders and trade unionists from throughout the Caribbean inaugurated the first Caribbean Labour Congress in Barbados. No British Virgin Islanders attended this congress. One noteworthy Virgin Islander, however, did attend the second Caribbean Labour Congress, held in Jamaica in 1947. I. G. Fonseca, the son of David Fonseca, traveled to Jamaica, where he also unexpectedly got his first taste of popular protest. Immediately following the congress, he remembers, participants staged a nonviolent demonstration in favor of West Indian federation. Also in 1947, H. R. Penn (who was to become Fonseca's political rival), representing a more conservative slant on the emerging BVI political scene, attended the Closer Union Conference in St. Kitts to discuss federating the Windward and Leeward Island Colonies. There, he put forth a resolution calling for the reinstatement of a Legislative Council in the BVI. It passed unanimously. Upon his return to the BVI, however, Penn found Commissioner Cruikshank not too keen on the proposal. So, Penn asked Fonseca to call a public meeting in the Anglican Schoolroom, to inform all interested of the resolution and the commissioner's response (see Penn 1990:24–25). But the struggle found voice, as before, through the USVI media. A 1949 St. Thomas *Daily News* editorial read:

> A rumbling sound is coming out of the British Virgin Islands which may soon attract the attention of No.10 Downing Street. Having tasted freedom and the pursuit of happiness served the American way [during World War II], the younger inhabitants of Tortola are clamoring for a liberal form of government which gives them voice in their own affairs. (Quoted in Harrigan and Varlack 1975:158)

It is important to point out that the emerging leadership of the British Virgin Islands grew from the class of people for whom the period of out-migration and Prohibition had been a real boon. These men were for the most part lighter-skinned merchants and traders with family ties in Anegada, Virgin Gorda, East End, and Road Town.[12] Fitzpatrick (1980:11–12) reminds us that the international crisis of capital during the interwar period and carrying over into World War II led to a decline in metropolitan interest in the colonies: for the metropolis, this was a period of consolidation and retrenchment. The vacuum created by white flight to the metropolis and the subsequent indigenization of colonial state bureaucracies created space for the rise of a quasi-nationalist bourgeoisie to emerge in the colonies. This was precisely the development in the British Virgin Islands, but with an interesting twist: whereas nationalist bourgeoisies in other parts of the colonial world could mobilize a mass of disenfranchised laborers under them in staging substantial popular protests (e.g., in Trinidad and India), in the BVI a bourgeoisie was coming into being without a proletariat in tow: the wage workers, for all practical purposes, were abroad, working in the military projects in St. Thomas.

The fact that the working class was abroad, in St. Thomas, provides an explanation for the increasing importance of the St. Thomas press in the late 1940s in expressing the BVI bourgeois's positions on political self-determination. "Leaders" at home in the BVI had no one to lead; but they could find voice through their professionalized comrades in the USVI media, who provided the mass of BVI laborers with news and information on affairs across the channel. I. G. Fonseca, especially, was well positioned in relation to the mass media, as the owner of the only radio repair and phonograph shop on the British side of the Virgin Islands, Fonseca's Radio and Record Centre in Road Town, a store he took over from his father at about this time. This position gave him contacts among the young progressives in the St. Thomas media, who supplied him with both popular music recordings and political savvy. It also gave him insight into the workings of the communications and wire services. Elites' media expertise became quite significant with the slowdown of military operations in the late 1940s after the end of World War II, when those British Virgin Islanders who had left as subsistence farmers and had become, after their own fashion, "proletarians," came home.

"Freedom": A Liberal Revolution?

"Things came to a head in a curious manner," write Harrigan and Varlack (1975:157) in the introduction to their account of the first (and only) major "nationalist" popular uprising in British Virgin Islands history. The story they tell has become legendary in the BVI and runs as follows. T. H. Faulkner, an Anegadian fisherman, came to Road Town with his pregnant wife. H. R. Penn relates, "He was a drinking man, and began talking to the people by night in the old market square . . . telling them how Anegada was neglected and how Dr. Joseph, the only doctor here at the time, had not visited that island for several months, thus forcing him, a poor fisherman, to have to charter a seaplane to bring his wife to the hospital" (Penn 1990:25). Harrigan and Varlack pick up the tale: "He lambasted the government night after night. Others who had been waiting for this 'psychological moment,' or who had noted that he was not arrested"—a common fear that prevented people from speaking out against the government—"came forward" and added their voices. "There was now no stopping a movement which gripped the imagination of the vast majority of the natives, and had the solid backing of Virgin Islanders in the American islands and in the United States" (Harrigan and Varlack 1975:157).

I. G. Fonseca and Carlton de Castro took Faulkner's spark

and harnessed it, calling for a wide-scale demonstration demanding that the Crown remove Commissioner Cruikshank from power. Fonseca's experience in Jamaica and with the St. Thomas media made for a well-planned and well-executed event. De Castro went all over the islands—from Jost Van Dyke to Virgin Gorda—holding meetings and drumming up support. Faulkner pulled together people from Anegada. And Fonseca, from his base in Road Town, contacted his friends in the St. Thomas press and convinced them to come to Tortola in preparation for the big event. He related to me:

> I organized the newspaper people to get here, you know. And I told them all about this demonstration and so; and I chartered a little, a seaplane to land in Road Town Harbor. And now the twenty-fourth of November 1949 was Thanksgiving Day in the United States, and the plane came with about, let's see, the pilot and carry about three passengers [. . .]. They agreed to share the news together when they go back to St. Thomas. And so I paid sixty dollars and forty cents to charter the plane, and when I tell people about this they say, "but why the forty cents?!" I say well you see what happen was, it was a holiday [in the United States], it was Thanksgiving, and that forty cents was for the immigration, the immigration fee, forty cents. So I paid that out of my pocket, I got the plane to come, landed right here Road Town Harbor, got the newspaper correspondents; and Reuters [. . .] of London, the correspondent didn't come but they shared the news with him, those that went back. And the interesting thing and the important thing is, that the next morning the news came out in newspapers and came out in Fleet Street in London [. . .]. Well, the news came out about this march, this demonstration in the British Virgin Islands, a demonstration for a new constitution, and the news went around the newspapers of England.

On November 24, 1949, fifteen hundred people marched through the streets of Road Town calling for the commissioner's removal and delivering a manifesto of their political agenda and demands. The protest came to be called the Freedom March, and the manifesto read:

We, the people of the British Virgin Islands, theoretically a free people by reason of the fact that we are supposed to be British subjects and Citizens of the British Empire, are today in numbers assembled as a Demonstration of Protest against certain conditions under which we have hitherto been forced to live. Our history since the beginning of this century has been one long tale of political oppression by a Government which, being our own local government and not constitutionally 'of the people' nor 'by the people' at least should have been a Government 'for the people.' But the events throughout the decades that are past, and more especially the events of the latter part of this present decade, that is to say, the mismanagement of our public affairs during your own tenure of office as Commissioner administering the Government, have forced upon us the conclusion that we are governed for the benefit of a certain few; and as a consequence Government instead of being for the people has been against the people.

One of the purposes of this demonstration today is for us to try to achieve a measure of political freedom for ourselves and the generations of the future. Our aim is, that we, the politically enslaved people of these British Virgin Islands, should henceforth be free British subjects in truth and in deed. We refuse any longer to be virtual slaves of a Government in which a few officials call the tune while we, the taxpayers, pay the piper. We refuse to go on paying our taxes and revenues for others to spend and to waste as they see fit; others who have no regard for us and our public needs and no interest in us nor our welfare. Since we are always to pay the piper, we are resolved in future ourselves to call the tune. We are imbued with a desire to decide our local affairs our own selves. We have outgrown that undesirable stage where one official, or an official clique, makes decisions for us—decisions which usually prove to be in favour of officialdom and with which we are compelled to abide. We are seeking for the privilege of deciding how our monies are to be spent and what shall be our Presidential laws and policies. We are disgusted and weary of the oppressions of the years. We are ashamed and indignant over the matter, that, though the people of the British Virgin Islands belong to a democratic British Empire, we are, in fact, afflicted and saddled with a form of government akin to dictatorship. We are engaged in a great struggle for our liberation. And in this struggle we assuredly do not stand alone. IN GOD WE TRUST. As a Christian population we feel that Almighty God is by our side, is behind and before us. He is able by His guidance to help us, His people, through as He has helped others through in the past. Standing by our side is the balance of British Virgin Islanders who are resident in the United States and its possessions. TODAY WE ARE MARCHING TOWARDS FREEDOM. And we will continue to march until that Freedom has to us been secured. We will no longer remain contented with conditions as they are. We have endured, and endured, until our powers of endurance have failed us. We are to be freed from the yoke we have been carrying. We are asking for Freedom. We are seeking Freedom. WE DEMAND FREEDOM.[13]

It continued, listing complaints against the commissioner under four headings: "You have sinned against Us the People in Diverse Ways, so that Our Grievances against You are Sundry and Manifold"; "You have left Undone the Things You Ought to have Done"; "You have Done the Things You Ought not to have Done"; "And there is no Confidence in You." A "nation" was being born.

Chapter 2

The Muting of Distinction and the Making of the "BVIslander": 1950–90

Local state apparati came into being as the British Virgin Islands gained legislative autonomy and a separate colonial status from the greater Leeward Islands Colony, of which it had been a subunit until the 1950s. This chapter documents the rhetoric that surrounded the institutions of statecraft from the moment of their inception. The state was conceptualized as an "organism" and as a "machine" separate from and owned by the "people." Following from this conceptualization, state and legal processes led British Virgin Islanders to consolidate themselves as a people. Other previously significant markers of identity—island of origin, skin tone, party affiliation, class—lost much of their relevance. The tourist industry, beginning with the revolution in Cuba and subsequent closing off of that island to U.S. tourists, was a boon to BVIslanders. It muted class distinctions and led to the immigration of large numbers of other Caribbean peoples. This immigration also encouraged the muting of distinctions among BVIslanders and the consolidation of British Virgin Islander identity by leading BVIslanders to distinguish themselves against immigrant "others."

Equality and Difference: Disputing and "Studying"

Ethnographic literature on Caribbean peoples frequently makes reference to an ideology and ethos of equality. Much of this literature generally takes note of Caribbean people's attention to public

67

behavior and appearance (Fisher 1976; Reisman 1974; Abrahams 1968; Wilson 1973; see Williams 1991:285 and chap. 4). Brackette Williams has recently argued that ideas about equality implicated in Caribbean people's concern with public appearance and status must be understood in terms of "politicoeconomic structures" and "local conceptions of morality, patterns of social interaction, and modes of status competition" (Williams 1991:285). Williams suggests that such status competition occurs in the context of "norms of egalitarianism, solidarity and reciprocity as well as norms of hierarchy, competition, and individualism" (1991:94). These norms appear to conflict. As Williams shows, however, there is no necessary contradiction between egalitarianism and individualism when both are seen as part of a liberal worldview fostered by liberal state practices. I open this chapter with a small sketch of BVIslander patterns of interaction that demonstrates the coexistence and ultimate reconcilability of ideas about equality and ideas about individual achievements. Like Williams, I turn to the everyday street-level contests over status and especially over public appearance, and I draw on BVIslanders' perception by and interactions with "outsiders," to highlight BVIslander approaches to status and equality.

BVIslanders frequently use expressions based on the verb *to study,* such as "I ain' studying you!" or "Don' study her". The first is used when someone complains that the speaker is giving him or her a hard time or is being too nosy. The second is used when someone complains to a third party that an individual is causing him or her some trouble, is teasing, or is suspected of spreading gossip about the complainant. In both cases, the verb *to study* means essentially the same thing as the U.S. English *to pay mind,* as in "don't pay her any mind" or simply "don't mind her." Expatriates from Europe and North America cite this BVIslander expression as "proof" that BVIslanders are "always looking at everyone else," "by disposition are suspicious," are "paranoid," and "notice everything." Expatriates suspect that BVIslanders' use of the expression *to study* indicates that BVIslanders are *always* in a state of "studying" others. What is said negatively by BVIslanders ("*don't* study her") is taken by expatriates to indicate an everyday condition of social life in the BVI.

BVIslanders are more concerned with status equalization than they are paranoid, which is evident in the frequently heard statement that "there are no classes here," or else "there used to be no classes, but we're getting some now." Because of their concern with status, BVIslanders do take note of other people, especially when someone new comes into their community. "Studying" is for BVIslanders a positive everyday condition in a way significantly different from how expatriates interpret it.

BVIslanders complain that white people and many American blacks are sloppy and lack "style." People often comment on how they dress, especially how women dress. The worst thing for a woman to do in the BVI is to wear a "shapeless" or "unstructured" dress. People are expected to be neat and pressed. BVIslanders like sharp lines and shoulder pads, not flowing waves of loose fabric. Cleanliness, manners, and even morality are judged on the basis of the style and fit of one's clothes.

At the same time that BVIslanders measure up the white and American black expatriates in their midst, they complain that such people are nosy and pry into other people's business—a complaint certainly justified in the case of the visiting anthropologist. This judgment is the basis of BVIslanders' labeling such people—including, upon occasion, myself—"rude" and "disgusting." One person related the following story.

Ann, a BVIslander, was throwing a dinner party for a group of relatives and their partners. Among those invited was the American black girlfriend of Ann's cousin. To make the event special, Ann had gone around to her sisters and her mother asking for things to borrow: she got one linen tablecloth each from her sisters, several china serving plates from her mother, two sets of silverware from a sister and cousin, and more china dishes from her sisters' and cousins' collections. She also brought out crystal glasses and china dinner plates from the cabinet where she usually keeps her "special" things. The table was nicely laid out. The cousin's girlfriend, upon arrival, exclaimed to her hostess, "Oh, but Ann! These are such lovely things!!" She continued, "Oh, this is such lovely china! Where did you get it? How much did you pay?" and "You must tell me where you got these linens!" To Ann and her husband, these were unspeakably "rude" questions that verified what they had suspected all along—this new girlfriend in the family, like all Americans, was "disgusting."

A BVIslander named Marcia tells this story: Her sister lives in St. Thomas and thus has access to more and better clothing stores than she does. (The woman telling the story here paused to berate the quality of the clothes available from the "Syrian," or Arab-owned, stores on Tortola.) Whenever her sister gets tired of a particular dress or outfit, she'll send it to Marcia in Tortola. Marcia related to me that an American friend of hers always used to comment, "Marcia, that's such lovely dress! You always dress with such style. But how can you afford such clothes on your salary?!"

BVIslander friends gave me the following characterization of white expatriate social events in the BVI. Everyone will be gossiping; "everyone has a story to tell about everyone else." People will be traipsing all over the house, peeking into all of the rooms and commenting on the decor, asking the hostess questions like "Where did you get this?" and "How much did you pay?" People will comment on the rooms, "Oh, but it's such a small bedroom! How do you manage" or, alternately, "What a large kitchen! I wish I had a nice big one like this."

To BVIslanders, it is the whites and American blacks who are always "studying" other people and, more important, who are always making it known that they are doing so. This is what BVIslanders see as rude. The means of BVIslander status equalization *is* to study everyone but, in contrast, not to let on that you are doing so, for to let on that you are studying someone is to imply that you think that some inequality of status exists in the first place. Hence, when people use the expression *to study,* they often do so in the negative— "I *ain't* studying you, so go about your business." This statement effectively means, don't think you're special and that I'm paying you any mind, because I'm not and therefore you're not any more special than anyone else.

Men engage in this kind of status equalization, too. When a group of men gets together for round after round of drinks with the hapless 130-pound anthropologist, one man buys all the drinks for the others and will usually keep doing so throughout the binge. The other men are not supposed immediately to make a "return" for the drink, because to do so would indicate that they are "keeping track" of or "keeping the score" on their host's buying. Keeping the score would indicate that they are waiting for status inequality to obtain among them. Instead nothing is spoken, and next time someone else will buy the drinks, but without so much as a "I'll get this round" or "Let me pay this time."

It works much the same way for buying things for other people; one does not expect immediate return payment. To ask for it is an insult. It suggests that you don't really trust that the person can actually pay up, or that you think they will not be able to pay in the future. Similarly, one does not offer immediate payment; this would suggest that you do not appreciate the gesture of having something bought for you, or that you think the person doing you the favor is stingy, greedy, selfish, or petty.

These observations on status are related to the way BVIslanders resolve little disputes that sometimes arise. Alvin was helping Emile dig up a stump on Emile's property. While they were working, Emile accidentally swung his cutlass and hit Alvin on the back of the shoulder. Neither of the men said anything at the time; they "let it pass." Later, Alvin realized that the blow had seriously bruised his shoulder and that subsequently, he had favored the unbruised muscles in his arm more heavily and that this had led to muscle strain. But he never said anything about this to Emile. Later that week, however, Alvin asked Emile to make him some fish pots out of chicken wire that Alvin provided. Emile did this, under the expectation that Alvin would pay him. Alvin made it clear to others that he had no intention of paying Emile when he asked Emile to build him the fish pots. He never did pay Emile. Emile, for his part, apparently complained to one friend, but to no one else. The affair was dropped, and the two men continue as friends and helpful neighbors.

The North American expatriate who first related this story to me did so to "prove" that BVIslanders "repress" everything, and that this is a reason for their "paranoia." However, rather than make a fight over status—who "owes" whom what, a position that starts from the assumption of inequality—Alvin chose to wait for an opportunity to set things straight. A BVIslander I told this story confirmed this interpretation, and added, making a washing motion with her hands, "You see? One hand washes the other, we say." What goes around comes around.

A traditional (Eurocentric!) legal anthropologist might use this example to argue that BVIslanders use a form of dispute resolution as an alternative to those provided by the state (the courts, the laws, etc.). They might even see it as a form of resistance to courts and the law, since people are not going to the law to settle differences.[1] However, this logic of status equalization is not all that dissimilar from the logic of liberal egalitarianism. The kinds of subjects engaged in such "alternative" dispute resolution scenarios are already the subjects of a liberal state, a state that has been integral in muting class and race distinctions and establishing and furthering the interests of "equality." The participants in this state do not necessarily need courts because they already know how to act to ensure a fair, equal, and balanced outcome. This is not to suggest that disputes do not arise which people go to courts to settle. Cases that do make it to court become as popular as soap operas. But there is more talk about bringing people to court than there are actual court cases (cf. Greenhouse 1986; Greenhouse, Yngvesson, and Engel 1994).

The task of this chapter is to chart how state formation—where the state is imagined as an entity apart from the people, even as nearly all the people who count as "the people" work for the state—is crucial to the equalization of differences and the muting of distinction in the BVI and perhaps the wider Caribbean. With state formation, such distinctions became less important to the people who came to call themselves "BVIslanders" over the course of this century.

As BVIslanders and colonial officials constructed an administrative apparatus for the BVI separate from that of the other Leeward Islands colonies, they created economic and political opportunities for most BVIslanders and helped consolidate BVIslanders as a group distinct from other Caribbean peoples. Indeed, it was not until the 1950s that the terms *British Virgin Islander* and *BVIslander* came into widespread use. The administrative trappings of statehood—honorific titles for legislators, a mace symbolizing the presence of the sovereign in the territory, debates over legislative costume—together with the new technologies of statecraft—postage stamps, radiotelephones, office supplies as mundane as letterhead paper—forged the "British Virgin Islands" itself as a political entity, a "machine" operating in the interests of its "people." The demise of the political party system forged a strong connection between these people and the state: intermediaries such as parties or interest groups fell by the wayside in the new political milieu, and the category "BVIslander" took on a new ontological status.

Statecraft and Subjects

Harrigan and Varlack argue that the movement for some form of self-government in the British Virgin Islands was aided in large part by the general "retreat from Empire" of postwar Britain, and also that agitation in the BVI itself, while impressive, was not inspired by "particularly deep" political sentiments (1975:160). Regardless, early in 1950, following the mass protests in 1949, the governor of the Leeward Islands Colony appointed a committee to discuss legislative autonomy for the BVI, and in the same year, on that committee's recommendation, the Legislative Council of the Leeward Islands brought into existence the Legislative Council of the Virgin Islands and allowed for two of the four elected members of the new Legislative Council to serve on an Executive Council. Elections were held for the first time in November 1950.

This chapter concerns shifts in political discourse during the 1950s and 1960s, as politicians in the British Virgin Islands and the general public changed their ideas about the best scenario for the BVI's future political status—from uniting with the American Virgin Islands, to affirming long-standing connections to the eastern Caribbean islands yet opposing federation with them, to asserting the necessity of complete BVI autonomy from both the other Virgins and the Eastern Caribbean—while they formed a BVI state and began to call themselves "BVIslanders." This shift was obtained through the progressive bureaucratization—and no small degree of glorification—of state practices in the BVI, practices that brought every BVIslander into the purview of the state both as an object of state discipline and as an active participant in state building. The creation of electoral districts for the BVI and the formation and dissolution of political parties competing in the elections offer windows into the ways that distinctions among BVIslanders that emerged in the first part of the twentieth century began to lose their significance. The tourist boom of the 1960s mitigated many old class inequalities, and an ever-expanding civil service provided jobs for BVIslanders traditionally excluded from the political center.

"The state" and "the people" came into being in the British
Virgin Islands during the same historical moment and were envisioned as opposed, separate entities: the state as a machine that is
universally useful and that can be used by anyone or any people;
the people as unique, special, and distinct from all other peoples.
"The people" also constitute a third entity, "society," which is envisioned like "the state" to be a totality. "Society" is taken to constitute the "true" organization of the people, while "the state" is
taken to be an artificial and opposing entity. In arguing against
positivist and formalistic notions of "the state" and "the social,"
Ernesto Laclau and Chantal Mouffe (1985) draw attention to the
connection between a conception of society as a closed structure
subject to the actions and tinkering of individual subjects and a liberal understanding of the state as an entity made by individual
persons in the image of society (cf. Strathern 1985). According to
the logic these authors seek to dismantle, the state is conceived as
an autonomous object created of, by, and for individual subjects,
which, like society, is subject to individuals' reformations and
reconstructions. In spite of these tinkerings, however, the state
remains an entity apart, a thing, a positivity, a "sutured and
self-defined totality," like "society" itself (Laclau and Mouffe
1985:111). Laclau and Mouffe unseat these conceptions of state
and society by pointing toward the antagonisms that highlight
both the contingency of state/society as well as its never-closed-off,
always-in-process nature. The modern state/society they seek to go
beyond was articulated quite vividly, they note, by Benjamin Disraeli in the middle of the last century. Disraeli worked to fit the
unruly field of the social into the "positivist illusion" that antagonisms and differences could always and without disruption of
order "be absorbed in the intelligible and ordered framework of
society" (Laclau and Mouffe 1985:130). The liberal democratic
state, conceptualized as a positivity, an object in itself, an ordered
and ordering machine functioning according to principles of reason and individualism, was for Disraeli precisely the means to seal
the "two nations"—the rich and the poor—into one (see Disraeli
[1845] 1964). The one nation would emerge when people became
propertied and from their position as "possessive individuals"
(Macpherson 1962) formed a true political community based on
the mutual obligation to preserve property, and not the false com-

munity of mere "aggregation under circumstances which make it rather a dissociating than a uniting principle" (Disraeli [1845] 1964:65).

Laclau and Mouffe direct their critique against both liberal and Marxist theorists of the state, who stress the state's autonomy as an objective entity, and demonstrate that these theorists assume a conception of "a sutured society," closed from disruption (1985:139). In contrast, Laclau and Mouffe seek to "renounce the hypothesis of the final closure of the social" for they maintain that this conception of state/society "autonomy" is itself "a form of hegemonic construction" (139). I invoke Laclau and Mouffe not to explore their alternatives for democratic politics, but to use their critique of existing democracy to highlight the invention of "the state" and "society" in mid-twentieth-century British Virgin Islands political discourse. This discourse hinged crucially around the notion of a state and a society as totalities, as objectively real things unto themselves, external to the people who nevertheless make them up because they are always subject to individuals' tinkering and fine-tuning. Metaphors of the state as a "machine" (cf. Mitchell 1988) and of both society and state as progressing through inevitable "stages of development" are rife in this discourse and help form a modernist conception of state and society central to a liberal ordering of the world. At the same time, much like recent political rhetoric analyzed by Laclau and Mouffe (1985:170), the liberal understanding of state and society that began to be articulated at midcentury depended upon invented and decidedly nonliberal "traditionalisms" invoking supposedly "ancient" connections to other Caribbean islands and the British Virgin Islands' particular "heritage" of British political and cultural institutions.

The discourses enabling the fiction of a "BVI society" and "BVI state" as sutured totalities—metaphors of the state as machine, imaginings of BVIslanders as all equal participants in the state-machine, and so forth—themselves are "articulatory practices" which constitute as they invoke social relations (Laclau and Mouffe 1985:96). These practices stitch together a seemingly whole fabric of the British Virgin Islands as a territorial entity whose polity maps neatly onto a place and a people. Yet as they do so, they leave out large swatches of cloth, the antagonisms and contradions made evident by the absent presence of immigrants in the discourses creating state and society.

The State-Machine

The elections of 1950 were held under an "at large" system—electors from the entire territory voted to select the four from a slate of nine candidates who would serve on the Legislative Council. Five of the candidates ran without a party affiliation. The men behind the Freedom March put together a political party to contest the elections. Calling itself the Progressive League (echoing the names of both New York and St. Thomas political organizations), the party put up four candidates and saw two of them—I. G. Fonseca and Carlton de Castro—elected to office. The two candidates winning the highest number of votes were nominated to the Executive Council, and these two turned out to be I. G. Fonseca and H. R. Penn, both of Road Town. C. Brudenell-Bruce, an Englishman, won the fourth slot on the Legislative Council. All of the elected legislators were members of Road Town's merchant elite.

As Harrigan and Varlack note, the new Legislative Council did "not set the world on fire" and was "more in the nature of the learning situation for most of its members" (1975:162). What the members of this new legislature learned, however, were the fundamentals of a new political discourse and an approach to both "state" and "people" that would figure in all subsequent popular and political discourses in the British Virgin Islands.

BVI elites had come out of World War II demanding autonomy or union with the U.S. Virgin Islands. This latter option made sense in the context of the mass migration to St. Thomas during the 1940s and the importance of the St. Thomas mass media to BVIslanders. Now that some degree of autonomy had been achieved, however, and gains were to be had from closer associations with the Commonwealth, elites turned their attention to the eastern Caribbean islands to the south. While one commentator in the 1960s felt confident in pointing out that "links with the other British islands were so slight as to be almost non-existent" during the 1940s (Proudfoot 1965:6), the Legislative Council in 1951 saw fit to delineate what it then felt were immemorial, almost primordial connections to their southern neighbors. In passing a resolution to remain outside of a proposed federation of the British Caribbean islands, the Legislative Council emphasized its ties to St. Thomas and the United States, yet also argued that deep ties to the British Caribbean existed:

> Whereas the Legislative Council of the British Virgin Islands after due consideration of the Report of the British Caribbean Standing Closer Association Committee of 1948–49 feels unable to concur with the findings and recommendations in regard to the British Virgin Islands whose geographical position and close economic connections with the Virgin Islands of the U.S.A. have precluded any considerable intercourse between them and the other British West Indian islands:
>
> Resolved: —
>
> (i) That this Council after much reflection has come to the conclusion that the British Virgin Islands should stand outside the proposed Federation, the economic disadvantages being too great, and the political partnership too slender to make their participation effective or even useful.
>
> (ii) That this Council, however, wishes to express the view that total severance of an ancient and historical connection cannot be entirely envisaged, and requests that some provision be made within any Federation that may be arrived at by which the Virgin Islands may continue to make a Federal contribution as is now done in the Leeward Islands Federation of which they are now a unit [as a Presidency within the Leeward Islands Colony], to enable them to have access to administrative and technical advice and guidance, and to obtain certain specific services which so small a Colony must inevitably require, and must seek from closer quarters than the Secretary of State for the Colonies [in London] under whose jurisdiction they prefer to remain. (Minutes 9/14/51)

There are several ambiguities and tensions expressed here that would remain prominent elements of BVI political discourse for the next four decades. First, the legislators claim their historical connection to St. Thomas and essentially deny one with the British Caribbean, but then turn around and postulate an "ancient and historical connection" with the British Caribbean. Second, they ask to stay out of the proposed federation, yet want access to it and its "technical" resources in exchange for whatever "contribution" the BVI makes to the federation. Third, they wish to remain under the direct governance of the secretary of state for the colonies in London, yet they complain that he is too far away to do them much good. Ultimately these are tensions surrounding the limits of sovereignty and autonomy. They also reflect ambiguous identifications—with the U.S. Virgin Islands, with the British Caribbean, and with the United Kingdom. It is during the 1950s that legislators and the people who elected them begin to carve a space for themselves out of and between these three separate identities and, in a creolizing practice of both mediation and purification, constituted the three entities as separate, forceful, and powerfully real.

The term *British Virgin Islander* comes into widespread use during this decade, and *BVIslander*—an empty category, and infinitely signifiable, with both the *British* part of the term and the *Virgin Islands* part of the term reduced to initials, bare traces—emerges in the 1960s. The reduction of *British* and *Virgin* to initials reflects the ever-increasing ambiguity of British Virgin Islands identity as at once British, Virgin Island (encompassing the U.S. Virgins as well), and Caribbean, and none of these things. It is during the 1950s that British Virgin Islanders begin to worry about "outsiders"—St. Thomians, English, and other colonial Caribbean peoples—purchasing land. New land laws tried to define exactly who was an "outsider" and who was not, in this Virgin Islander, British, and colonial Caribbean place. The three zones from which BVIslanders draw their identities—and which, in their act of citing them, take on new meaning as stabilities—increasingly took on the character of resources to be used strategically, as BVIslander subjects took on the character of liberal subjects, rational, strategic maximizers. Identity becomes a matter of choice, reason, and— with the rise of tourism and the offshore banking industry—marketability. This is a discussion I will return to later.

There are other elements of a nascent political discourse evident in the resolution to stand outside of federation. The legislators refer to the British Virgin Islands as a "unit" in the Leeward Islands Colony. The language that casts institutions, organizations, and peoples as "parts" of larger "wholes" came into common use in the BVI during the 1950s and continues to this day. In 1950, the BVI was a "unit" of a larger administrative apparatus. In the 1990s, small divisions of different branches of the civil service are styled "units"—the Development Planning Unit, the Caribbean Studies Unit, and so on. Units are parts of larger wholes; they are singularities making up a totality. Each unit has its function to perform. The rhetoric evokes images of an organism and a machine.

We see a hint of this organism/machine discourse in the resolution quoted earlier. This discourse depoliticizes politics and power relationships. It holds the "state" to be an entity separate from the "people" who work "for" it or work "on" it, trying to make it work more "efficiently" and "effectively." Since the goal is efficiency, any assistance people receive that pushes toward this goal is welcome, for such assistance is not taken to be an expression of broader power interests. Observe, for instance, the final sentence of the quotation. The BVI is a small colony, far away from the metropolis. This location places constraints on the development of an efficient administrative apparatus. Hence, the BVI would like to maintain access to "administrative and technical advice and guidance" from its federation neighbors. The advice and guidance would be granted solely to help the BVI's own administrative and technical apparati, and not in the interests of maintaining federal relations, since the BVI will remain outside of the federation. Assistance and guidance are technical, not political, issues.

When the state becomes an object, and a mechanical/organic object whose functioning must be made efficient, the relationship between the BVI and the three loci of power and meaning it skirts between and creates—the United States, the United Kingdom, and the British Caribbean—becomes one of expediency, not politics. It is also a relationship not expressly about "identity"—except insofar as the BVI possesses "ancient and historical" connections with each of these three loci. BVI identity becomes precisely the shuttling back and forth between the three loci, as it continually re-cites and thus re-sites them, in the interest of expediency and efficiency. In the same meeting of the Legislative Council where the quoted resolution was passed and the desire for remaining under the domain of the secretary of state for the colonies was expressed, the Legislative Council decided that "the keeping of Government accounts in United States dollars would simplify and render the accounting work of the Treasury infinitely more efficient" (Minutes 9/14/51). The issue is efficiency, not identity.

There is a desire expressed in 1950s political discourse to keep the three loci separated from "the people" of the British Virgin Islands and to use their resources only in the interest of solving the state's "technical problems." In 1951 the government of Montserrat, another unit in the Leeward Islands Colony, presented a ceremonial mace to the Virgin Islands Legislative Council. The mace symbolizes the presence of the sovereign of the United Kingdom in the Legislative Council. It has been on continuous display in the Legislative Council Chamber ever since— except for a brief time after an incident, discussed later, when a member of the council broke it in two—and is brought out every year on the queen's birthday, where it takes the place of the queen herself in the Queen's Birthday Parade. In 1951, the Legislative Council split into two camps over the issue of how exactly to word the note of thanks to Montserrat for this fantastic gift. H. R. Penn and C. Brudenell-Bruce, who had cozier relationships with the British in the BVI and were sometimes called the "tea-room boys" by their more populist political opponents, voted to thank "the Government, the Legislative Council and the people of Montserrat." Their opponents I. G. Fonseca and C. L. de Castro objected and voted to thank only "the Government" since, as Fonseca recalls, it was not a gift from "the people" at all, who had no say in the matter whatsoever. When the alternative wordings were put to a vote, Fonseca and de Castro's won.

The ambiguity of BVI identity and its relationship to the emerging BVI state played itself out in this vote about the mace. On the one hand, in being given the mace, the BVI was being recognized as a state within the colonial Commonwealth, a unit of empire on its own. For a place that had been part of a bigger colony administered from Antigua for most of its history, this was an important moment. On the other hand, as Fonseca and de Castro were careful to point out, the mace was a gift from a government to a government; "the people" themselves were not involved. "The state" exists apart from "the people." Both the people and the state are entities unto themselves. Affairs of the state do not necessarily impinge upon the peoplehood or the identity of the people. Peoplehood is something that exists all on its own, for it springs from the people themselves. It is through contradictory articulations of people and state that both people and state come into being as separated and separate entities, even as they come into being in the same moment and even as each depends upon the other for its meaning and force.

The state-as-machine metaphor was most clearly and power-fully articulated in a speech made by the commander in chief of the Leeward Islands Colony (then acting governor), P. D. Mac-donald, when he addressed the Legislative Council of the Virgin Islands in 1953. If the sentiments he expressed were greeted with some skepticism by the members of the Legislative Council, the language he expressed them in soon all but took over Legislative Council debates and popular conceit. Macdonald argued that only with the proper machinery of government would the BVI "develop," stage by stage, into a modern society.

> The question to which I wish to draw your attention this morn-ing is that of the organization of your Government. It would be pleasanter and easier for me to review and discuss other topics—road development, water development, industrial development, agricultural development, and so on. But—and I cannot sufficiently emphasize this point—every develop-ment in your Presidency will succeed or fail precisely to the extent to which the governmental machinery is capable of implementing the plans which we all wish to see undertaken, and of giving effect to the advice tendered by your Commit-tees. Shortly after my arrival in this Colony, someone with con-siderable knowledge of the British West Indies suggested to me that, whilst the passage of the Colonial Development and Welfare Act and the provision of funds thereunder had been a boon to these colonies, it also produced an adverse effect, particularly in the smaller territories. Somewhat surprised, I enquired the reason for this view and it was suggested to me that the implementation of the schemes had placed too heavy a burden on the smaller administrative machines, thereby causing disruption in the administrative machinery. I think there is some truth in that. I think that the work of the admin-

istrative machine is too often taken for granted; if it is to function efficiently and economically, and fulfil its purpose in the light of the changing scene [*sic*]. It is often insufficiently realized that the ordinary day to day routine administrative work provides the foundations for progress and achievement. (Minutes 4/21/53, Appendix, ¶7)

Max Weber couldn't have put it better! The day-to-day work of the administrative machine is what makes progress toward modernity possible. If you try to do too much with a machine that is not ready or is too small—that is, one that has not yet "developed" or grown enough to handle a new workload—the administrative machine will not function properly and may in fact impede development by breaking apart altogether. These sentiments are eminently "reasonable." They are eminently modern. Macdonald concludes:

I am a convinced believer in the very material benefits to be derived from reorganizing the government machine. I have done it in my new office and elsewhere in this Colony and you would be surprised at the response which it has called forth. It has paid handsome dividends in speed, efficiency and pride of work. After all, if you are a motor racing driver anxious to win a long race, you chose your car and engine with the greatest care and bring the engine to the highest pitch of efficiency for the race. All machinery needs overhaul, streamlining and refurbishing regularly—whether it be inanimate or one comprised of human beings. (Minutes 4/21/53, Appendix, ¶12)

Macdonald's speech of twelve paragraphs contains the word *machine* or *machinery* a total of fourteen times. Machine metaphors were popular in earlier colonial periods, especially as Europe was in the process of industrializing (cf. Mitchell 1988), but they became even more popular after the triumph of cybernetics during World War II and ergonomic systems approaches to organizational behavior during the 1950s—approaches that figured equally prominently in Parsonian and other neo-Weberian social science.[2] One hears echoes of Parsons (and Durkheim) in Macdonald's description of a well-functioning civil service:

An efficient governmental machine is, I suggest, comprised of two elements: a contented, hard-working Civil Service; and a properly organized service, where each officer is fully aware of his duties and responsibilities, no less than aware of a realization of the part which he or she must play as an essential unit in a larger machine. (Minutes 4/21/53, Appendix, ¶9)

The machine was the hallmark of all things modern, of the new world opening up after the technologies of war were brought home to raise standards of living and the quality of life. Macdonald recognized that his listeners—who were more concerned about fever ticks decimating their livestock and other agricultural problems besetting the subsistence sector—might not see the relevance of the modern machine to their simple, peasant lives (Minutes 4/21/53, Appendix, ¶5). But Macdonald forgot that the British subjects of the British Virgin Islands—who were anything but peasants—had already had quite a bit of experience with machinery and machine metaphors, on their boats and "motor launches" during periods of trade and migration, in the sugar factories of Santo Domingo and the munitions plants of St. Thomas, and in their political organizing (with "cells" and "units" of civic leagues and political parties with complicated organizational structures). BVIslanders also had had experience with the everyday apparatus of statecraft, by way of marriage, birth, and death certificates, government seals, deeds, and land titles. To mix metaphors (and highlight the gendered implications), the ground was quite fertile for Macdonald's machine.

It bears repeating that the machine was conceptualized as separate from the people. As the civil service expanded, however, more and more people became directly involved in the mechanics of the machine, and the symbols of statecraft became increasingly important to BVIslanders. As the BVI was gradually separated off from the administrative structures of the broader Leeward Islands Colony and later federation, BVIslanders began to see significance in the fact that their territory was fast developing its "own" machine. Accordingly, they coddled it, nurtured it, and participated actively in its numerical growth—as more people became civil servants—and symbolic growth—as new trappings of autonomy took on symbolic significance.

To be sure, there were still conflicts—as there continue to be—between what were perceived to be the interests of "the people" and the interests of "the state." These made and make sense because of the conceptualization of state and society as separate, potentially conflictual, entities. For instance, disagreement between rivals Penn and Fonseca flared up when Penn proposed "improvements" to the "machinery" of land and house tax assessment and collection. Fonseca, fearing these "improvements" would mean higher taxes, argued that the proposed changes "touched the very vitals of the people of this Presidency; it went straight to their front door" (Record 1/21/55, Appendix). Against Penn's "machine," Fonseca places people's "vitals" and "homes." "Modern machines" and the conception of state and government as distinct from people arose in the BVI together with "romantic" ideas about people and personhood. The vitals of the people do not exist without the machine of government; indeed, the romance of the people comes into being together with the administrative machine.

"A Colony In Its Own Right"

In 1954, in the name of "constitutional advance," the Legislative Council repealed the act that had brought it into existence and drafted a new constitution, the Virgin Islands Constitution and Election Ordinance (1954). The new constitution increased the number of elected legislators to six and divided the British Virgin Islands into five territorial electoral districts. Two representatives were to come from the Road Town district. Districts were constructed solely with an eye toward "geographical considerations and such other factors as may affect the facility of communication between various places within the polling division" (Virgin Islands Constitution and Elections Ordinance No. 7 of 1954, ¶37 §4). Although districts were created according to geographical constraints, and not "natural" communities of interest, districting seems to have both created new regionalisms and reawakened dormant ones. Harrigan and Varlack suggest that "the introduction of constituencies created tiny pockets of self-interest each pressing with xenophobic fury to elect a 'local' man regardless of his qualifications for office" (1975:163).

Districting occurred immediately before a large step in the "constitutional advance" of the British Virgin Islands when the Leeward Islands Colony broke apart. The BVI was no longer a "presidency" of a larger colonial unit, as the subunits of the Leeward Islands Colony were styled. It was instead a colony in its own right with its own "administrator" as the Crown's official and direct agent in the territory. On July 1, 1956, when the Leeward Islands Colony ceased to exist, the BVI state achieved autonomy from all but the British administrative structures. The date has been a holiday—Colony Day or Territory Day—ever since. On that day, the BVI acquired its own official seal, kept in the Administrator's Office (formerly the President's Office), "where, in future, all documents requiring ensealing would be sealed . . . instead of having to be despatched to the Governor's Office in Antigua" (Record 7/10/56, 2). In honor of its new status, the Legislative Council drafted a statement affirming its allegiance to the queen, under whose jurisdiction it now more directly fell:

WHEREAS, by Act of the United Kingdom Parliament the ancient Federation of the Islands constituting the Leeward Islands Colony was dissolved with effects from the 1st July, 1956; and Whereas, in consequence of the dissolution of the Federation, the Virgin Islands which comprised one of the four 'Presidencies' of the Leeward Islands have regained from that date their former status as a separate Colony with a greater degree of self-government than they have hitherto enjoyed; and Whereas this Council, having regard to the events which have led Her Majesty's Government to create the Virgin Islands as a separate Colony and, to the assurances which have been received that the wish of the inhabitants will be respected in their choice to develop, with the assistance of Her Majesty's Government, along the path of self-government and economic progress as a territory outside the British Caribbean Federation, desires on this historic occasion to affirm its loyalty to the Person and Throne of Her Majesty Queen Elizabeth the Second: RESOLVED that this Council humbly affirms its loyalty and allegiance to the Person and Throne of Her Most Gracious Majesty Queen Elizabeth the Second, and that the terms of this resolution be conveyed to

the Secretary of State for the Colonies for transmission to Her
Majesty (Record 7/10/56, 3)

This affirmation of loyalty contains the elements of the political
discourse discussed earlier: the state is separate from its inhabitants, who desire a state that is at once autonomous and connected
to the Crown. Such a structure will facilitate "progress," for it turns
all intervention of the Crown in BVI affairs into a matter of "assistance," not political interest or power. The people are a unity separate from the state they will build and which will serve them and
their interests.

Indeed, the administrator's speech on this occasion emphasized the very technologies that made possible the conceptualization of BVIslanders, from Jost Van Dyke to Anegada, as a unified
people. G. P. Allsebrook, the new administrator, noted that "this is
an historic occasion, not because of any monumental piece of legislation to be enacted, or for any spectacular event, but because it
is the first Sitting of the Council to be held since the British Virgin
Islands became a separate Colony" (Record 7/10/56, Appendix).
In commenting upon the ceremony honoring new colonial status,
Allsebrook commented that

> a special tribute must be paid to Mr. Fonseca, the Second
> Member for the Second District for arranging the programme
> [of the ceremony] and for having it recorded and relayed the
> next day over radio-telephone link to the out-islands. Mr.
> Faulkner, the Member for the First District, has informed me
> that the broadcast over the telephone net work was clearly
> heard in Anegada by a large gathering. (Record 7/10/56,
> Appendix)

He concluded, "I extend my hearty congratulations to the new
Colony and wish it, its Councils and people, every happiness and
success and in doing so express the hope that the new form of
Administration will prove to be in the best interests of all" (Record
7/10/56, Appendix).

With the new administrative structure came such symbolic
niceties as a new council chamber, complete with mahogany tables

and chairs for legislators, a new flagpole to fly the Union Jack outside the chamber, and, more practically but equally symbolic, the transference of funds for aid directly from the United Kingdom instead of through Antigua (Minutes 6/25/57; Record 7/9/57). One former legislator, Leslie Malone, recalls that direct aid from the United Kingdom provided a rationale for standing outside of any attempts at refederation, since the BVI would have its own administrative pathways to receive and channel aid, and also permitted the BVI to maintain economic and political ties with the U.S. Virgin Islands, since there were fewer agents of the Crown close to home to argue against it. In other words, direct aid from the United Kingdom allowed BVIslanders once again to maintain their balancing act between the United Kingdom, the USVI, and their Caribbean neighbors.

BVIslanders also acquired their own public holidays. Besides the July 1 holiday commemorating separate colonial status, named Colony Day and later renamed Territory Day, the Legislative Council argued that St. Ursula's Day (October 21) should be a holiday and that the British Labour Day—which they maintained "has little significance in this Colony"—be done away with (Minutes 7/9/57). The BVI was very much "having it both ways"—accumulating all the symbolic trappings of independent nation-statehood, such as national holidays, even while it maintained and even celebrated its colonial relationship with Britain through its recognition of Colony Day. This is a further instance of BVIslanders' creolizing practices, which draw on as they mediate and invigorate elements from apparently divergent domains. One further symbol of independence: during the same meeting in which they debated public holidays, the first meeting held in the new Legislative Council Chambers, the members of the Legislative Council received approval from the secretary of state for the colonies in London to refer to themselves as *Honourable.* Mr. Fonseca, Mr. Penn, and the other members became "The Honourable Mr. Fonseca" and "The Honourable Mr. Penn." With the symbols of nation-statehood in place, development could not be long in coming. Indeed, in 1958, the first technical adviser on tourism came to the territory to make an initial report on the prospects for tourism development (Minutes 3/11/58).

Districts, Parties, and Personhood

But as it unified the British Virgin Islands into its own territorial political entity, separate colonial status brought with it, and highlighted, divisions within that territory. The bulk of the debates in the Legislative Council during the 1950s were not about constitutional advance, symbols of state, or relationships with the United Kingdom, the British Caribbean, or the USVI. They were about the mundane affairs of "development"—the construction of cattle dips, cisterns, drainage systems, roads, water pipes, electrical systems, radio-telephones, and so forth. They are also about disputes between elected legislators and appointed colonial officials, especially over "government" appropriations of land that did not meet with the approval of the elected members of government. Through debate about these technical matters of development, regionalisms were articulated and given material validity for members of the legislature as for the people of the British Virgin Islands. "Development" came to some areas sooner than others. One member of government complained that some parts of the territory were being connected to water services and that other parts were being neglected: "The people of West End needed water too" (Minutes 4/21/53). H. R. Penn complained that a jetty had been constructed at West End but that construction had not even begun on a jetty for Baugher's Bay, in his district:

> [A] definite promise was made to the people of Baugher's Bay by the Public Works Department . . . [I have been] requested by the people of Baugher's Bay to make the strongest possible protest and to inform the Government that if action [is] not taken quickly to commence the construction of the jetty they would remove the sand and gravel [deposited by Public Works for the construction] for their own uses and would cease further cooperation with the Government. (Minutes 1/19/55)

Of course, much of this rhetoric was political posturing. But it was posturing of a new sort, directed not against a "Government" read as the United Kingdom or colonial lackeys in Antigua who sometimes neglected the BVI, but against a "Government" taken to be BVIslander and which sometimes met the needs and represented the interests of some districts at the expense of others. In the process of articulating these concerns, legislators using this rhetoric called attention to regional disparities within the BVI itself and called into being regional differences and regionalist peoples, new lines of fracture to replace the old class and race ones.

The district system, however, did not seem to meet the needs of the regionalist peoples it created. People felt that legislators only visited their districts at election time, or only voiced concerns about the development of their district when they felt like earning points at home. At the same time, people saw the beginnings of graft and patronage in the district system, when legislators fought for infrastructure and jobs in their districts only when they saw other districts receiving the same. The limits of the district system, it was felt, had been reached. It was time for the BVI to move on and to "advance" to the next "stage" of its development.

There were some calls in the British Virgin Islands for constitutional change, but the impetus came directly from London in a move resented by BVI politicians and people because it brought into relief their ambiguous colonial relationship with Britain. In 1965, the secretary of state for the colonies appointed Mary Proudfoot of Oxford to conduct an investigation into the workings of government in the BVI. The "Proudfoot Report" (Proudfoot 1965) has been a benchmark against which BVIslander politicians have gauged "constitutional advance" ever since. It was met with skepticism and resistance—Harrigan and Varlack recall a winning calypso entitled "The Proudfoot Bubble" in protest of the report's recommendations (1975:169). The Legislative Council in the end accepted most of the recommendations, however—another example of its speaking with an autonomous and independent voice words that come from England. This example reflects the perennial ambiguity of its creolized colonial nationalism.

The British colonial officials and advisers like Proudfoot whose job was to determine the fate of the BVI held liberal ideals of democracy and participatory self-government. Proudfoot stressed the "evident ability and seriousness" (Proudfoot 1965:10) of British Virgin Islanders and their right, as people of "reason," to govern themselves. She argued that "the British pattern of government—a Legislature and Executive, a small cabinet group, however styled, can . . . work [in the BVI] as well as—perhaps better than—it now works at Westminster" (11). Furthermore, she added:

> I think it is important to remember that British political insti-
> tutions, adapted, of course, to particular circumstances, are
> part of the heritage of the people of these islands, who are fel-
> low citizens of ours, and, like us, members of the Common-
> wealth. We should not seek to offer them at this or any other
> stage in their development, "solutions" which we ourselves
> would certainly not have found acceptable. The few who are
> politically articulate will not accept them today. The many,
> who will gradually become articulate, will certainly reject
> them tomorrow. (Proudfoot 1965:11–12)

Proudfoot's assumption here was that BVIslanders, like all reasonable people and members of the Commonwealth, would eventually come to articulate liberal ideals on their own—since it is only
"natural" to do so—and would therefore not accept paternalistic
colonial policies or governmental structures that treated them as
second-class subjects.

Based on her report, Proudfoot seems to have been acutely
aware that, as an outsider and an agent of the Crown, her opinions
on constitutional advance might lead BVIslanders to feel that they
were being granted illusions of autonomy from on high. That
would lead to resentment and would cause BVIslanders to feel that
the colonial power did not yet deem them fully capable of governing themselves and, by extension, of being truly complete and
rational human beings. Proudfoot especially worried about the
problem of what to name elected members of the legislature
under a new constitution:

> On the one hand I wish to avoid the danger that in designat-
> ing these men "ministers" I would lead them, in the end, to
> feel that they had been given the trappings, but defrauded of
> the realities of power. On the other hand, the term "minister,"
> as understood in the British Virgin Islands, does carry with it
> the implication of a power and a status different from that of
> a "member." (Proudfoot 1965:11)

Proudfoot did, however, recommend the change in title from *member* to *minister,* citing the "psychological" benefits the term carries (1965:11). She did not recommend the term *chief minister,* however, which she saw as "belong[ing] to the next stage" of government since the term "seems to imply, in the minds of the local people, full internal self government" (11).

Noting that the district system imposed by the 1954 constitution had not worked too well—having sparked what she considered petty regional rivalries (Proudfoot 1965:10)—Proudfoot sought to redraw district boundaries, and according to different principles. She did not recommend abolishing the district system and reverting to the at-large system of the 1950 elections. Her concern was that the at-large system would make "'government' seem even more remote than it does at present" and also that the districts, in the absence of other forms of local or community government, are the only outlet for community-level concerns to be voiced (15). Ultimately her goal was that of democratization—to bring "government" to the "people" and to bring "people" closer to "government"—for only with this close identity of people and state could self-government be justified and advanced. This *linkage* between people, state, and self-government, which depends on the *distinction* between people and government, is the logic of liberal democracy that the second half of this century saw inculcated in BVIslanders' everyday practices and self-perceptions.

To draw a connection between people and state, however, some people previously cut off from "government" needed to be brought into the fold. The first legislature was made up of men from Road Town. The district system remedied this imbalance somewhat, and Proudfoot wanted even greater integration to occur. To effect this change, she first decided that Road Town should be divided into two districts, each electing one member, instead of being one large district that sent two people to the legislature. Proudfoot invoked democratic common sense: "There seems no reason at all why the people of No. 2 District [Road Town] should, as at present, cast two votes, and everybody else one" (Proudfoot 1965:15).

Proudfoot paid special attention to Virgin Gorda, Anegada, and Jost Van Dyke, which she noted had been most detached from the affairs of state under way in Road Town. She thought Virgin

Gorda should be a district unto itself and noted for Anegada and Jost Van Dyke that, because these islands had close economic ties with the USVI, "It might be an advantage to have them more closely linked with Road Town, and thus more directly under the eye of the government" (16). The connection between democratization and surveillance is made quite explicit: everyone must participate in the new political milieu—it is essential for the functioning of government—and the government is watching to ensure it!

The 1966 report of the British Virgin Islands Boundaries Commission followed Proudfoot's document closely, recommending that the number of districts be increased from five to seven and that districts should be roughly equal in population, "except where, in the Commissioner's opinion, it is desirable to disregard mere equality in numbers on account of special considerations such as natural community of interest, physical features, transport facilities and the practicability of members maintaining in contact with electors in sparsely populated areas" (British Virgin Islands Boundaries Commission 1966:1).[3]

Besides spurring on the BVI Boundaries Commission to draw district lines, the Proudfoot Report led to a constitutional conference that put into place the great majority of Proudfoot's recommendations for the restructuring of government (British Virgin Islands Constitutional Conference 1966). While that was occurring, the BVI was witnessing the beginnings of an economic boom. The United States closed off Cuba to U.S. tourists shortly after the revolution in 1959, and Americans craving the once-thriving Havana nightlife scene sought new resorts throughout the Caribbean, especially Puerto Rico and St. Thomas. The British Virgin Islands captured some of this trade, and when, in 1964, Laurence Rockefeller opened his "Rock-Resort" at Little Dix Bay on Virgin Gorda, foreign investments in the territory soared—along with land prices. Immigration, formerly a scarce trickle, became a small flood. The Legislative Council enacted protective land legislation and also, in 1963 and 1966, passed two ordinances aimed at the "indigenization" or "localization" of certain sectors of the economy, the Trade Licenses Ordinance (No. 1 of 1963) and the Pioneer Services and Enterprises Ordinance (No. 4 of 1966). Both were a boon to new local businesspeople, and both helped solidify local economic activity, creating miniature monopolies in the small but significant printing, leather, ice, sail-making, stone, and tile industries. Similar processes occurred elsewhere in the colonial world and, as Fitzpatrick remarks, led the emerging small business classes to a dependence on, and a degree of identity with, the state (1980:42). In the BVI, these measures helped local political leaders consolidate their constituencies and helped provide the appearance of local political control in spite of continued colonial relations.

Protectionist and "indigenist" policies served to prevent extractive foreign interests from gaining a foothold in the colony and also helped "demonstrate" the ability of colonized and formerly colonized peoples to "manage" their own "economic resources" as rational individuals. Members of the BVI Legislative Council, as a bureaucratic class responsible for technical matters more than political leadership and already focused on administration rather than governance, bolstered their political power and the illusion of their political autonomy through this assertion of rationality. They also achieved popularity with the electors. Trade licensing and pioneer industries regulations sparked favoritism, graft, and patronage. Some saw the corruption and favoritism entering into the political and economic scene as a bad thing, especially as time went on and the tourist industry took off. But the system was one from which all could potentially benefit, and most people accordingly supported it and the leaders who brought it into being. The political platforms of the parties that formed as a direct result of the Constitutional Conference of 1966 all made "localization" and "indigenization" of industry an integral part of their campaigns. Indeed, the peculiar character of political party formation in the BVI cannot be understood outside of this "indigenized" economic context.

Norwell Harrigan (1990), the local BVI historian, has repeatedly stressed the chimerical nature of BVI political parties, and his assessment of party dynamics has been taken up by other local commentators (cf. Romney 1992; Rhymer 1992). The political system ushered in by constitutional changes in 1966–67 provided for a "ministerial" form of government, in which political parties would vie for a majority of seats in the Legislative Council so that they could form the Executive Council—made up of elected members for the first time—and select from their number a chief minister to be appointed by the governor. Three parties formed for the first election under the ministerial system—the Democratic Party (DP), the United Party (UP), and the People's Own Party (POP)—and candidates ran for office under these party rubrics and as independents. Parties could claim no constituent base, however, and only really mattered to the political process during the formation of "government." As has been the case since the inception of the ministerial system, political parties existed in name only. Politicians changed political party affiliation at the drop of a hat in order to gain a ministerial seat. For instance, Q. W. Osborne changed his allegiance from the People's Own Party to the United Party, and finally became the "strongman"—indeed, by the early 1970s, the *only* man—of the Democratic Party. People today remember this as a baseball joke—Osborne made a "Pop-Up Double Play" (POP to UP to DP). To take another example, Willard Wheatley, who would become chief minister after the 1971 and 1975 elections, began his career as an independent, changed his affiliation to the DP, then the UP, then the Virgin Islands Party (VIP)—a new party that formed in 1971—before becoming once again an independent and finally, in 1983, returning to the UP.

Although Harrigan argues that no one actually paid much attention to the various manifestos and party platforms put out by the political parties over the years, I would like to draw attention to the rhetoric of some of them because they exemplify aspects of BVI political discourse and themselves help explain the failure of the party system. These manifestos constitute real data, but not necessarily on parties themselves. When I questioned people about parties, they invariably told me that parties were not at all significant to their political views or voting behavior. This response is in itself significant.

The catchwords of all of the party manifestos are *democracy, freedom,* and *progress.* Each manifesto is written in the shadow of the political language of the United States. The United Party's constitution opens with rhetoric lifted from the Preamble to the United States Constitution:

> WE the People of the British Virgin Islands United Party . . . in order to form a perfect union within our country, to promote the General Welfare of its people, to ensure domestic tran-

quility of these Islands, to secure the blessings of liberty and
determined to establish and defend DEMOCRATIC GOVERNMENT
in our Country: ARE RESOLVED TO COMBINE OURSELVES AND OUR
EFFORTS TO ACCOMPLISH THE FOLLOWING AIMS AND PURPOSES AND
DO ORDAINED [*sic*] AND ESTABLISH THIS CONSTITUTION FOR THE
BRITISH VIRGIN ISLANDS UNITED PARTY. (British Virgin Islands
United Party 1967)

Ironically, but not surprisingly, each United Party (UP) manifesto
printed from 1967 to 1990 sports on its cover a Union Jack. The
manifestos for the Virgin Islands Party (VIP), in contrast, display
Lady Liberty holding up her torch.

The VIP manifestos show a certain evolution in their rhetoric.
The first, from the 1970s, merely states the intent of the party to
further progress and democracy. The second, however, from the
1980s, and after several electoral victories under its leader, H. Lavity Stoutt (chief minister in 1967, 1979, 1986, 1990, and 1994 until
his death in 1995), implicates "the people" in the party's successes:

> The Virgin Islands Party is continuing to assist the people of
> the British Virgin Islands in the major economic and social
> advances of the Territory in the 1980s. Over the last 20 years
> we have all worked together to create the beginnings of a
> modern society and economy. (Virgin Islands Party 1980)

The third manifesto, from the 1990s, maintains an even closer
connection between the party and "the people":

> The Virgin Islands Party has represented the people of the
> British Virgin Islands in their own land and has preserved its
> position in their community for nearly thirty years. . . . The
> Virgin Islands Party, as the British Virgin Islanders' political
> base and guardian will go forward over the decade of the
> nineties to strive to consolidate the very substantial achieve-
> ments it has helped to make for you, the people.
> The Virgin Islands Party comes from the roots of you, the
> people, and is driven by you, the people. The Virgin Islands
> Party, by its deep links into every strata of the society of the
> British Virgin Islands is attuned at all times to your concerns

and anxieties as they arise. The Virgin Islands Party through
its long experience of the art of Government in this Territory,
both in office and opposition, is able to respond through and
with you, the people, to the new challenges that time must
and does bring and can set them into the overall framework of
what has been achieved and the direction in which you, the
people, wish to progress. (Virgin Islands Party 1990)

The manifesto first envisions a distinction between "the party" and
"the people" whom it has served. But then it implicates the party in
the aspirations of the people themselves—it has reached into
"every strata of society" and it knows and even anticipates the
needs of the people "as they arise." It works not only "with" the
people, but "through" them. According to the manifesto, the party
is the "political base" of all British Virgin Islanders.

The VIP manifesto reflects sentiments and attitudes that the
majority of BVIslanders find it hard not to approve. The party
claims an identity with "the people." To be against the "Virgin
Islands Party" is to be against "the Virgin Islands." And everyone in
the British Virgin Islands is a "V.I.P."—a very important person—
whose individual needs can be met directly by the state. For those
who would try to suggest alternative political views, this rhetoric is
difficult to argue against.

The rhetoric of the VIP manifesto captures changes over time
in conceptions of personhood. From distinctions created through
ideas about race and class, the BVI developed as an entity made up
of people who think of themselves not through racial or class categories, but first and foremost as individuals. These individuals vote
not according to party, but according to personality; with the
"localization" of economic opportunities and the possibilities for
graft and patronage, they find encouragement to vote not from
social obligation, but for their own individual advancement. With
the demise of race, class, and party, "BVIslanders" became a category of people who are more similar than all of the ways in which
they might be different from one another. The conception of
"BVIslanders" as similar individuals opened up possibilities for
what I here gloss as graft and patronage, but which are mischarac-
terized as such.

The Changing Shape of the Civil Service and the
Body Politic

In the last section I touched on economic prospects created for BVIslanders with indigenization campaigns and the rise of the tourist industry. Here, I dwell on a concomitant shift in opportunities for BVIslanders to serve as functionaries of the state and on the use of political power for individual achievement. Parties may not have had a tremendous impact on BVIslanders, but the maneuvering for ministerial positions within the system that required political parties did. Put simply, ministers could get people jobs in the civil service. And, with money from tourism, the BVI was able to greatly expand its civil service. Along the way, the expansion of the civil service worked to mute differences in privilege and power among BVIslanders. It did so, in part, through the electoral district system.

Prior to ministerial government in 1967, most civil servants came from the traditional power centers of the British Virgin Islands—Road Town, Anegada, and the Valley on Virgin Gorda. When Willard Wheatley came into power as chief minister in 1971, however, he and his government made a conscious effort to distribute civil service posts away from these centers and toward Wheatley's own district in East End. Between 1966 and 1973, East End went from contributing 9 percent of the territory's civil servant to contributing 23 percent, outstripping Road Town in 1973.[4] This trend continued until the administration of H. Lavity Stoutt in 1979, when the numbers of civil servants from Road Town and East End remained at their past levels, but increasing numbers of civil servants were drawn from Stoutt's district in West End. By 1988 civil servants were coming from the whole of the territory in about equal proportions, with the more populous areas of Road Town, East End, and Anegada/Virgin Gorda contributing slightly more than the "country" and ridge regions of Tortola. The overall pattern was one of ever-increasing diffusion of civil service posts for people from throughout the territory to the point where, at present, most BVIslanders can name at least one member of their immediate family, if not their own household, who works as a civil servant.

This diffusion of civil service posts resulted in a change in graft and patronage relationships. Previously, if one wanted to cut a road to one's land—a very common need that people turned to the state to meet—one would ask one's elected representative. If that representative was not in good favor with the representative in charge of roads, the good citizen might never see the road built. One man from Road Town remembered, "I wanted cement for my road, but the man in charge of those things was the man from Virgin Gorda." Today, however, matters are simpler and much less about region (and not at all about party, if they ever were). When a neighbor of mine was planning to pour a concrete driveway up the steep slope to his newly constructed house overlooking Road Town, he called up the minister of communications and works on the telephone, and within a couple of months workers from the Public Works Department showed up to help lay the concrete and put in water pipes up the slope. The minister was not my neighbor's district representative.

Diffusion of civil service posts allowed most BVIslanders access to the resources of the state—usually in the form of labor, technical advice, and construction work, precisely the kinds of technical issues the state originally served to resolve. The state machine was now available for all citizens to use. "Graft" and "patronage" are essentially the same thing as "equality" for those whom such relationships serve.

Re-membering Immigrants

The fact that BVIslanders have come to be constituted as status equals means that the actions they take and behaviors they evince, even if they seem to be self-serving or "clannish," are interpreted in terms of "support" and "contribution" and are accorded value. Since everyone is an individual with needs to fulfill, and "everyone" works for the state—that machine that exists to meet the needs of its individual citizens—everyone has access to what are commonly called "graft" and "patronage" relationships. Hence it makes little sense to call these relationships of patronage since such a term implies that there are those whose interests are not served by special relations with people working for the state. Among BVIslanders, indeed, there are very few who could make this complaint. Among immigrants, however, it is another story altogether.

The fiction that all people participate in the state and the state exists to serve all equally, establishes the literal presence of the state in people's lives. It makes the state "matter" (Butler 1993), both in the sense of having import and, crucially, in the sense of being a real entity, a solid totality. The state appears as a machine that exists to serve those who serve it. But when immigrants are "re-membered," when their bodies are forced into the discourse, it is evident that "all discourse of fixation is metaphorical: literality is, in actual fact, the first of metaphors" (Laclau and Mouffe 1985:111). The "objectivity" of the state and society is a materialization, an effect of a half century of techniques and practices "by which discourse produces the effects that it names" (Butler 1993:2).

The absent presence of immigrants in the articulatory practices making up British Virgin Islands state and society points up the limits of the "objective" state-machine and BVI society. Immigrants compel a questioning of the totality that the BVI society and state appear to be. The practices whereby BVIslanders gain verification of their status as members of a sutured and homogeneous society and state depend on the exclusion of antagonisms that appear to come from "outside" state and society. These antagonisms, elements of "disorder" from the point of view of the closed-off totality of state and society, are called forth by recognition of immigrants. When immigrants are taken into account and accorded a place as speaking subjects—when they are "re-cognized"—the fiction of fixity fades away and "the social" evaporates. Immigrants, in their attempts to "join" BVI society, speak the language of choice and preference in opposition to "nature" and the law that makes it. For when the social is dispersed and the state's fixity melts away, the "facts" underlying them—"nature" and "choice"—matter most forcefully.[5]

Chapter 3

Stereotypes and the Immigrant Problem

British Virgin Islanders stereotype Guyanese immigrants of Indian descent as "greedy," "clannish," and "crafty." BVIslanders see themselves, in contrast, as "making contributions" to the community and "offering support" to their peers. This distinction between making contributions and being greedy can be seen in terms of a discourse of inequality that rationalizes people's success or failure by referring to their motivations for action. Like all rationalizations of inequality, these always come after the fact, and it would be fruitless to assess their predictive value. More important, perhaps, the idea that BVIslanders act out of "generous" motives while Guyanese act from "greed" supports liberal understandings of what it means to be a "good citizen" and a "good person." "Good citizens" are conceptualized as a group of normative "individuals" who are defined as similars and equals. "Bad citizens," different and unequal, are cast as unable to stand alone as true individuals and therefore unable to contribute to the social good. Hence, their actions, which may be identical to those of "good citizens," are attributed to self-interested, greedy, or clannish motives.

In stereotyping Guyanese Indians as greedy, BVIslanders echo other African-Caribbean peoples who traditionally have held similar beliefs about Indian-Caribbean people (Williams 1991, Ehrlich 1976, Skinner [1955] 1971, Vertovec 1992).[1] Indeed, accounts of African-descended people's assessments of Indian-descended people as crafty or moneygrubbing litter not only Caribbean ethnography but Caribbean literature—one thinks of the works of Shiva Naipaul, Sam Selvon, and perhaps especially Edgar Mittelholzer's

101

(1950) humorous satire of Trinidadian race relations, *A Morning at the Office* (see Yelvington 1995). Brackette Williams has suggested that stereotypes of Indian-Caribbean people derive, in part, from plantation-era labor hierarchies and the Anglo-European hegemony that maintained and justified them. Building on Williams's work, I suggest that these stereotypes are overdetermined by a complex set of significations that include colonial history but are not limited to it. Stereotypes of people as greedy and clannish are always in flux, for they do not simply or unproblematically map onto "ethnic" groups. This fact challenges a reading of stereotypes as translations of colonial labor hierarchies. They are also parts of a moral discourse about people's worth as individuals and the worth of their actions, a moral discourse that only occasionally concerns ethnicity or race but more often local and interpersonal power struggles. As such, they are mutually constituted by other stereotypes, sometimes ethnic, sometimes not. And they are implicated in materializations of "natural facts" that only occasionally seem to be connected to colonial history and "ethnicity" or "race." Sometimes the natural facts are linked to a sense of "heritage," as history embodied in individuals (cf. Austin-Broos 1994); other times, the natural facts are articulated to "race" or "ethnicity" as intrinsic "natural" attributes, and other times to individual personalities or personalistic dispositions. Each of these elements—the colonial legacy, discourse on moral worth, and "nature"—is its own nodal-point, bringing together diverse practices and significations. Only when "nature," moral assessments of action, and the colonial legacy stitch themselves together do they crystallize an "ethnic" discourse linking some people to greed and clannishness and others to their flip side, "contribution" and "support." In certain circumstances, the insertion of the body of the Guyanese immigrant into everyday discourse makes "ethnic stereotypes" materialize.[2]

While I was in the field, I spent most of my Sundays with Tortola's Sanatan Dharma Satsang, a loose organization of Hindu Guyanese immigrants in the territory, who held worship services and cricket matches most weekends. Whenever I did this, I spent much of the remaining week explaining myself to BVIslander acquaintances, who could not understand why I would want to hang out with such "disgusting" people. BVIslanders who had a greater understanding of my project eventually assumed that, as an anthropologist, it was my job to live among the "natives" and learn their ways, and that the Indians, since they were "alien," "exotic" and non-Christian, besides, were the closest thing to "primitives" on the island. None considered the possibility that I had made friends in the immigrant community or enjoyed myself with them.

During this time, the ethnographic and literary resonance between BVIslanders' stereotypes of Indians and other Caribbean people's stereotypes of Indians led me to consider Brackette Williams's argument about the origins of ethnic and racial hierarchy in Guyana, to see whether the argument made sense in another Caribbean context. And here I began to find some points of discord between the argument Williams made for Guyana and the argument I could make for the BVI. In the end, I found I agreed with the main thrust of Williams's argument. She maintains that "it is in the ideological rationalizations of contribution to economic and cultural development . . . and their links to assumptions about just allocations of economic rewards, burdens, and power . . . that the roots of an understanding of local conceptions of ethnicity, place, and the rights of ethnic groups must be sought" (Williams 1991:132). Williams has identified an important element of a key capitalist hegemonic construct in the Caribbean, that of "contribution" to community, and has shed light on how ideological arguments about "contribution" generate local understandings of difference. But this construct is not solely determined by the colonial legacy.

One of the central claims of Williams's argument is that current conceptions of ethnic and racial hierarchy derive from nineteenth-century plantation organization of production and its ideological rationalizations. Current stereotypes, based as they are on ideas about work and contribution, reflect the histories of slavery and indentured labor. For instance, in the nineteenth century, those "who enjoyed the highest status not only worked the least but also acquired their material worth and their social position by forcing others to labor for them" (Williams 1991:55). Williams explains young men's desire to find jobs that allow one to appear carefree and that allow room for socializing by pointing toward the historical position of the overseer who appeared to work little, to command authority over others, and to reap the benefits and rewards of a particular economic situation as if it were his birthright. Today, as a result of this particular history of labor, Williams argues, the African-Guyanese conception of independence focuses on "controlling the amount of time one must spend working rather than socializing and, when working, the constraints imposed by job-related obligations and regulations" (64).[3] Indentured Indians' insertion into the plantation regime after African emancipation and Africans' partial rejection of plantation work led Indians to economic adaptations centering around kin networks and rural agriculture. Today, the Indian-Guyanese conception of independence focuses on "their contribution and, thus, their right to enjoy the privileges of membership in a unit (for example, domestic group or, more broadly, kin group)" (64). Hence stereotypes of Indians as "clannish." Williams concludes that "past attitudes continue to inform current views of the relations between different forms of work and such factors as racial or ethnic identity, and the social and moral worth of an individual" (55).

The historical argument is a neat one, and persuasive. But does it fit the British Virgin Islands, where current stereotypes of African-descended and Indian-descended people are so strikingly similar to those Williams recorded in Guyana? Several factors lead me to hesitate. For one thing, the BVI does not have the same history of plantation agriculture, slavery, and indenture as Guyana. Settled by Quakers in the eighteenth century, the British Virgin Islands did not possess terrain suitable for large-scale plantation agriculture. Several planters did hold small plantations of sugarcane and cotton worked by slaves. But by the 1760s the British Virgin Islands' Quakers had freed all of their slaves and settled them on lands given to them in perpetuity (Jenkins 1923; McGlynn 1980; O'Neal 1983). Other whites continued to keep African slaves, but slaves were attached to small private estates, not large plantations. More significantly, however, the British Virgin Islands never witnessed the arrival of indentured Indian laborers. Indeed, many British Virgin Islanders I spoke with claimed never to have even seen an "Indian" before the first Guyanese immigrant arrived in the late 1960s. The time-depth of racial and ethnic hierarchy in Guyana simply does not exist for the BVI. Past hierarchies could not therefore map onto present-day ones. How, then, do we account for the similarity of stereotypes?

We can dismiss several possible explanations rather quickly. Perhaps British Virgin Islanders learned the stereotypes of Indians they presently hold from African-Guyanese immigrants. But very few African-Guyanese immigrants have come to the BVI. In my time there I met only two, and I actively sought them out. Perhaps British Virgin Islanders learned these stereotypes during their own periods of migration abroad. While some British Virgin Islander men did travel to Trinidad for work in the oil fields in the first half of this century and did meet some "Indians" there, there was no migration of BVIslander workers to Guyana at any point during this century or the last. Perhaps British Virgin Islanders learned these stereotypes from the mass media or from their schooling and textbooks. This possibility is more plausible, but it puts an important twist into the argument that traces historical continuities between present stereotypes and past labor hierarchies. It would suggest, not that past attitudes inform current views of the relationship between contribution, work, identity, and moral worth, but that certain current conceptions of what past attitudes might have been inform current views. How is a past imagined to help present hierarchies make sense?

Clearly the historical legacy is a part of the problem of stereotypes, but perhaps plays a more complicated role (Segal 1993). I argue that the imagining of the colonial past outlined by Williams only crystallizes an "ethnic" stereotype when in solution with a discourse on the moral worth of people's actions and a materialization of "nature" after the law.[4] After first outlining the pattern of Guyanese immigration to the BVI, I will turn to the moral discourse by which BVIslanders and others make sense of people's actions.

BVIslanders imagine themselves as similar in a way much more fundamental than all the ways in which they are different when they construct themselves as legal citizens and when they argue that they, unlike immigrants, "contribute" to the life of the territory. At the same time, BVIslanders envision a realm of natural difference that the formal legal equality granted by citizenship mitigates. Noncitizens' inequality is not, however, lessened but affirmed by law: the law levels distinctions between BVIslanders because it purports to reflect their deepest "natural"/national similarities, but places an unbridgeable chasm between BVIslanders and immigrants whose root natures are "different" from those of BVIslanders. These deep natural differences are seen to derive from "blood" or "race" and also from "place" or "territory." Some natures are better than others. BVIslanders fit Guyanese immigrants into a discourse in which people with bad natures are unable to fulfill their needs without assistance, either from others or from supposedly unfair advantages that their natures confer. The subordinated seem to be subordinate because they have bad natures. At the same time, when subordinated people attempt to rise in social position, their bad natures are seen as conferring unfair advantages: they are not bound by morals or conventions, as people with "good" natures are, and will climb up the social ladder by pulling others down from it. Good persons, by contrast, are seen as having natures that allow them to meet all their needs and then enable them to "contribute" to the greater social good. Immigrants, as needy people, always appear to be acting self-interestedly to meet their needs whenever they attempt to contribute to the social good. So immigrants, by definition, never truly "contribute" anything at all. The "nature" of immigrants determines their motivations. They always appear to be self-interested and greedy. Needy, greedy people do not have the nature it takes to be a good citizen.

Guyanese Immigration to the BVI

Since the 1960s, significant numbers of Guyanese immigrants of South Asian descent have come to the BVI in search of jobs in construction and the service sector. BVIslanders and other Caribbean peoples refer to Guyanese people of South Asian descent as "Indians" or "East Indians." In the BVI, "Guyanese" has become synonymous with "Indian," since so few Guyanese of African descent have immigrated.

The 1980 census reported the presence in the territory of 98 "East Indians" and 39 "Hindus." By 1990, these numbers had increased to 507 and 348, respectively. At present, Guyanese represent the third most numerous immigrant group in the territory (after St. Kitts–Nevis and St. Vincent, respectively), and "East Indians" represent the third most numerous "racial" group (after the census categories "African-Negro-Black" and "White," respectively). The Indian immigrants in the BVI can be divided into five waves or groups, based on their geographical origin and the circumstances surrounding their migration.[5]

The first wave, a group of Guyanese immigrants, came in the late 1960s when a Guyanese company contracted by the government began work on several large-scale construction projects. Many of these first immigrants subsequently left the territory for the United States, Canada, or a return to Guyana. Two families remained and, throughout the 1970s, helped about thirty of their friends and relatives come into the territory by finding them jobs, taking care of immigration papers, putting up the bond deposit required of all immigrants, and helping them find a place to live. Since that time, there has been a slow trickle of Guyanese immigrants into the territory, growing into a small flood by the 1980s.

The second wave, another group of Guyanese immigrants to the BVI, consists of people who arrived in the early 1980s. Almost all of the second-wave immigrants were from the county of Berbice, and most had been wage laborers in rice and sugarcane fields before migrating. Many quickly found a place for themselves in the rapidly growing tourist service sector. Meanwhile, a prominent BVIslander, finding that he could employ Guyanese Indians at significantly lower wages than he could BVIslanders, hired many of these new immigrants and became known in some circles as "the Guyanese Ambassador." Quite a few men found jobs in construction, transportation, and dock work; women not engaged in tourist services found jobs as cooks, seamstresses, and clerks.

By 1985, these second-wave immigrants were joined by a third Guyanese group, this one composed of former teachers and civil servants, many of whom found jobs in the BVI as teachers, accountants, civil servants, and secretaries. One of these, who had some religious training in Guyana, and under the patronage of one of the two families who had arrived in the 1960s, set himself up as the local pandit. He took up residence in an apartment owned by the matron of that family and began to hold regular *hawans* and *poojas*[6] in his house. By the late 1980s, new arrivals from Guyana quickly learned that they had to strike up a good relationship with this matron and pandit if they were to make it in the BVI. The Department of Immigration, in fact, helped foster this almost clientistic relationship by sending recently arrived and often confused immigrants to see the matron, who paid their immigration fees and agreed to sponsor the new arrivals during their stay in the territory. This arrangement contributed to an impression among BVIslanders that all the "Indians" coming into the territory were related to one another. By the early 1990s, new immigration officers tended to assume as a matter of course that arriving Indians were relatives of the matron.

In the late 1980s, a fourth wave of "Indians" came into the territory. Not all of the people in this group were Guyanese. One was from Suriname, some were technicians and agricultural experts from Guyana, and others were from the Indian subcontinent itself. At present, Pakistan, Bangladesh, India, and Sri Lanka are each represented in the BVI. All of these fourth-wave people are educated urbanites with a strong interest in what they call "Indian culture," referring mainly to musical, dance, and literary traditions. During the time of my fieldwork, these individuals were constituting themselves as a block with the Surinamese individual and Guyanese extension officers, against the pandit and the matron. One member of this newer group was trying to generate interest in a Sanskrit course, and the group was raising funds to build a temple and cultural center.

The fifth wave, finally, includes a group of very recent immigrants, most of whom are young men in their twenties and late teens who have found employment as laborers in enterprises ancillary to the tourism industry, such as sail making, boat repair and maintenance, shipping, and transport. These young men move between all of the groups listed above and seem not to hold deep allegiances to any one of them. Most, too, consider themselves "Madrassi." That is, they hold that they are descendants of indentured laborers from "Madras," the place-name Guyanese Indians give to the south of India. Madrassi are marked racially by other Guyanese Indians, who consider them "dark." They are also marked by their low class position and by their religious worship centering around "Kali Devi." According to one Madrassi youth, "Kali Devi do wild things": making devotions to Kali can entail animal sacrifice and spirit possession. Madrassi youths were eager to gain my friendship in the hopes that I would be able to find them American wives or help them migrate to the United States, legally or illegally.

The first three groups of immigrants make up the core of the Guyanese immigrant community as it is organized under the local pandit. I spent almost every Sunday with these people, either at worship or at a cricket match. The pandit holds *hawans* nearly every week during which a *pooja* for a particular god-manifestation is observed. The pandit holds services only when someone agrees to sponsor them, however. During my stay, people sponsored *hawans* to observe birthdays, to congratulate a newlywed couple, for a sick person, before embarking on a journey—or to say farewell to the anthropologist. Services were frequently pre-empted by cricket matches as most of the Guyanese men play in one of the local leagues—a purely immigrant affair, since British Virgin Islanders do not play cricket but rather American base-ball—where they compete against teams made up of immigrants from other Caribbean places.

To sponsor a *hawan,* an individual pays the pandit between twenty-five and thirty U.S. dollars and buys food to feed the people who attend. Attendance varies from twenty to fifty people, includ-ing men, women, and children. The minimum food requirements include ghee, sugar, candied fruit or raisins, and flour to make *prasad,* a sweet dough offered to the gods and to the congregation. Most sponsors also provided curried chickpeas (*channa*), potatoes, fried bread (*nan*), Kool-Aid, fresh fruit, and occasionally sweet rice pudding (*kir*). The most elaborate *hawan* I attended included cur-ried chicken, curried spinach, and curried goat as well as the aforementioned items.

In addition to *hawans,* the pandit held religious services for five holidays during my stay—Diwali, Ramnaumie, Hanuman-jayanti, Phagwah, and Holi.[7] Holidays were a source of tension between the pandit's followers and the members of the fourth group of Indian immigrants, who on more than one occasion held their own services separate from pandit's and drew significant numbers of his followers away from him. Indeed, the Diwali cele-brations of this group featured music, dancing, plays, and moun-tains of food, and they drew a crowd of nearly two hundred people even after they had been rained out and postponed a day. Most of those attending were people who normally followed the pandit. These Diwali celebrations also attracted other Caribbean immi-grants, plus a few BVIslanders and expatriate white residents.

BVIslander Stereotypes of Indians

The diversity of and conflicts within the Guyanese immigrant community go unrecognized by British Virgin Islanders. Merely mention the word *Indian* in a group of BVIslanders and you are likely to hear the following kinds of statements: "They save the rust from the pennies," they are "grabbaricious," "They'll eat tuna fish and rice every day just to save pennies." It seems everyone has a personal story to tell, too. Variations upon the following are common:

> They come with nothing and then try to get your job when you're not looking. I was working a Festival booth as a favor, for nothing. A Guyanese comes and asks how much I am making. I tell him nothing. He says, "Nothing! You crazy?" But if I was making money, you know he'd go to my boss and say he work for half as much! That's how they are.

Of course, there are many BVIslanders who do not express prejudice against Indians with the vehemence of those whose words I discuss subsequently. Quite a few BVIslanders are, as they put it, "curious" about "things they don't understand," and want to learn more about Indians, especially their religion. As one BVIslander told me, "We are ignorant; and we need to learn about these people so we can live with them." At the Diwali celebrations, several BVIslanders quietly looked on from the sidelines, and were shy to speak about their reactions to the celebrations. Some, not without trepidation, sampled the sweets and snacks for sale. Their young children, however, took to the sweets with gusto and were delighted by the spectacle of the celebrations—the costumes, the decorations, the music, and especially the "Indian" dancing.

Furthermore, some BVIslanders claim that much of the ill will expressed toward Guyanese immigrants comes not from "native" BVIslanders, but from immigrants from other Caribbean places. Those who have not obtained citizenship see Guyanese as a threat to their jobs and their residence status. Those who *have* acquired citizenship legitimate their status by emphasizing the hard work they put into getting it. They do not want Guyanese people's "thrift," "selfishness," or "craftiness" to aid them in getting citizenship status any more easily.

BVIslanders who have had some education abroad, or who have frequent dealings with immigrants from other Caribbean islands living in the BVI, will sometimes refer to Indians as "coolies." Interestingly, other Caribbean immigrants claim that BVIslanders do not use the word *coolie* because they are too simple-minded, too childlike, or too parochial to know it, or even to "realize" the "threat" posed by Indians. I have heard quite a few BVIslander teenagers use the epithet, however, but only among themselves and never to an Indian's face. BVIslander teenagers in general stay away from their Indian classmates and view them as incomprehensible. Once when two Indian boys got into a tussle, a BVIslander youth restrained another who was setting out to break it up. "It's an Indian thing," the one boy told the other, "you can't understand it. Best leave it alone."

BVIslanders complain that Indians are "clannish," that they "stick to themselves" and never get involved in community activities: "You never see them at funerals, they never come to Red Cross." There is a common myth that the early immigrants rapidly set themselves to gaining passage for as many of their relatives as they could. There are rumors that Indian teachers have helped Indian students in their classes cheat on exams. One BVIslander exclaimed, "They are always trying to help their own to get ahead, and it's the local [i.e., BVIslander] students who suffer!"

Then there is the matter of their religion. Most of the Guyanese Indians in the BVI are Hindu, and about a quarter of them are devout. BVIslanders tend to assume that all Indians are Hindu. The Hindus in the BVI are followers of Sanatan Dharma, one of the more orthodox of the Hindu sects in the Caribbean and the one that places a heavy ritual emphasis on the manipulation of physical objects in propitiating various manifestations of God (see Vertovec 1992). They use flowers, sticks, mango leaves, and other "natural" objects in their worship, as well as ghee, incense, bells, and conch shells. These are all offered to the god-manifestations who are present at the *pooja* in the form of decorative paintings. When I first attended a Hindu *pooja* in Tortola, my hunch was that Methodist, Anglican, and fundamentalist BVIslanders would see the colorful paintings of the god-manifestations as a form of "heathen idolatry." I was rather surprised, then, when I learned that BVIslanders see Hindu worship as "obeah," a kind of West Indian magic or witchcraft. A BVIslander is struck more by the use of plants and leaves than by the use of images of the gods, since obeah was practiced using similar "natural" objects. When I asked one BVIslander whether obeah was still practiced in the BVI, he responded curtly, "It is against the law."[8] Since this response occurred in the context of a discussion on Hinduism, I took his tone to indicate that Hinduism, "really" a form of obeah, should be against the law, too. To make matters worse, the BVIslanders who have seen the word *Sanatan* on Tortola Hindu Organisation advertisements tend, at first, to read it as *Satan*. The only interfaith council in the territory, meanwhile, is the BVI Christian Council. The Tortola Hindu Organisation, needless to say, is not invited.[9]

BVIslanders who have had more than passing contact with Guyanese immigrants usually point to their dietary practices or table manners as evidence for both their thriftiness and their "disgusting" habits. When I mentioned to a group of BVIslanders that Hindu worship on Tortola is always followed by a meal of tasty Indian food, a BVIslander within earshot retorted, "Them Guyanese food? Chick peas and rice? Is that a meal?" Guyanese table manners come under attack, too: "They picking up their food in their fingers and shoveling it into their mouths like someone going to come and take it from them. Greedy, man, greedy!"

These stereotypes are strikingly similar to those reported in the literature on Guyana and elsewhere in the Caribbean. It is important to emphasize that they are referential; like all stereotypes and identity categories, they make sense in a field of discourse and are mutually constituted by other stereotypes and identity categories. To fully understand them, then, we must examine the flip side of "greed."

"Making a Contribution"

Conflicts among people in the British Virgin Islands tend to involve moral judgments of a person's or group's character based on an opposition between "support"—a local term—and what could be glossed as "self-interest." Some descriptive phrases that indicate the opposite of support include "being clannish," "being greedy," or "having a dirty heart." With the exception of the last, which I heard only in conversations with Guyanese immigrants, these phrases are used by BVIslanders and immigrants to the BVI alike. Both groups also use the verb phrase *to make a contribution* to indicate "giving support," the opposite of being self-interested.

Of course, the opposite of "support" includes characterizations of people's moral worth that reflect the stereotypes of Indian-Guyanese that Williams reports and that BVIslanders voice. Indians are seen as being "greedy" or "clannish," and, as one woman put it, "they do not make contributions to the territory." These expressions constitute stereotypes of Indians as an "ethnic group." However, the behaviors these phrases are supposed to reference, and the phrases themselves, do not simply and do not always constitute an "ethnic" stereotype. Rather, they are part of a discourse shared by Indians and non-Indians in the BVI and perhaps elsewhere in the Caribbean that people use to make moral judgments about others regardless of their "ethnicity" or "race" and that only in special circumstances come to signify purportedly "ethnic" or "racial" characteristics or dispositions. That in itself would suggest that stereotypes of Indians as greedy are overdetermined.

BVIslanders and others frequently measure immigrants in terms of the "contribution" they have made, or failed to make, to the general life of the territory. Sometimes, "making a contribution" is a grand, showy, newsworthy affair, as in cases where wealthy North American or European expatriates donate large sums of money for the construction of school additions, bridges, hotels, or other big projects. More frequently, "making a contribution" entails participating in one of the territory's many civic organizations, such as the Red Cross, Girls' Brigade, Toastmasters Club, Rotary Clubs, Lions Clubs; one of the territory's established churches or church organizations; or any activity that results in a furthering of the territory's interests in tourism and "national development," such as participation in the annual August Festival commemorating emancipation. Attending funerals of prominent BVIslanders can be considered "making a contribution" and can help an outsider establish a favorable reputation among BVIslanders. Even being critical of the government in letters to the editors of local newspapers can be considered a "contribution" to the territory's life, although it may likely generate debate on whether the critic ought to be granted citizenship or ought to be deported. One now-deceased longtime contributor of invective to the editorial pages was famous for his boldness; in his last series of letters to the editor, he demanded citizenship for his "birthday present." He never got it; but he is still remembered as a "character" and as having "contributed some good laughs" to the territory.

He was not alone, however, in expecting citizenship in return for his "contribution." Indeed, immigrants from other Caribbean places, North America, and Europe who have "made their contributions" frequently reap the reward of citizenship. Whether someone has "made a contribution" is cited by immigration officials and people on the street alike as a (if not *the*) primary consideration in the government's decision on whether to grant someone citizenship. One white immigrant commented negatively about other whites who never make a contribution: "You have to do something, do something in the community, in order to make your way in. A lot of white people say, 'I'm too busy!' They're just takers, they take, they line their pockets and leave. Some of them haven't even tasted mango! It could be Hong Kong, they don't know. People like it when you do something for the community, it's a good way to make yourself known, so people know you and you get in." Many of the so-called "Syrians" living in the BVI—people from Lebanon and the West Bank, and founding members of the BVI Islamic Society—have acquired citizenship, and many "made their contribution" in the form of financial donations to organizations such as the Red Cross.

Community organizations make up the bulk of BVI social life. BVIslanders frequently point out that they "don't go out visiting." One of my most difficult adjustments to doing fieldwork in the BVI was acclimating myself to a nine-to-five schedule, since usually by dinnertime everyone would behind the closed doors of home. There is little of the street life I had experienced during earlier fieldwork in the less-developed island of Dominica. In the BVI, all extrafamilial social life happens in the context of church and the many community organizations. Almost all cultural, dramatic, sporting, educational, or other recreational events are put on by these organizations. Many BVIslanders and some Caribbean immigrants to the BVI belong to several. Often, a person will participate in church activities, belong to one of the major community organizations, and help out with one of the clubs for children.

There are two chapters of the Rotary Club—one is more

"establishment," made up of older businessmen and politicians and closed to women. The other, "Rotary II," is made up of the 1960s generation of more "progressive" individuals and is open to women. Both Rotaries have the highest status of all of the organizations. A close third is the solidly middle-class, mainly female and mainly well-established immigrant Toastmasters Club. There are several chapters of the Lions Club. In addition, there are "ladies' clubs," the Red Cross, several self-help groups (Al-Anon, Overeaters Anonymous, etc.), yachting clubs, a philatelic society, a hibiscus society, a humane society (these last two made up almost wholly of white expatriates), countless church groups, children's organizations such as Girl Guides, Girls' Brigade, Boys' Brigade, Girl Scouts, and Boy Scouts and various athletic organizations for both children and adults. Several of the immigrant groups have set up their own clubs, such as the United BVI Latin Association (for Dominicans and Puerto Ricans), the Dominica Progressive Society, the St. Vincent Society, and so forth. African-Guyanese immigrants have a Guyanese Society that is unofficially closed to Indians and that supports the Guyanese People's Nationalist Congress (PNC).

Community organizations are very important in the BVI. For a territory of eighteen thousand people, the telephone book lists thirty-two churches and clubs besides those already noted. At the time of my fieldwork, an additional sixty-five were listed by the Public Library. All told, there are probably nearly three hundred such organizations servicing the population (the majority of which are informal and unregistered). Yet there are no labor unions.[10] Unions are based on an ideology of category membership, or membership based on one's placement in a particular social category (i.e., "workers"). Without exception, the community organizations of the BVI are guided by an ethic of individual responsibility. For instance, the Toastmasters Club, I was told, stresses "the individual's ability to communicate effectively, to be able to stand up before a group and speak his mind without any note cards, to be able to speak for himself." Girl Guides and Girls' Brigade, similarly, stress individual ingenuity, creativity, and responsibility for one's actions. Rotary is about success in business and competitiveness—it is, I was told, an organization of "managers," of "the men at the helm."

"Making a contribution" is a voluntary act effected through one of the community organizations. One comes to a community organization as an individual, and out of one's own goodwill one gives what one can. "Giving of one's time" equals "giving to the community"; it means "being a good citizen" by "making a contribution" to the national life. When one "contributes," one demonstrates one's autonomous, nonneedy and independent "nature." It is no accident that immigrants who "demonstrate" autonomy and whose actions subsequently become defined as "making a contribution" generally do acquire citizenship. Immigrants who disavow any prior attachments and identities are often "taken in" by BVIslanders.

Many BVIslanders and non-Guyanese immigrants maintain that Indians have made no contribution to BVI society. One Trinidadian woman told me that all the Guyanese had ever done was "to build the roads." I asked why building roads was less of a contribution than driving over them to get to a Red Cross meeting. She replied that they had *had* to build the roads, because "that's what they were *paid* for, that's why they were brought over in the first place!" Her characterization of BVI government labor policy is not far off the mark—Guyanese laborers were recruited in the past by government officers for manual labor, especially during the first wave of Guyanese immigration. What struck me, however, was the contrast this person drew between labor for a wage and "making a contribution." Implicitly, she held that labor is not a "contribution" because one does it for pay, or out of "self-interested" motives, not "altruistic" ones.

For BVIslanders, Indians will not make good citizens because they "take care of their own" and are "selfish." Being selfish is different, however, from being an "individualist," since every selfish act of an Indian has "clannish" motives. The discourse of contributions casts Indians as thinking "a victory for one is a victory for them all." The success of an Indian student illicitly aided by an Indian teacher, for example, is the success of the "clan." They do not "contribute" to voluntary community organizations. Instead, they "hoard" all the wealth they earn. An Indian can be very successful as a businessman due to his "wiles"; but in not putting something "back" into the community, he demonstrates (according to BVIslanders) that his greater commitment is toward Indians as a group. "They are only interested in their own," says one informant. I once pointed out to a BVIslander that many Indians put a great deal of time, money, and work into the Indian cultural celebrations that are open to the public. In that sense, I argued, Indians *did* contribute to the wider cultural life of the territory. "And where does the money go, the money that they raise at those things?" she demanded. I replied that it probably went to cover the costs of putting on the event. "You see! This proves what I am saying," she said, "they only support their people!"

Motivations for Action

Judgments about people based on their support and contributions do not only occur across "ethnic" or "racial" lines. Guyanese immigrants frequently used evidence of a Guyanese person's support of others for deducing moral worth. And Guyanese immigrants used evidence of support—or lack of it—to cast judgment on British Virgin Islanders and other immigrants. In doing so, they occasionally voiced stereotypes of African-Caribbean people that echo African-Caribbean stereotypes of themselves.

At a cricket match between two Indian teams, a Guyanese observer noted that the Indian teams had "more support" than other teams. The Indian teams were playing on the grounds of the elementary school while, across the street in the A. O. Shirley Recreation Grounds, with about six times the space and seating of the school field, two teams made up of immigrants from St. Vincent, Dominica, and St. Kitts were competing as part of an official tournament. At the Indian game, about 150 people—Indians and non-Indians—had gathered and were milling around and enjoying a big barbecue put on by the Indian teams to raise money. Across the street, about thirty people watched the "official" game from their seats in the bleachers. The low attendance was taken as evidence of the other teams' lack of "support." People didn't support them, I was told, because "for them it a money ting." In this case, then, my Indian informants attributed African-Caribbean cricket players' lack of support to their emphasis on the monetary rewards of the game and their "greed" to win.

At the same game, a Guyanese schoolteacher remarked to me

that immigration to the BVI created new social networks that people use to "gain support," especially support in financial matters. Immigrants used their new contacts to send remittances home to family in Guyana and to rely on for favors in times of crisis. The possibilities for gaining "support" are valued as positive aspects of an otherwise often bleak immigration experience.

"Support" crosses race and ethnic lines. One Indian-Guyanese man assisted a former student of his, who is African-Guyanese, in her effort to immigrate to the BVI. And one Indian-Guyanese woman shopkeeper, waxing nostalgic on the "racial harmony" she claimed existed in Guyana, told a story of harmony and mutual support between blacks and Indians in Guyana, sharing in worship. She described a *jag*, a religious gathering where "people come from all over and sit on tarps on de gron' and listen to de big gurus and pandits, and dere's lots of food. It's not like here, Bill: de negros deh know about dese tings and dey come sit, too, right don on de gron.'"[11] In her narrative she drew an explicit contrast between blacks in the BVI and blacks in Guyana: those in Guyana "support" Indians because they "know about dese tings," that is, they have knowledge of and respect for Indian customs, while those in the BVI are "ignorant" and so offer neither respect nor support. It is the "ignorance" and "dirty hearts" of BVIslanders that cause conflict between Indians and blacks in the BVI, she contended.

The opposite of support is not simple bad-naturedness, it seems, but rather support gone wrong or support for the wrong reasons. People are said to have "dirty hearts" or be "clannish" when their efforts to gain or give support appear to be based on their own self-interest. One rather candid Indian-Guyanese seamstress told me that she sometimes feels that she herself has a dirty heart, because she frequently "hails" or calls greetings to anyone she sees who "looks Indian, so I always think they must be Guyanese," in order to "get in with them" and gain their support. Indians in the BVI use the Hindi word *korhi* to describe people whose efforts to give or gain support are undergirded by selfish motives. When I asked for a definition of the term, I was told, "Them too korhi—[means] them can't do anything right, them can't do nothing without corruption and troublesomeness."

Understanding Inequality in the Caribbean

Judgments based on people's supposed motivations behind giving or gaining support are identical whether the person being assessed or the person making the assessment is a BVIslander or a Guyanese immigrant. The problem with seeing these as "ethnic" stereotypes is that everyone uses them to describe anyone else. Williams's "colonial legacy" argument works to explain stereotypes, but not unproblematically, and not necessarily in a place like the BVI where the specific colonial legacy Williams's argument relies on is an imaginary one. "Ethnic" distinctions are overdetermined, by colonial history as Williams suggests, but also by a moral order that explains inequality in terms of nature and the objectification of that nature as determining motivations. Indeed, the colonial legacy Williams describes is also a materialization of a "natural history," that is, a "heritage" that is part of the objectification of determining and determinate nature that purportedly creates motivations and justifies inequality.

Numerous scholars of the region have seen Caribbean peoples as, on the one hand, egalitarian individualists working to mitigate status differentials and, on the other hand, hierarchically organized persons attempting to maintain status distinctions (Wilson 1973; Mintz 1966, 1974; R. Smith 1970; Olwig 1993), but few have explored the liberal legal foundations of Caribbean societies structured in relations of dominance and subordination (cf. Williams 1991; Olwig 1993; Lazarus-Black 1994; R. Smith 1992, who do). Jayawardena (1968) has argued for the importance of separating formal equality from substantive equality in this context. He defines *formal equality* as the equality guaranteed by liberal legal norms and *substantive equality* as the "humanitarian" equality of all persons as human beings. Jayawardena argues that the history of labor exaction in the Caribbean, which denied formal equality to slaves, indentured laborers, and free plantation workers alike, encouraged Caribbean peoples to imagine themselves as inhabiting a world of substantive equals (perhaps as a form of resistance). In a world of substantive equality, people see others who have "gotten ahead" in life as having done so in either an appropriate way or an inappropriate way. To succeed in an appropriate way, one must not advance one's position at the expense of any other, for to do so would be to deny or destroy the substantive equality of all persons by lowering the status of people with whom one had previously enjoyed status equality. People are seen to have succeeded in an inappropriate fashion if they have done so at the expense of others.

In a world of substantive equality, however, it is not always easy to determine whether one has advanced without injury to others. People thus interrogate others' motivations for actions and deduce from motivations whether an individual intended to harm others along their own paths of progress. The metaphor of the "dirty heart" points up an important determining element crystallized in the discourse of motivations. The root of motivations is held to be an interior force or quality, a "nature" deep in the person. An assessment of a person's inner qualities, his or her true character, thus represents an assessment of the person's success. A person with "bad" inner qualities will have advanced at the expense of others; one with "good" inner qualities will have advanced because of those qualities and will therefore deserve his or her riches.

How do people in societies structured by liberal legality determine others' motivations? My contention, following Bourdieu (1977), is that they do not do so purely through observation of people's actions. The same actions are judged by different people differently: those at the top of a hierarchy usually do not cast their own motivations for action in the terms that those at the bottom might cast the same motivations. People at the top claim they got there because of their hard work, born of their virtue. People at the bottom claim that people at the top got there because they are liars and cheats and that only those at the bottom have any real virtue. Different people can ascribe different motivations for the same actions. One's position in a hierarchy of ranked statuses determines the value and virtue one ascribes to others' actions and motivations. Assessments of people's motivations flow not from values ascribed to individuals' actions, but from the value that is assumed to inhere in individuals based on their social status.

BVIslanders see themselves as always-already "above" immigrants in a hierarchy of ranked statuses, and they have institutional verification for their status in the form of citizenship. BVIslanders' position above immigrants gets articulated and justified in terms of BVIslanders' "virtues," made evident by their "contributions." Because they are at the top, they must by definition be virtuous. Their rank as "BVIslanders" guarantees that their actions will be valued and underwrites their motivations as emanating from "good" inner qualities. Being at the top, BVIslanders have nothing to gain from dastardly deeds or nefarious doings; whatever they do, in contrast, is cast as "contributing" to the social good. Immigrants, in contrast, especially Guyanese immigrants, are at the bottom. This social position is attributed by BVIslanders to their "bad" inner qualities; after all, if they had virtue, they would rise to the top. Yet their "bad" inner qualities also pose a threat: the thing to fear most from people with bad natures is that they will use their bad natures to get ahead at others' expense and destroy order. If they are seen to advance at all, their advancement is attributed to their craftiness, greed, and clannishness.

Guyanese immigrants participate in the same discourse. They judge BVIslanders to have achieved their social status through clannishness, craftiness, and greed. They also occasionally judge each other in these terms as well. That makes sense because both the dominant and the dominated share a social world in which making assessments of others' motives can be used to one's advantage whether one is dominant or dominated.[12] One can use such assessments to claim substantive equality and to point the finger at those who lack virtue. Immigrants contest domination by recrafting and reiterating the dominant moral vision (cf. Collier 1988:208). And they do *not* do so "with a difference" (Bhabha 1984; Nelson 1995)—when they reiterate the dominant moral vision, they do not alter it or reformulate it into concerted resistance. Laclau and Mouffe (1985:141–42) argue, and Nelson demonstrates ethnographically (1995), that for subordination to mutate into an antagonistic relation to the dominant order, it must be rearticulated by the subordinate in a discourse external to the dominant order—here, a discourse of "human rights," for example, or a discourse of immigrants' difference *as a group,* would contest BVIslanders' discourse of contribution and greed. But Guyanese immigrants, sharing a moral world with BVIslanders and able to influence people's moral assessments of themselves by participating in it, do not reiterate their subordination as the subordination of immigrants as a class; theirs is a discourse of individual motivation and individual worthiness.

Hence, the stereotype of people who get ahead as "greedy" is not an ethnic stereotype per se. Rather, it is part of a moral discourse for assessing people's actions, a moral discourse reiterated by Caribbean peoples as they negotiate (or creolize and materialize[13]) the liberal legal orders left them by colonialism. It materializes "ethnicity" only when it is brought together with understandings of status distinctions as "natural" or "racial"—when a BVIslander marks the body of an Indian. And its materialization of ethnicity is denied and disavowed by those whose bodies it marks. The facticity of the racially marked body is crucial to the crystallization of "ethnic" stereotypes. The moral assessments people make revolve around notions of "nature," and nature, as I show in the next chapter, is linked to both "kinship" and "race"—hence the concern with Indians' clannishness. Citizenship law emerges as a key site for the crystallization of "racial" difference read as natural and as "in the blood." These differences, taken as natural ground, can then be articulated to motivations for action and can "explain" why Indians are "greedy."

Chapter 4
Race, Place, and Citizenship

The debate over who has claims to legal and cultural citizenship in the quasi-national community of the British Virgin Islands has been at a slow boil for the past twenty or so years, but it bubbles violently from time to time. My fieldwork was during one of these more active periods. Old-time residents of the islands claimed that only those descended from "real" British Virgin Islanders had a claim to citizenship. And they had the law behind them. Others, mostly children of immigrants, maintained that citizenship should be granted based on birth within the territory of the BVI. They were spurred on by the Calypso King of the BVI, himself an immigrant, who sang that "where we're born" ought to determine where, in a truly deep sense, "we're from."

When assessing others, BVIslanders and immigrants appear to make judgments based on putative motivations and then from motivations deduce people's moral worth. The previous chapter argued that assessments of individuals' motivations flow not from values ascribed to individuals' actions, but from the value that is assumed to inhere in individuals based on their social status. This discussion suggests that a status hierarchy is at the basis of judgments about people's "dirty hearts." But aside from the obvious status differential, and hence presumed value, between citizens and noncitizens, it leaves the origins of status hierarchy unexamined. If moral assessments of people's actions flow from relative valuations of people's social status, we need to account for the social statuses that appear to be given in the natural order of things by those making such assessments. The discourse of motivations exists alongside a discourse of "natural difference" that explains the character of people's motivations for action. Social status is overdetermined by imaginings of colonial history, by a moral order that stresses the equality of persons and explains inequality with reference to people's "natures," and by the objectification of those natures as determining and determinate "facts."

BVIslanders and immigrants conjure up a domain of "nature" in their debates over who has claims to citizenship. For citizens who never emigrated, the law helps construct the nature of identity in terms of descent, blood, and "race." For immigrants and their children, the law lends its emphasis on region and jurisdiction to construct identity in terms of supposedly preexistent places. The next chapter concerns return émigré British Virgin Islanders and immigrants who disavow their "difference," for whom the law enables notions of individual ability and individuality that appear to make place- and race-based identities superfluous. Here, however, the focus is on how conceptions of belonging and identity based, on the one hand, on place and, on the other hand, on descent work to naturalize inequalities. The law is critical to the creation and maintenance of these competing identities and the inequalities that they cover over or remove from debate.

Race and Place in the Law

Lawyers and legal historians debating criteria for determining nationality and citizenship have struggled with what was termed as early as 1918 the "race or place" problem: Should citizenship and nationality follow from parent to child, or should they depend on the place of the child's birth? (See Baty 1918–19.) These legal scholars have tended to view "race or place," the *jus sanguinis* (law of the blood) and the *jus soli* (law of the soil), as separate, distinct, and ultimately alternative criteria. Several have gone about trying to suggest a third option, such as a "jus educationis," or a legal principle that would determine nationality or citizenship based on a child's country of education (Baty 1918–19; Randall 1924). In contrast to the traditional legal literature, this chapter argues that the jus sanguinis and jus soli are themselves mutually constitutive—not really separate options at all—since each is implicated in the other. The fact that both work so well for racist reasoning in liberal societies should lead us to wonder about their mutuality, as should the point made by Liisa Malkki that concepts such as "motherland and fatherland . . . suggest that each nation is a grand genealogical tree, rooted in the soil that nourishes it" (Malkki 1992:28). Different bloods come from different soils, and different soils are different because of the different genealogies they generate and support.

Sociolegal scholars are beginning to pay attention to the ways in which law constitutes inequalities: the inequalities it is supposed to help mitigate, to "level the playing field" and grant equality of opportunity, and the inequalities it claims it is helpless to redress (Collier, Maurer, and Suárez-Navaz 1995; Fitzpatrick 1987; Merry 1991, 1992; Yngvesson 1993; Danielsen and Engle 1995; Lazarus-Black and Hirsch 1994). The argument advanced here is not that liberal law enables people to "use" conceptions of nature or identity in their struggles for equality or their struggles to maintain dominance but, to the contrary, that liberal law is constitutive of a "nature" that people see as a resource to use or a determining factor for their social statuses and identities.

The idea that liberal law creates a determining nature seems at first to be counterintuitive, but returning to the roots of liberal legalism sheds light on the nature made material by liberal law. Arguing against the medieval and Renaissance idea that natural and social laws were one, both written by the hand of God, and that God positioned people into different social ranks, Thomas Hobbes declared that "nature hath made all men equall" (Hobbes [1651] 1994:86). In so doing, Hobbes articulated what was to become a central tenet of liberal law: that all "men" were equal by nature.

The "man" as conceived by Hobbes was a "proprietor of his own person and or capacities, owing nothing to society for them" (Macpherson 1962:3). This modern concept of the person made possible a different understanding of the relationship between social rank and individual ability. Whereas people in medieval times were supposedly assigned a social status by God, which they could fulfill well or poorly according to their abilities to refrain from sin and temptation, modern people supposedly acquired their own social status based on their inner capacities and the uses to which they put them. The medieval person had to resist sin to realize his station in life. The modern person had to work hard using the capacities with which he was endowed by nature to acquire his station in life (see Collier, Maurer, and Suárez-Navaz 1995).[1]

Hobbes's dictum that "nature hath made all men equall" presupposes a realm of nature apart from and prior to the laws men made to regulate themselves. The persons imagined by Hobbes owed nothing to society for their social and economic positions, but rather were constituted by a "nature" now endowed with creative capacities whose laws could be discovered by experimental science (see Latour 1993; Shapin and Schaffer 1984). If individuals failed in their ambitions, if equality remained elusive, liberal ideology left only "nature" to account for it. If nature, conceived as determining and determinate, had made men equal, only it could make men unequal.

The Enlightenment thus witnessed a separation of things that in the Renaissance were one and the same: the laws of nature and the laws of men. Men can "uncover" the secrets of nature (Keller 1993), but when they do so, they are merely "discovering" something that has been always-already there, waiting to be discovered. In the liberal conception, nature has an ontology, a thingness unto itself, separate from the laws of men. "Natural facts" simply exist, and people construct social and cultural worlds out of them. Law in this conception exists as a creation of men to regulate themselves, to mitigate the inequalities created by nature, inequalities that the law is incapable of completely erasing because, according to the ideology of liberal law, they are given in the natural order of things.

Verena Stolcke has identified the ethos of equality and the persistent inequalities generated by market forces as one of the key contradictions of liberalism. She has argued that notions of "race" as inherited inferiority have papered over this contradiction by casting inequality as the result of the "natural" failings of individual people. If individuals fail despite the promise of equality of opportunity that liberal societies offer to all, and if their failure is not attributable to some "irrational" choice of their own not to succeed, then according to liberal logic, "this . . . [has] to be due to some essential, innate and therefore hereditary deficiency. The person, or better even, his or her biological endowment, rather than the socioeconomic context, [is] to be blamed for this"

(Stolcke 1993:33). This is the principle behind the "old racism" of the nineteenth century and most of the twentieth.

The logic of the so-called new racism, where persons are not deemed inferior by virtue of heredity but merely "ethnically" or "culturally" different and unassimilable, similarly naturalizes inequality in liberal societies. Stolcke traces a continuity between the old and new racisms (1993:33–34; Stolcke 1995; Balibar 1991). She identifies in the rhetoric of the new racism a concern with "population" that brings heritability and the attendant conceptions of gender and reproduction that "produce" populations back in (cf. Foucault 1980). In addition, the new racism adds a dimension of spatiality: people have no choice over where they are born or enculturated, just as they have no choice over their genetic endowment. Since these are qualities beyond "choice," they are the only factors through which liberal societies can explain inequalities that appear "natural" because unchosen by those suffering under them.

Peter Wade (1993) has argued that much current theorizing about the constructedness of "race" implicitly relies on a distinction between nature and culture according to which nature is a given substrate out of which people build meaningful cultural distinctions deemed racial. Analytical definitions of race that assume race to be a cultural construction after certain natural facts—either phenotypic variation or genotype—reproduce, Wade argues, the very distinction between nature and culture that empowers racialist thinking and racial categories in the first place as having some basis in "natural" facts. Wade concludes, "[I]t is not the original, 'natural' distinction between genotype and phenotype from which derives the supplementary, 'cultural' distinction between the significance and insignificance of race, but precisely the latter which makes possible the former" (1993:30).

Wade follows Donna Haraway's admonition against taking nature as the stuff from which culture fabricates itself. Haraway has argued against the "productionist logic" wherein "nature is only the raw material of nature appropriated, preserved, enslaved, exalted or otherwise made flexible for disposal by culture in the logic of capitalist colonialism" (Haraway 1989:13). Wade points out that in discussions of "race," analysts often "refer to a level of biology ('phenotypical variation') that is presented as neutral and

undifferentiated": "what is in fact highly structured and historically specific is presented to the reader as unstructured and general" (Wade 1993:19).

"Race," Wade notes, is not always about phenotype. In scientific discussions it is also often linked to a "'deep' level of biology" (1993:27)—the level of heritability, biogenetic relatedness,
"ancestry," and "descent." He rightly points out that "descent" and
biogenetic relatedness are ultimately "about" kinship. And as
Yanagisako and Collier (1987) argued, kinship is constituted in
Western worlds along with another purportedly natural domain—
the domain of sex and sexual reproduction. Analysts have seen
"sex" as the raw material from which Westerners create the "cultural" domain of gender. Yanagisako and Collier point out that
"the fundamental units of gender—males and females—and the
fundamental units of kinship—the genealogical grid—are both
viewed [in scholarship on gender and kinship] as existing outside
of and beyond culture" (1987:29; see also Delaney 1986). Gender
and kinship studies both start from the same set of assumptions
about what are presumably "natural" differences—the supposed
"facts" of sexual reproduction. Studies of race relying implicitly on
some notion of phenotype or genotype similarly begin from the
supposed biological "facts" of sex and reproduction.

"Nature" in the interrelated and mutually constituting discourses of race and sex has the status of an object-domain, a given
world of things and facts, resources and constraints, that all peoples find self-evident and given in the world. Nature is just "out
there"; it is universal; all peoples must deal with "it" as they go
about making cultural life for themselves. How has the separation
between nature and culture been made meaningful and powerful
in Western contexts? Why does "nature" come to be privileged as
more objectively real than "culture" (cf. Latour 1993)? As Paul
Gilroy suggests, we need to be attentive to "the ideological work
which has been done [on supposedly natural racial signifiers like
skin color] to turn them into signifiers in the first place" (Gilroy
1987:39). Much of this ideological work occurs through the techniques of law. Legal distinctions made among "races" and "places"
make possible and constitute as immutable objects those "facts"
which supposedly "underlie" them—the realm of biogenetic relatedness and the realm of physical space.[2]

Island Identity and the Law of the Blood

After we had spent a long afternoon in the Government Archives, my friend Paulie gave me a ride up the hill to my apartment. We passed the Legislative Council chambers, situated immediately next door to the British Virgin Islands High School. Sporting the flag of the British Virgin Islands as well as the Union Jack, the Legislative Council chambers stands as a symbol of both local legislative autonomy and continued colonial rule. My friend had to drive slowly and carefully, through the crowds of students crossing the street to the playing field for after-school athletics. We were at a dead stop a couple of times, and during one of these moments Paulie commented on the bodies swirling around us. She asked me if I could tell which students were immigrants and which were locals. I told her I couldn't unless I know the student personally, and she said that she could always tell "just by looking" if a student was a non-BVIslander. One young woman we passed was wearing tight, torn jeans. Paulie pointed to her and said to me, "No BVIslander would wear jeans like that." She continued to explain that you can tell non-BVIslanders by their "see me here!" attitude; they are "bold and brassy, with wide eyes and silly smiles." She also said that non-BVIslanders look "lower class," but then qualified her statement: "I used to think it was class, but they have that look in their faces besides. Even their children born here have that look." She refers to the children of BVIslander and non-BVIslander unions as "half-breed BVIslanders" or "children of mixed marriages." They "don't know where they belong to" and become hostile because of their "confused" identity.

Paulie is one of the majority of BVIslander citizens at midlife who did not go abroad during the 1960s for education or employment. She and others like her have witnessed firsthand the influx of immigrants who have radically reshaped the BVI. And they have closely watched the activities of an upwardly mobile, foreign-educated emerging class of elites coming back "home" to the new British Virgin Islands.

Like most of the other former and present colonial possessions of the Caribbean, the British Virgin Islands owes its existence as a territorial entity to late–nineteenth- and early–twentieth-century legal jurisdiction. Recall that, from 1773 until 1956, the

British Virgin Islands of Tortola, Anegada, Jost Van Dyke, and Virgin Gorda, together with the islands of Anguilla, St. Kitts, Nevis, Montserrat, Antigua, and Barbuda, made up the Leeward Islands Colony. Colonial administration was centralized in Antigua, with local legislatures in each of the subunits of the colony and a federal legislature in Antigua. Defederation of the amalgamated Caribbean colonies in the 1950s and decolonization of most of the Caribbean from the 1960s to the 1980s challenged a regional West Indian identity forged in colonial rule and especially in regional labor movements at the beginning of this century. This was not, however, a simple case of distinct "island identities" coming into being out of a regional "West Indian" identity, for the 1950s witnessed the start of a period of intense emigration from the Caribbean to London, New York, Miami, and Toronto. For those who emigrated, West Indian identity retained its salience. For those who did not, jurisdictional division, its symbolic trappings like flags and its practical manifestations like passports, suggested new categories of persons based on new administrative units and later, independent republics. Island identities became significant to those living at home. Those abroad bound together in their sense of West Indianness in the face of white northern metropolises.

At home in the British Virgin Islands, the assertion of island identity intensified as the local legislature drafted laws facilitating the rapid development of luxury tourism in the Caribbean. A 1953 Hotels Aid Ordinance (Cap. 249) and several land acquisition ordinances enabled wealthy business entrepreneurs to begin construction of tourist facilities and the infrastructure to support them. This development required skilled and unskilled labor, much more than the BVI had to offer, and so within a decade of gaining local legislative autonomy, the BVI became an important destination for immigrant laborers from St. Kitts, Nevis, and others islands. But now these newcomers were aliens in a sense they had not been before, when Virgin Islander and Kittitian alike were not only fellow British subjects but also fellow citizens of the Leeward Islands Colony.

Defederation created new categories of persons out of the space of jurisdictional divisions, and in the late 1950s and 1960s the BVI Legislative Council went about passing laws drawing boundaries between these new categories of persons. The legislature passed a number of employment and landholding laws that disfavored immigrants and justified these laws by referring in legislative debates to the new immigrants as "outsiders," "foreigners," and "people who do not belong to this territory." Immigrants to the BVI, former members like BVIslanders of the now-defunct Leeward Islands Colony, became "nonbelongers."

Jurisdiction created difference based on space. But in 1981, British Virgin Islander identity took on a new character, when the British Parliament enacted wide-ranging changes to citizenship policy for the United Kingdom and its colonies, including the British Virgin Islands. Previously, people with citizenship rights in the United Kingdom and any of its colonies were "Citizens of the United Kingdom and Colonies," or, simply, "British subjects." Citizenship rights were transmitted either by birth to a citizen father (the jus sanguinis) or by birth within a British territory (the jus soli). The 1981 British Nationality Act, first, abolished the all-encompassing citizenship category, and second, replaced the jus soli with the jus sanguinis. According to the 1981 Nationality Act, a person's citizenship depends upon that of his or her mother and/or legal father (see Maurer 1996, 1995a).

As critics at the time of the debates surrounding the 1981 British Nationality Act were quick to point out (White and Hampson 1981; White, Evans, and Hampson 1981; White and Hampson 1982), the new emphasis on legal fathers and mothers, by inscribing into law the principle of the jus sanguinis, "racialized" British citizenship. One of the effects of the act was to exclude colonials from full membership in the British nation (see Dummet and Nichol 1990:chap. 13). As Paul Gilroy observed, the new British Nationality Act of 1981 solidified a "cultural politics of 'race'" for British citizenship (1990:280). The 1981 British Nationality Act effectively denied British citizenship to the children of immigrants to Britain from newly independent nations of the Caribbean, Africa, and Indian subcontinent. The law thereby encouraged the equation of "Britishness" with "whiteness."

In the BVI, the Nationality Act also had consequences for conceptions of "race." British Virgin Islanders had placed an emphasis on paternity and descent for figuring social status and identity at least since the turn of the century. Now, however, discussions of "race" have more to do with identifying the immigrants and "out-siders" in their midst than figuring inequality among those who call themselves BVIslanders. Ideas about shared substance passed down patrilines figure rather prominently in current BVIslander conceptions of race and class. BVIslanders say that they can tell the "name" of a person—the patronymic, or what BVIslanders fre-quently call "title"—by looking at their "face." Furthermore, family names go hand in hand with class identities and statuses, since it is generally known which families own what businesses and proper-ties, which families historically have been "big money people," and which have been from the "country." A popular expression, although one some BVIslanders would consider "rude" because it calls attention to class differences between BVIslander families, is "Title get you anything."

In the British Virgin Islands, where "name" or "title" equals "*patro*nymic," family resemblances are figured through connec-tions to real or presumed male paternal ancestors. Women do make contributions to one's biological inheritance—however, they generally contribute "bad" substance that detracts from the recog-nizability of paternal inheritance. One man from a family known for light skin and "good [i.e., wavy] hair" explained to me that his "bad hair," dark and kinky, resulted from "all the women" in his particular family line who had married in and "corrupted"—his word—the family features. If it weren't for all those women, he suggested, he would be more easily "recognizable" as a "Smith" [pseudonym].

The equation "face = name" allows BVIslanders to make assumptions about people based on characteristics deemed racial. When BVIslanders guess someone's "title" by looking at her or his "face," they take into consideration features like skin tone, hair texture, eyes, nose, and chin. Certain types of features, people claim, are associated with certain families. It would be foolish for me to deny that "family resemblances" exist in so small a place as the BVI, with so few surnames easily identifiable as long-standing "British Virgin Islands" names (between forty and sixty, depending on who does the counting). But there is a lot of guesswork involved, and people frequently come up with the wrong "title" of the person they are trying to place. One teacher admitted to me that if a student "looks" like a BVIslander, she'll often just start listing "BVIslander" names until she hits the right one. The question "Who you for?" asks, "What family do you belong to?" This teacher, when she is about to scold a child, will often begin by asking: "Who you for? Rhymer? Dawson? Hodge? . . ." and so forth, until she hits the mark. Then, she might continue, "Oh, I know your father and mother and they will not enjoy what I'm going to tell them!" Family resemblance is in the eye of the beholder, and the beholder often looks through the lens of "paternity" and "descent."

Paternity and descent were powerfully consolidated and naturalized by the 1981 British Nationality Act. When BVIslanders go about making sense of immigrants, they now have new racialized notions of identity to draw on. Children of immigrant mothers and citizen fathers, hence, are "children of mixed marriages," or "half-breed BVIslanders." Although women contribute "nature" to these "mixtures," what it means to be a "BVIslander" has become a question of "descent" and "paternity," for women's natural contribution only confuses rightful (and *legal*) biological inheritance, identity, and status. Phenotypic characteristics gain their meaning through ideas about "BVIslander" family names, and not, I would argue, the other way around. You can't tell by looking who is from what family, although people frequently try and sometimes succeed.[3]

The jus sanguinis thus lent its emphasis on "blood" to newly configured understandings of exactly what "British Virgin Islanders" were: under the Nationality Act, they became a group defined by deep and lasting ties of descent, a community of blood. Children of immigrant and citizen unions, thus, became "half-breeds," and British Virgin Islander identity became quasi-racialized. The Nationality Act fostered conceptions of immigrants as "outsiders" and "aliens" who are "inherently" different from BVIslanders because they are made up of different stock. The law encouraged people to demarcate the community of BVIslanders from Caribbean immigrant others as if such groups of people were given in nature and hence incontestable by law.

Responses to the Nationality Act

Of course, the fact that one's identity as an "alien" is difficult to contest under the law does not mean that immigrants to the BVI do not contest it (see Maurer 1996). Immigrants, like BVIslanders, possess island identities forged in the rise of statecraft and legislative autonomy. But many also come with a West Indian identity, as many are on a migration circuit that encompasses the eastern Caribbean, Miami, and New York. These people sometimes make claims to belong by virtue of their being "West Indians."

Notions of heritable identity are not the only ones through which immigrants and BVIslanders think about their participation in the BVI colonial state. People refer to BVIslander citizens as "locals" and to immigrants and their children as "outsiders." Belonging to the territory thus is put in a spatial idiom. Immigrants deploy place-based identities to contest the new BVIslander "race-"based identity. In doing so, they often explicitly invoke the unrestricted jus soli, or law of the soil, of the United States and Canada, where many of them have borne children. Immigrants routinely make contrasts between the "unfair" citizenship law of the BVI and the "commonsense" citizenship law of the United States or Canada.

Others, born within the British Virgin Islands but legally "immigrants" because their parents are not citizens, have taken to using the expression "born here" to assert their sense of belonging to the territory in which they were born. Where the discourse inspired by the Nationality Act emphasizes the supposedly natural flow of identity through blood lines, the immigrant counterdiscourse emphasizes the supposedly natural connection between place of birth and identity. In 1991, Benji V, an immigrant from St. Kitts, was crowned Calypso King of the BVI. He won the competition with a song entitled, "Where We Born Is Where We From." The song posed an explicit challenge to BVI citizenship policy by claiming "Where a baby first is born / That country should be his own / He should have the rights / Like anybody born in the same region / So if a mother born in Antigua / And she children born in Tortola / Where we born is where we from." Other lyrics include, "And if a child need a passport / He should achieve one without a storm"; "If a woman from England goes to Canada / Born a baby, that baby is a Canadian"; "No child knows where his mother will put him out / He is innocent, he doesn't know his whereabouts"; "It could be land, sea or even in the air / All our babies, they have to born somewhere."[4]

The kind of move the Calypso King made in challenging the Nationality Act was echoed throughout the BVI in the summer of 1991. A horse race I attended featured Prospect versus Kentucky, two horses which, according to the commentator, were "born of foreign parents right here in the BVI, so they're local horses." Of course, were they *people* they wouldn't legally be "local" at all. But as in the song, the take-home message was that birth in a territory should be the basis of citizenship in that territory-cum-nation, regardless.

The "born here" idea resonates for immigrants with regional West Indian notions of identity. Like the phrase "born here," expressions of "West Indianness" figure identity in terms of meaningful places. The idea that place confers identity begs the question of how spaces become imbued with meaning and are taken to engender congruencies of feeling and interest (see Gupta and Ferguson 1992, Keith and Pile 1993). Like the idea of descent, place returns notions of difference back into a domain of "nature," where nature is understood in opposition to "choice." Just as a child cannot choose who its parents are, so it cannot choose its place of birth and thus cannot choose its place-based identity.

Furthermore, the discourse of "place" as determining identity also naturalizes inequalities. If one's belonging comes by virtue of one's being "born here," then what of those who are *not* born here? Are they not entitled to rights? To a sense of "belonging"? In naturalizing spatial difference, the immigrant discourse and the jus soli it draws on have the potential to lend their concern with the natural facts of birthplace to new inequalities among immigrants and their children.

Making Natures

The immigrant response crystallized by Benji V's calypso touches a debate in Western law over the nature of nationality and citizenship, or more precisely, just how that nature materializes through legal practices. The British Nationality Act of 1981 holds forth the old idea of the law of the blood for determining membership in a political unit. The song "Where We Born Is Where We From," by emphasizing the fact of birth in a particular place, exposes the law of the soil. Where the jus sanguinis naturalizes ideas about blood and descent and makes these "facts" crucial to national or territorial belonging, the jus soli naturalizes ideas about the division of the world into supposedly self-evident nations and territories. Both are richly constitutive—together they help create two of the most powerful ideas in current Western discourses about belonging and national identity: the idea of race, and the idea of place. Lest we romanticize the "outsider" response to the British Nationality Act, we need to recall that "where you're born is where you're from" echoes the same deeply conservative and protectionist sentiments expressed by many Anglo-Americans on the U.S.-Mexico border (see, e.g., Chavez 1992).

The natures constructed in citizenship law provide the cultural explanation for the perceived neediness and dependency of immigrants like the Guyanese, whose actions appear always self-interested because they are the products of natures different from those of autonomous and upright BVIslanders. Citizenship law constructs BVIslanders as legal equals and as all partaking of the same racial and territorial nature. Immigrants are denied legal equality because their racial and territorial natures obstruct the rational fulfillment of their needs, rendering them constantly needy and always dependent, unable truly to contribute to the national life as individuals without hidden self-interested motives. The natures concocted in citizenship law underwrite what it means to "contribute" and justify inequalities as natural facts.

Furthermore, as discussed in the next chapter, citizenship law in the British Virgin Islands wove together ideas about place and race at the same time that it allowed BVIslanders to cough up an identity that became highly marketable in the world of investment banking. Together with the justification of immigrants' inequality in terms of "natural" differences, this creation of a BVI identity is evidence for a broader set of processes that have become increasingly important in the Western capitalist world, as ideas about race and place weave themselves ever more closely together in the creation of modern and marketable identities. We need to attend to the deep naturalization of these identities, without reproducing the "nature" from which they gain their authority.

Chapter 5

Immigrants between Legislated and Chosen Identities

One of the great difficulties in studying immigration into the British Virgin Islands is deciding upon a terminology. Although citizen BVIslanders call themselves "belongers," and people who are not citizens are frequently called "nonbelongers," the legal term *belonger* does not mean "citizen," and some people who legally belong are often called nonbelongers. The term *expatriate* leads to another confusion, for some people take it to mean "white," while others take it to mean "foreign" and to include non-white Caribbean migrants. Some people refer to "expatriate white people," but I never heard the expression "expatriate black people" or "expatriate West Indians."

Another problem is the highly charged relationship between Virgin Islanders from the U.S. side of the Sir Francis Drake Channel and Virgin Islanders from the British side. People from the United States Virgin Islands will refer to themselves as "Virgin Islanders," and people from the British Virgin Islands call themselves "BVIslanders" or "British Virgin Islanders." But many in the BVI feel that only people on the British side have rightful claim to the name "Virgin Islander," since the USVI was the Danish West Indies only eighty years ago and because the British Virgin Islands has always been the "Virgin Islands." One of the civic organizations in the BVI devoted to furthering the cultural and political development of the territory goes by the name "Virgin Islanders for a Better Virgin Islands" and avoids the use of the "British" marker altogether. Indeed, some BVIslanders are vociferous in their call to drop the *B* from *BVI*.

People in the USVI who have familial connections to the BVI, meanwhile, frequently try to conceal them since, in the USVI, the BVI is associated with backwardness and the USVI with "modern" living and "civilization"—in the form of Kentucky Fried Chicken, Kmart, and McDonald's. In a St. Thomas shop with a couple of BVIslander friends, I asked the cashier if he would accept a personal check from a Tortola bank. He glanced at my two friends with a devilish grin, and said to me in mock disbelief, "You mean it have [i.e., there are] banks in Tortola?" I showed him my Chase Manhattan Bank checkbook, and he commented, "Oooh, Chase! They'll go *anywhere!*" One of my friends, who had been watching this interaction with some amusement—the anthropologist was being tested, and was being tested on how good a Tortolian he could be—turned to the cashier and asked, looking at him over the top of her half-glasses in schoolmarm manner, "Who are your people?" He said, "Me, I a Thomie [St. Thomian]!" She held her stare, and raised her eyebrows a notch, and asked, "You sure you not Carrot Bay [a north coast Tortola village]?" Then she turned to me and asked, "Bill, doesn't he sound like Millie [a mutual friend who is from Carrot Bay]?" I said, "Yes, he does!" and the two of us burst out laughing. I had passed the test, and the cashier, caught in the act of concealing his "true" identity, shamefacedly admitted that he had "cousins" in Carrot Bay and that he had been raised in Tortola.

Labor and Immigration: Local Views

I was told by a BVIslander lawyer that the Netherlands Antilles has just as much immigration as the British Virgin Islands, but not nearly as much "confusion" about who "belongs" and who does not. That is because, he claimed, "the Netherlands Antilles calls them 'migrant laborers' in the law books. Why can't we call them this too?" Instead, immigrants to the BVI find themselves caught in a web of words and labels—*nonbelonger, immigrant, migrant, down-islander, off-islander, island man, garot, outsider,* and the hotly contested term *born here* used by children of immigrants and BVIslander youth alike. Immigrants are also caught in BVIslander stereotypes of them. One BVIslander told me, "The average Latin person is very clannish; and they don't have complimentary things to say about us! They boast, 'I come from a bigger place!' and so I ask them, 'So why you come here?!'"

Why do immigrants come to the British Virgin Islands? Immigrants and BVIslanders alike explain immigration in terms of a discourse about labor and work, a discourse that paints immigrants as hardworking and BVIslanders as lazy. Immigrants want to make money and see the BVI as a "stepping-stone" in their endeavors. And BVIslander employers make migration worthwhile, because they are reluctant to hire BVI labor. Many private-sector employers view BVIslanders as lazy and unmotivated workers who have been living off the civil service system for too long. One well-educated middle-aged BVIslander involved in migration issues summed up the position of many BVIslanders regarding immigration when he related to me the following:

> The Government was making moves to control the flow of immigrants. The U.S. had been very tolerant but [viewed] the BVI as one of the crevices through which people come in to the U.S. from the southern islands and the Dominican Republic. Dominicans used to come across the Mona Passage to Puerto Rico and get into the U.S. that way; but the INS has stepped up its efforts there. So, now people go to St. Martin, or to Curaçao and then to St. Martin, and then come here as a stopping-point on the way to the U.S. It's the people who have an interest in keeping people coming through the Virgin Islands—the landlords, especially, who rent apartments, like Purcell [a community adjoining Road Town where many immigrants have settled]. The employers, the building contractors—sometimes one half of the labor force for building contractors or more than one half come from the other islands. They couldn't function without them!!—these people [employers] do not work hard to close the gaps!

The same man continued,

> On the one hand, we need the labor. On the other hand, we worry about a drop in the economy which would cause widespread poverty among migrants because immigrant people [who] come here own *nothing*, so if there's an economic col-

lapse, there'd be an army of unemployed who can't go to the hills and grow subsistence because they don't have land.

Immigrants, too, participate in the discourse that casts their labor as necessary to the BVI economy, but they put a slightly different spin on it. I once observed a telling interaction in a shop owned by a "Syrian" I'll call Asad, a Palestinian migrant whose clientele is made up almost entirely of down-island immigrant women. Two down-island women were in the shop comparing shoe prices and trying to find the best bargain. Asad's shoes sell for anywhere between $19.95 and $29.95 and are among the least costly in the BVI. But the women were complaining to him that his prices were too high and that this was a "big ting" for them since the labor and immigration departments were "getting hard" on immigrants. The discussion turned to immigration policy. One woman said, "Labour and Immigration have no heart; they won't let them work someplace else. They have no heart!!" She was referring to a recent change in policy that mandated that immigrants who lost their job would have to leave the territory before reapplying for a work permit and taking another job. Previously, immigrants could simply have their new employer sign their work permit.

Asad identified with the plight of these women. He pointed to the women and said to me—as the women, who continued to look at the shoes, nodded their agreement—"She make, OK, she make five hundred dollar a month; she pay rent, buy shoe, dress, and then—"he clapped and wiped his hands together in the air, wiping them clean—"that's it!! How Labour expect them to make a living when they can't find [i.e., they're not allowed to look for] other job?"

He continued, linking his situation to theirs, "It's like with me: Tortola think Syrian stores—[aside, to me, with a chuckle] they call we 'Syrian,' you know, but we not Syrian!—Tortola think all the Syrian stores make all the money . . . but Tortola doesn't realize! It have eleven Syrian stores in Tortola—if they leave, Tortola going back one hundred years! One hundred years!! Because, OK, see,"—he began calculating on his fingers—"I pay for this store one thousand four hundred dollar rent a month, and landlord wants to raise rent to four thousand a month." The women interjected to express disbelief and shock. Of course, Asad was trying to convince the women that he was not doing so well himself and that they shouldn't complain about his prices! I asked him, meanwhile, who his landlord was and learned that it was a very prominent public official. "I could get shop like this for one thousand two hundred in St. Kitts. Tortola doesn't realize—I pay rent, I have my merchandise, maybe worth one hundred thousand dollar in merchandise; so I pay ten thousand to twelve thousand a year for customs, and I pay lights, water, tax—all go to Tortola; Tortola doesn't *think;* Tortola just want to make more money! Look at that building they putting up," he gestured toward a new construction site. "Who working over there? Not they own people! Why not the local contractor thing, and so, being employed [i.e., Why doesn't Tortola use local contractors with local labor]? Tortola want to make money but doesn't want to put its own people to work!"

Other immigrants commented on the contradiction between labor policies that make life hard for immigrants and local resentment of immigrant labor, on the one hand, and the necessity of immigrant labor, on the other. A Vincentian told me that he feared for his life at the hands of jealous locals: "Dey tink I takin' de bread out dey mouts." A BVIslander who was with us commented that, even so, immigrant laborers were not to be trusted because they would always try to get more money somehow. This man commented that many immigrants just want to have fun and not work, and told a story about a "Spanish" (Dominican) man who first asked for five hundred dollars and then wanted two thousand dollars. And "you turn your back and they start to dance and drink." At the same time, this man complained, immigrants bring their friends around whenever one of them is given a job. "You tell them you don' need another man, but they coming around here for work and you turn your back and they start working and then demand pay!"

BVIslander youth are often blamed for the current state of affairs. Elders say that the young are lazy and want "the good life" but do not want to make any effort to "advance themselves." In part this perceived lack of effort is because of the money to be made off of immigrants in the form of rent. One twenty-year-old man told me that his dream is to "retire at thirty-one" from his civil service job and then live off rents from apartments. In fact, he had just begun construction on his family land. He said, "I got my apartments going up, make my money." Older BVIslanders also sometimes comment that BVIslander youth have too good a life and that it makes them lazy. There are echoes here of the discourse on contribution and greed, where BVIslanders are conceived as persons whose hard work has allowed them to meet their own needs and who can now spend time contributing to the community, while immigrants are seen as needy persons whose work is always self-interested since they are always trying to catch up to others. BVIslander youth, the products of twenty to thirty years of relative prosperity, have had their needs already met by the work of their parents and so start from a condition of completely satisfied wants and do not see the reason or motivation for industry.

Return Émigré BVIslanders

Like immigrants, BVIslanders returning home from abroad emphasize identities derived from place. Having lived in West Indian communities in Miami or New York, return émigrés come back to the BVI with a strong sense of being "West Indian." This sense of identity profoundly impacts the ways they go about making a life for themselves in their "homeland."

Return émigrés complain that their fellow citizens do not want to work hard and have little commitment to their jobs because they expect family ties to protect them from redundancy. A civil service department head complained in conversation that she had a difficult time motivating her workers. "They don't want to work!" she declared. She explained that her best workers are immigrants, but that "our people," that is, BVIslanders, "don't want to work." Like others in her position, this woman has taken to hiring immigrants over British Virgin Islanders.

When return émigrés hire immigrants, they are seen by their British Virgin Islander compatriots as greedy, as traitorous, as not fulfilling family obligation or "national" commitments. For BVIslanders, it makes sense to see these return émigrés as having gotten to the top of the economic ladder through nefarious means, by stepping on others or using unfair advantages. But these return émigrés explain themselves by referring to "good business

sense": they claim they are not expressing national or racial preferences, or dastardly scraping their way to the top, but are merely
looking for the best individual workers.

Their discourse casts difference in terms of individual abilities. Employers simply look for the best person for the job. If a
BVIslander is not the best person, lacks the necessary skills, is not
a "good worker," then the employers will look elsewhere for someone else. Some employers invoke West Indian regional identity to
justify this: "We are all West Indians, after all." Of course, this discourse removes from view the production of the qualities the
employer is looking for in a worker. These qualities are seen as
existing before the prospective employee applies for a job. They
are also seen as existing before the law, while covering over the
work of the law in constituting individual abilities at the same time
that it constitutes them as prior to the law (Collier, Maurer, and
Suárez-Navaz 1995). In this case, the laws of citizenship, immigration, and labor determine in part who applies for jobs and how
their abilities look "on paper" to prospective employers, so that
inequalities that emerge between those who gain employment and
those who do not seem to be the result of natural differences in
ability, even as labor and citizenship laws structure the groups of
people who apply for jobs in the first place.

In the aforementioned conversation, Justine said that it's
"hard to motivate people, you have a staff meeting and things are
good for a week or so, and then they're back to their old ways." She
brought up the "born here" category, stating: "It's because they say
'they born here' that they feel they don't need to work hard." Her
friend Lisette, a woman who had also returned home to the British
Virgin Islands after having been trained abroad, admonished her
for saying that Tortolians don't want to work:

> *Lisette:* Who gives you trouble? You have other people working
> for you?
> *Justine:* Most of them, the ones who give me trouble is *our* peo-
> ple, Miss Lise! It's *our* people! They don't want to work. Our
> people are too lazy!
> *Lisette:* No, no . . . don't say that, you mustn't say that—
> *Justine:* But Miss Lise, it's true! It's our people don't want to
> work! They just want to sit and do nothing.

Lisette: No, it's not that . . . You need more people, you need a bigger staff is all.

Justine: Well . . . that's certainly true . . .

Justine sets herself above BVIslanders—"our people"—because of her frustration with the quality of their work. Her employees, meanwhile, think that she is bossy, that she steals the ideas of her staff without acknowledging them, that she is only in her present position because of nepotism, that she delegates but at the same time wants her hand in everything. To her employees, this behavior is "inefficient." But Justine thinks of herself as a member of the group of bright young intellectuals who got their education abroad and who now are coming "home" to "make a contribution," and who should rightfully come into the top positions in the territory. These people feel thwarted by "closed-minded" and "intolerant"—her words—BVIslanders. She will likely burn out and go back into "exile," abroad to the USVI or the United States. Lisette perhaps more clearly views this latter possibility as a risk and a bad thing for the BVI, since Lisette obviously valued foreign-educated people above others—if they all leave, if they give up, then Lisette's own return to her "home" was for naught. I think this concern partly accounts for her leading Justine to blame her labor-relations problems on an inadequate number of staff and not on any intrinsic attribute of BVIslander staff people. Near the end of the conversation, Justine asked me if I had heard the term *Bh.D.* "They think they should have everything because they have a Bh.D.—a 'born here' degree!"

Making "Belongers"

The Legislative Council attempted to use the legal category *alien* in the early 1960s to stave off a perceived English "takeover": after neglecting their colony in the Caribbean for much of the century, white English people were now coming with hopes of earning a fast buck in the tourist business and in land speculation. At the time, both Britons and BVIslanders had the same citizenship, and so people from the United Kingdom could not legally be restricted from buying land under a law that placed restrictions on "aliens."

This is not to suggest that BVIslander lawmakers did not try to prevent such persons from buying land, and indeed they often did so with success. Since citizenship policy comes under the purview of London and not Road Town, the BVI Legislative Council played with various legal rewordings of existing laws in order to place some checks on the activities of their fellow citizens from across the Atlantic. The category *nonbelonger* was born in these legal games of trial and error.

The British Virgin Islands in the late 1960s was witnessing intense economic development with the construction of several luxury tourist facilities. Building the Rock-Resort on Virgin Gorda required the development of that island's entire infrastructure, since piped water, electricity, and paved roads had not yet reached the whole of this island. The BVI labor force was too small to absorb the boom in construction, service, and middle-management jobs created, and as a result very large numbers of down-islanders—that is, people from other eastern Caribbean islands—began to arrive. Legislation designed to keep the English at bay served quite well to prevent immigrants from buying land and to keep them out of management positions and shunt them into service jobs and manual work. The large immigrant population led BVIslander lawmakers to see bigger problems looming on the horizon, as immigrants began to settle and put down roots in the BVI.

The term *belonger* appears for the first time in the 1969 Immigration and Passport Ordinance (No. 4 of 1969), which details the documents necessary for "persons not deemed to belong to the territory of the Virgin Islands" who wish to enter and reside in the BVI. The term *nonbelonger* appears first in the 1969 Non-Belongers (Restrictions as to employment or occupation) Ordinance (No. 5 of 1969). In 1970, the Legislative Council concocted a means of preventing speculation by English investors with a Restricted Persons (Commonwealth Citizens) Land Holding Regulation Ordinance (No. 9 of 1970), and thereafter speculation by the English was no longer seen as a threat. The category *belonger* served to restrict even more persons from purchasing land without a license than the restrictions placed on Commonwealth citizens, and so in 1977 the language of land law borrowed that of immigration and labor law, and the Restricted Persons Land Holding Regulation Ordinance became the Non-Belongers Land Holding Regulation Act (No. 31 of 1977).

Ever since the keystone legislation of 1969, a *belonger* is legally defined as (1) any person born in the BVI, (2) any person whose mother was born in the BVI, or (3) any "legitimate" child of a man born in the BVI. Belongers automatically have rights to purchase land and to work without restriction. Nonbelongers must apply for licenses to purchase land and must obtain work permits. Belonger status is not the same as citizenship. BVI citizenship policy is dictated by the United Kingdom, not by local legislation.

Although the terms *belonger* and *nonbelonger* entered the law books in 1969, they did not achieve widespread popular use until 1975, with the passage of a labor code.[1] Labor regulations then required that employers have proof of their prospective employees' belonger status and compelled every employer and employee to fill out various forms. Since every working person now had to have papers on file either with their employers or the Labour Department (or both), state power and practices came into people's everyday lives in a new way as all people of working age marked state-created categories of personhood on a form next to their name and sex (Foucault 1977; Collier 1996). "Belonger" and "nonbelonger" became identities when people who had come to the BVI as children reached working age and "discovered," as one high school teacher put it, "that they didn't belong." So, she continued, "they got restless and angry." Children born in the BVI of immigrant parents face a similar situation, for although they are legally belongers, they are not citizens, and because of the popular conflation of the categories *belonger* and *citizen,* these people, too, "discover that they don't belong."

Immigrants from the Dominican Republic faced a special problem under these new laws. Many of these people consider themselves "return migrants": they are the "illegitimate" children of BVI men who emigrated to the Dominican Republic in the first quarter of this century. They had grown up in the Dominican Republic thinking of themselves as "BVIslander-Dominicanos" and, upon "returning" to their "homeland," found suddenly that they did not "belong" unless they could prove the marriage of their parents and thus "legitimate" birth.

Making Citizens

While the *legal* meaning of *belongers* and *nonbelongers* has not changed, the *popular,* identity-infused definitions have, and as a direct result of changes in British citizenship policy from the 1981 British Nationality Act.[2] The British Nationality Act effectively denied British citizenship to the children of immigrants to Britain from both the still-colonial and the newly independent Caribbean nations, and thereby solidified a "racial" notion of "Britishness." In the BVI, however, the act was greeted by many belongers with pleasure, especially as political turmoil in the Dominican Republic and Guyana brought more and more immigrants from those countries and as the BVI achieved one of the highest standards of living in the Caribbean. BVIslanders found themselves reluctant to share the spoils of their economic prosperity, even with their "long-lost" Dominicano cousins.

The 1981 British Nationality Act laid down the principles by which citizenship rights thenceforth would be conferred in the dependent territories of the United Kingdom, including the British Virgin Islands. The act itself is quite straightforward. In part II, section 15, the conferral of citizenship is laid down for the British Dependent Territories, thus:

> A person born in a dependent territory . . . shall be a British Dependent Territories citizen if at the time of his birth his father or mother is—a) a British Dependent Territory citizen; or b) settled in a dependent territory. (British Nationality Act 1981, II §15[1])

The act's definition of *settlement* is somewhat tautological: to be "settled" in a dependent territory is to be subject to no residence, employment, or immigration restrictions (V §50[2]).

More important than "settlement," then, is the citizenship of one's mother or father. And *father* and *mother* are specifically and narrowly delimited by the act:

> For the purposes of this Act—a) the relationship of a mother and child shall be taken to exist between a woman and any child (legitimate or illegitimate) born to her; but b) . . . the

relationship of a father and child shall be taken to exist only
between a man and any legitimate children born to him; and
the expressions "mother," "father," "parent," "child," and
"descended" shall be construed accordingly. (British Nationality Act 1981, V §50[9])

Prior to 1981, citizenship rights were passed along *patrials,* or
lines of descent traced through legal and nonlegal fathers. Under
this earlier system, women could not pass their citizenship rights to
their children. The 1981 act was seen by some as affirming the
"natural" bond between mother and child, as women who were citizens for the first time were able to pass on their citizenship. For
men, on the other hand, the act shifted emphasis from "patrialty"
to "legitimacy." Now, men who are citizens pass on citizenship
rights to only some of their children—the "legitimate" ones born
to noncitizen or citizen mothers.

In other words, the new Nationality Act provided that citizenship pass on in a fashion almost identical to how belonger status
passes on in the BVI—but with one crucial exception: one's place
of birth can determine belonger status but has no bearing on citizenship. That means that persons in the BVI who have belonger
status because they were born there, but whose mothers or fathers
were not born there, are not citizens under the act. As noncitizens,
such belongers are not eligible for passports, cannot vote, and are
considered "outsiders" by BVIslander citizens. As a direct result of
the 1981 British Nationality Act, people living in the BVI have
recast the meaning of the identity categories *belonger* and *nonbelonger* to correspond with the meanings of citizenship contained
within the Nationality Act. *Belonger* as a category of identity has
come to mean "citizen"; *nonbelonger* has come to mean "noncitizen."

But the Nationality Act did much more to BVI ideas about
identity than cause people to recast its terms. In addition to providing that citizenship depend on "natural" mothers and "legal"
fathers, the act also created three kinds of citizenship (each of
which is passed on through mothers and legal fathers). Formerly,
people with citizenship rights in the United Kingdom and any of
its colonies were "United Kingdom and Colonies Citizens" or, simply, "British subjects." The 1981 Act abolished this all-encompass-

ing citizenship, replaced it with "British citizen" (for people in Great Britain itself), "British Dependent Territories citizen" (for people in places like the BVI), and "British Overseas citizen" (mainly for white people in former African colonies who desired that their "protection" under the Crown continue), and set up a system of passports for each kind of citizenship. It is a mistake, however, to see the act as creating just three categories of citizenship where there had been one, because each British Dependent Territories passport specifies the dependent territory in which the bearer of the passport holds citizenship. The Nationality Act thus created as many citizenship categories as there are dependent territories—in the Caribbean today there are six[3]—plus a category for "real Britons" and a category for people in former colonies who consider themselves "real Britons." This change had a real impact on the changing labor scene, as the British Virgin Islands moved from a primarily tourist economy to one increasingly dependent on offshore financial services.

The Nationality Act and Flexible Accumulation

In the midst of its changing legal landscape, the BVI Legislative Council put into place the legislative foundations for the offshore financial services business. Having a citizenship of their own allowed BVIslanders to construct a taxation system that could shelter the new classes of "foreigners" (i.e., the British) from British tax laws. The BVI became a tax haven.

People who use tax havens look for jurisdictions with political and legislative stability since offshore financial business relies on predictable banking, corporation, and tax laws (Roberts 1994). Hence offshore bankers and investors prefer to set up in places where political control is not likely to be contested by groups or parties with conflicting ideological or "ethnic" affiliations. One trade publication, for instance, advises offshore investors to avoid tax havens with competing ethnic and racial groups (Kinsman 1978:43). For BVIslander legislators, the British Nationality Act, which denied citizenship rights to half the territory's population, turned out to be a handy way to ensure this kind of political "stability." Government is "stable" since no voting block of downislanders or Dominicans could ever form. Partly as a result, and as

one member of the Legislative Council boasted in a recent interview with a finance magazine, "we don't have political parties or
trade unions" (*Euromoney* 1989:51). The conjuncture of citizenship
laws and political "stability" with the financial services sector exemplifies the processes David Harvey (1989) details in *The Condition of
Postmodernity*—a proliferation of categories of citizenship and
identity has contributed to the development of specialized financial practices at the same time that such practices have led to an
invigoration of local class and national interests.

It might seem to be an exaggeration to claim that the British
Nationality Act created a "proliferation" of citizenship and identity
categories, but it was experienced this way by BVIslanders and
other eastern Caribbean peoples. One prominent BVI barrister
told me that when the act came along, he and his colleagues
thought, "Ut-oh, now everybody [is] going to have a nationality of
their own!" Furthermore, the passage of the act corresponded in
time to the granting of independence to many of the United Kingdom's Caribbean possessions—between 1973 and 1983, eight new
independent states came into being out of the former British West
Indian colonies.[4] Thus, along with "British citizen," "British
Dependent Territories citizen" in its different varieties, and
"British Overseas citizen," also came "Antiguans," "Kittitians,"
"Grenadians," "Vincentians," and so forth, all as legal citizenship
statuses. Legal jurisdictions proliferated as well. A space that once
had come under the domain of only one legal regime—the Leeward Islands Colony—now consisted of several, some overlapping,
others "independent."

In the British Virgin Islands, the Nationality Act heightened
people's awareness of their citizenship, residence, and employment rights in different jurisdictions—what immigrants and locals
alike call "status." Today migrants especially connect "status" to
economic success. Guyanese immigrants say they long for status in
the United States because they think that adding U.S. status to
their BVI status will have a multiplying effect on their economic situation. One successful immigrant credits his multiple "statuses"—
in the form of work permits, residence rights, visas of entry and citizenship—for his prosperity: a Bermudian, he has "status" in the
United States, Bermuda, the British Virgin Islands, the Netherlands (Holland), the Netherlands Antilles, the United Kingdom,

Portugal, and the Azores. "With EEC integration," he says, "I will be extremely fortunate!" For immigrants, the possibility of economic gain from multiple statuses mitigates any feelings they might have to pressure the government to reform legislation affecting them. Thus, since the late 1970s and early 1980s, most BVIslanders and immigrants have valued having multiple "statuses," and many have gone about getting them.

Remaking Families

In order to obtain multiple statuses, immigrants use state practices to remake their families and thereby envision "family" and "kin" as entities that people construct through individual choices within limits set by "biological" or "natural" constraints. Children born out of wedlock who would have citizenship rights in the British Virgin Islands if their parents were married can pick up the necessary papers at courthouses in the countries of their birth or their parents' birth, have their parents "married" on paper. and take a trip to the local Registrar of Births, Deaths and Marriages to make up a birth certificate, or have the original register changed to indicate that they are now "legitimate" children. They can come back to the BVI, documents in hand, and petition for status. Some go even further. One BVIslander-Dominicana told me, "I didn't come here with just paper, you know—I came here with my father!" Her father then personally signed the official Birth Register when she registered her birth—at age twenty-nine—in the British Virgin Islands.

Although laws governing belonger status and the British Nationality Act suggest that rights are "passed through" mothers, immigrants invariably recreate paternity as they try to gain rights through legal practices. Remember that the children of BVIslander women are always BVI citizens regardless of the woman's marital status—so here rights are "passed through" mothers. But children of *immigrant* women are citizens *only* if the woman is married to a BVI man. The primary issue in deciding citizenship in these cases is "legitimacy," and here "legitimacy" is inseparable from "paternity."

"Paternity" (or "maternity," for that matter) is not given, natural, or self-evident (see Delaney 1991:15; Delaney 1986); rather, it is the effect of discursive practices that produce it as a natural and immutable category. The BVIslander-Dominicana who brought whom the law considered her father to the BVI for him to "claim paternity" by signing a birth register demonstrates that paternity in this case is inseparable from—indeed, is constituted by—state practices. Note also that "paternity" has tangible effects: it creates subjects who are citizens. Hence, legally and practically, men's contribution to procreation is an active one: it generates new citizens by distinguishing the "cultural/legal" identities men are seen to give their children from the "natural" ones women are seen to contribute.

When I said something to a BVIslander about "people who are now coming *back* to the BVI" from the Dominican Republic, she laughed and said that the people who left to go to Santo Domingo in the first place were "dark people from the hinterland." So, she said, "there's no way our men could have produced the blonds, the blue eyes we see coming in now, and they telling me they Crabbes [an Anegada family name]!" She said that it was possible that "the blue eyes [came] from Anegada maybe," but that there is no way to explain the light skin and "blond" hair of the "return migrants." Like many BVIslanders, this woman believes that "race" has to do with "paternity" and that since all the people who went to Santo Domingo were men, and supposedly dark men, the people coming "back" should be dark if they are "really" BVIslanders.

The idea that "race" is inherited through the male line informs a discourse about immigrant women. Many say that some Dominicanas are whores; some say that all down-islander women are whores. To people who think of them as prostitutes, immigrant women pose a threat to the orderly heritability of name, face, race, and class. On the one hand, BVIslander women worry that Dominicanas will steal their husbands. On the other hand, immigrant women fear that citizen men will take advantage of them.

Immigrant women thus face hardship in maintaining respectability and sometimes physical well-being. Stories circulate about men posing as immigration officers threatening immigrant women with expulsion if they do not have sex with them. Also, the Immigration Department requires that all immigrants give a refundable bond of several hundred dollars in case they do anything to warrant deportation. BVIslanders employing immigrant women as domestics often put up that bond and place strict controls on their servants' free time to guarantee its security. In one case I know of, the domestic is not allowed to leave the house, except on errands, and cannot use the phone. In 1986, male immigration officers were accused of attempting forcibly to remove pregnant immigrant women from the territory (remember, although not all children born in the BVI are citizens, they *are* all legal "belongers" with rights to work and purchase land). This incident prompted one local commentator to characterize his compatriots' alleged actions as a "Pharaoh-like hunt for pregnant mothers without rights of abode" (Rhymer 1986:5). The injustices leveled against immigrants also prompted one member of the Legislative Council to smash the mace, representing the sovereign, during a sitting of the council.

Ideas about the heritability of class, race, and national identity do not just keep immigrant women subordinate; they seem to be intimately tied to the offshore finance business. Let me quote from the offshore finance trade publication I mentioned earlier. The author, giving advice to potential investors on how best to choose a tax haven, writes: "*Racial* considerations are important in many of the havens. Several have widely mixed racial make-ups, a potential factor in the stability of the country" (Kinsman 1978:43, original emphasis). This account seems in line with BVI beliefs about the supposed danger of immigrant women to racial order. Brochures advertising the BVI to potential investors place a heavy emphasis on the islands' "British heritage" of "law and order." BVIslanders themselves also speak of "law and order" as the defining feature of BVI society and as something placed in serious jeopardy by the large numbers of nonbelongers in the territory. Marilyn Strathern has recently observed a similar deployment of an imagined British heritage in England: she writes that some white English political leaders have stressed that "recapturing traditional values"—notably, a "law-abiding citizenry" and "traditional families"—"will bring the bright future promised by (what the English fantasise as) American enterprise" (1992a:45). A BVIslander voicing his opinion of continued colonial rule reflected this belief when he told me, "We have the best of both worlds: British law and order, and the American dollar."

Since for BVIslanders, identity is heritable, their "heritage" of

"British law and order" ought not be put at risk. Immigrant women's sexuality must be controlled, either by marriage or other means, since heritability occurs through the male line and unmarried immigrant women have the potential to "confuse" these male lineages by giving birth to illegitimate children of different fathers, names, classes, and races. They have the potential to break down "law and order."

New citizenship policies have created a proliferation of citizenship categories and "statuses." New state practices help both locals and immigrants restructure their identities along the lines of a discourse of heritability. Their restructuring of identity makes class and race appear "genetic" (Austin-Broos 1988, 1994); it makes "paternity," and it makes paternity central to legal, economic, and social status. For BVIslanders, heritable identity takes an unexpected path as the offshore finance sector demands the "law and order" of "British heritage." For immigrants, this discourse of heritable identity compels them to remake their families, but as they do so they contribute to and "realize the structures of inequality that constrain their own possibilities" (Collier 1988:2). Remaking their families, they reinforce the commonsense understandings of paternity, family, and nation that provide the legal underpinning of the offshore finance business in the British Virgin Islands and that deny them status in the first place.

In a 1991 article, Mindie Lazarus-Black has shown that "certain rules and juridical processes of the . . . state are . . . constituent of local family ideology and practice" and that therefore "studies of kinship must encompass simultaneously the legal forms and forces of the state and the common sense understanding of kin which evolves in local communities" (Lazarus-Black 1991:119). BVI and British laws and state practices have helped people redesign kin and reshape identity directly, through belonger and citizenship laws, and indirectly, through the offshore finance business. At the same time, the presence of large numbers of immigrants has led BVIslanders and immigrants alike to think and talk more about race, class, kinship, and descent as they try to acquire different "statuses." Gender and sexuality have become central tropes in this talk, which is informed by an overarching discourse of heritability. Race, class, and gender, construed in terms of heritability, fit into as they structure people's conceptions of "nature" and "law and order." People's identities and their attitudes about belongers and nonbelongers thus seem natural and rational at the same time that they encourage the happy "coincidence" of the territory's "British heritage of law and order" with the offshore finance business.

Immigrants and the Land

The emphasis the law places on the legitimacy of children born to nonbelonger mothers fits neatly into local land laws and practices. By law and in practice, land frequently is inherited by groups of relatives in common. Long-standing BVI property laws require that all persons with claim to a piece of land be consulted before any other party holding a claim begins construction or development on the land. Although it frequently results in conflict, most British Virgin Islanders cite this pattern of land ownership as giving rise to their sense of independence as a people and a nation. As one man put it, all BVIslanders have "a piece of the rock" they can go back to in time of need. One elderly man held that the main difference "in character" between British Virgin Islanders and other peoples of the Caribbean is their independent-mindedness based on their history of land ownership: "We have always been an independent people. It was different from St. Kitts, Antigua because they were always dependent on plantations [even after emancipation]. [But] we are not servile, and [so] we should not sell it [our land]."

Illegitimate children of citizen fathers and noncitizen mothers who are born outside of the territory of the British Virgin Islands (for instance, in the Charlotte Amalie hospital on St. Thomas, as often happens for difficult births) cannot make legitimate claims to their fathers' land and, more important, cannot participate in the sense of independence that comes with it. As already noted, nonbelongers must petition the government for a "Non-Belonger's Land Holding License" before they can purchase land. This process involves an application stating the potential buyer's development plans for the land along with a commitment to complete any proposed development within three years of the time of purchase. Land so purchased cannot be sold to or inherited by another nonbelonger without application for another such license.

The land occupies a central symbolic place in discussions about the rapid development of the British Virgin Islands. Perennial conflicts born out of patterns of land inheritance helped convince the territory's leaders of the need to reclaim land from the sea when planning the development of the capital city, Road Town, in order to make the territory more attractive to investors and tourists. British Virgin Islanders point to this new land as a symbol of the islands' progress. They also discuss how, in keeping foreigners localized on this new space, reclaimed land helps protect the "virginity" of the rest of the islands. And indeed, these protectionist policies have checked uncontrolled foreign development and have helped the British Virgin Islands avoid the "Miami syndrome" blighting their U.S. Virgin Island neighbors.

BVIslanders frequently describe the islands' "virginity" as under siege by marauding migrants. The interconnectedness of three distinct themes of legitimacy—of birth, of rights to citizenship, and of claims to land—comes to the fore in belongers' statements about certain recently arrived groups of migrants. Belongers describe immigrants from Guyana as "hoarding and destructive of the environment." They "trespass," they "come on to your land without permission" with an eye to "strip the leaves from the plants" and "pick the immature fruits." In the water, they "take even the little fish" and the "tiny tiny snails from the reefs," all "to fill their greedy bellies." "They eat, eat, eat! Everything in sight! They would clear the land of all the plants just to eat!" As a result of all this feeding, of course, they generate a lot of garbage: "Their yards and their houses are full of trash." And they are renowned litterbugs: "Here is what a Guyanese will do: they'll set up a tent on someone's land without asking for permission, have a big party, and the next day leave everything, trash, bottles, papers, food scraps, everything but the tent on the ground."

Of Dominicans, one belonger woman said, "Dominicans have been coming in droves recently. There is communication now, by air, so no real problems in their coming here. But they cannot claim property unless their father wills it to them or gives it to them because they have no rights, because they are illegitimate." She continued, "The people who are coming are children of BVIslander fathers. It seems there were two brothels the men used to go to. But I suppose the fathers would have died by this time, so the people we are seeing are their grandchildren."

This interviewee, like others, articulates three themes of legitimacy—of birth, citizenship, and land. The official discourse of national belonging rests thus on the threefold nature of "legitimacy" as encoded in law and cultural practice and belief. Just as Guyanese do not respect the land or fair business practices, Dominicans do not respect moral convention or personal hygiene. Both violate "legitimacy" in its various aspects, as a result of their distinctive "natures." And both are therefore systematically excluded from full participation in the nation as citizens. As the official discourse stitches together the three threads of "legitimacy," it prescribes sexual morality in fabricating a sense of the nation and those who belong to it. Children born to nonbelonger women are citizens (and landowners) only by virtue of their mothers' virtue. Illegitimate offspring of nonbelonger women are stateless, because the state needs to protect itself from illegitimate incursions lest its "purity" be stained.

Getting Into BVI Society

The counterdiscourse that connects belonging to place of birth through the "born here" category is one route some immigrants take to claim legitimacy in the local arena. Others take a different approach to getting accepted into BVI society. Like return émigré BVIslanders, they emphasize individual achievements and choice to counter race or place-based ascriptions of identity. They set up "choice" and "individual" attributes as more important than "natural" or "given" categories.

One striking element of BVIslander stories about groups of immigrants who have "established" themselves on BVI soil is their incredible similarity. Two groups, in particular—the "Syrians" and the various expatriate whites—are discussed in nearly identical terms. One elderly man told me that

> Arabs who came here started out peddling small wares—cheap plastic things, knickknacks and what-nots, small manufactured goods. They would go from door to door offering

their items for sale. As they became more confident and made a little money, and when they had the good graces of the people here and had some regular customers who were friendly to them, they started selling their items to their customers on credit. This was the beginning of the end for BVIslanders—the credit indebted their customers to them, and so they were able to get favors and so forth when customers couldn't pay. This is how Arabs managed to get their foothold and open up shops. The people felt indebted to them because the Arabs had given them credit, and sometimes they couldn't pay anyway, so the Arabs were able to set up their businesses. They have always been better businessmen than we.

By comparison, a woman told me this story about expatriate whites:

One man arrived with only one pair of shoes, with holes in his shoes. Another man and his wife used to squat on land and grow vegetables, and pedal around on their bicycle selling vegetables from the basket of the bike. Some of us used to buy vegetables from them because we felt sorry for them. Well, they went on to start a wholesale business, starting small, and growing and growing. You can always tell the whites who have plans to make it big in the BVI, because they come and drive around old, beat-up cars. A BVIslander would never drive around an old car so, but the whites do so they can get ahead.

The message here is similar to the stories about immigration and labor discussed earlier, though here the whites and Arabs are not necessarily better "workers" than BVIslanders, but more savvy business entrepreneurs.

What interests me is not whether these stories are "true," whether Arabs and whites who came to the British Virgin Islands actually did establish themselves in this manner, but how these stories fit into the wider discourse on work and immigration through which BVIslanders and others assess the "immigrant situation" and its impact on the BVI. Indeed, the Arab and white immigrants tell very different stories of their coming to the BVI in which work or business figures little, if at all. Whites talk about wanting to "get away from it all," from the rat race of North America or Europe. They frequently buy property in the BVI to help their dream of living in paradise become a reality. Arabs explain their presence by referring to the difficulties of living under Israeli occupation. Most of the Arabs are not property owners in the BVI and never intend to become property owners. Several expressed a desire to return to the Middle East when "things quiet down over there." One youth who had lived in the Caribbean almost all his life recounted to me:

> Too much violence in Jerusalem. You have to fight because if someone take your land you don' just sit there and let them give it back to you, you have to fight and take it back. I don' want to be there because I have no choice—I have to fight. St. Thomas, it cost a lot of money, so I come here. Tortola is boring and quiet, but too quiet! Boring, but safe—no fighting. You come to Jerusalem, but not now, don't come now; in a few years when maybe less fighting. Jerusalem is bigger than the whole of Tortola and the university there is bigger than Road Town!

Arabs in Tortola were quite frank with me about how they go about gaining acceptance in the British Virgin Islands, where their shops are often burglarized because they belong to "outsiders." One shopkeeper said, "I have thieves, but I am not a greedy man so I show them. I call them over and see what they try to steal and say, 'Go ahead—take it. But don't do it again.' So they respect me."

Another, a devout Muslim, told me the stories from the hadith that he often recites to BVIslanders who mistrust him because of his faith and "the color of my skin":

> Mohammed had two uncles, and one had an African slave and the other did not. Mohammed went to the slaveowner and said, "You should free your slave, for all men are one before God. We are all God's people." The slaveowner said he would free the slave for five camels. Mohammed went and got five camels from the other uncle, and present them to the man with the slave. This man gave the slave to Mohammed. The African make as if Mohammed were his new master; but

Mohammed said, "No, brother, you are free." You see, he called him "brother" to show that we are all one family, one people. The earth belongs to God, and he placed us here as one family, one people upon the earth. So this is my country, my people, yes, my family; just as Lebanon is my people, my family, my country. Mohammed was the only prophet who freed the slaves.

On another occasion, this same man told me, "Islam is the religion of the future because it accepts everyone. Ishmael's mother, that woman, she was black, she was a slave, and Christianity and Judaism do not accept her, but we do."[5]

Other immigrants make much of the BVIslander practice of "hailing," or greeting people on the street. One learns quickly in the British Virgin Islands to hail passersby, even if one has never been formally introduced. Not to hail someone is to cause an affront. West Indian immigrants, who are used to hailing in their islands of origin, have few difficulties. Among the Guyanese immigrants, hailing is the main method of getting new immigrants into the Guyanese community. Some, however, especially from the larger islands and the big Caribbean cities like St. John's, Antigua, Kingston, Jamaica, and Port of Spain, Trinidad, sometimes "forget." One Trinidadian told me, "home, you forget to hail someone—no big ting. Here, everyone notice and next time you see the person not even look at you!"

White expatriates and African-Americans told me stories I thought were outrageously funny—because I often found myself in similar scrapes over the politics of hailing—about not knowing the "rules" of saying "good evening" and "good afternoon." One American in Tortola observed that Tortolians get very offended and "vexed" if you're white and don't hail them. He compared this with the United States, where if you were to say "good day" to everyone, "you're liable to be taken for a freak." He said that he thinks most Tortolians "turn off" to white people because, given their experience with tourists, they have come to expect whites *not* to hail them. As a consequence, this burly 220-pound fellow makes sure to say good morning "extra loud" in his booming voice whenever he walk into an office—"and everybody jumps!"

Shops are the site of conflicts over the politics of hailing, especially as many shops are tended by immigrants and many customers are tourists. When people walk into a shop, they are expected to hail the proprietor, and the proprietor is expected to greet them and, if she or he is not busy, offer help. When there is a BVIslander proprietor and a BVIslander customer, the customer will simply interrupt the proprietor if the proprietor is busy talking to someone else with a polite but firm "Excuse a while . . ." and ask a question. When there is an immigrant proprietor, however, BVIslanders sometimes use the occasion as an opportunity to catch the immigrant in a moment of being "rude" or "disgusting," as an excuse to find fault. Once I was in a shop tended by a Guyanese woman who was having a chat with me about Hindi kin terms. A BVIslander woman I knew came in and started browsing. After a few minutes of continuing her conversation with me, the shopkeeper said, "Excuse me, Bill," and addressed the woman with a "Can I help?" The woman, peeved that she had not received attention sooner, said, somewhat superciliously, "I thought you'd never ask." A similar incident could occur with a BVIslander proprietor and a tourist customer. The tourist will wait by the counter for assistance, even if the proprietor is sitting in a clearly visible place in the shop, instead of hailing the proprietor and asking for help. Hence, tourists are rude because they don't hail proprietors of shops. My students at the BVI Community College had a good laugh enacting these types of scenes for me during a role-playing game on hailing in gift shops. Their assignment had been to act out scenes of "cultural misunderstanding."

Hailing helps immigrants "get in" with BVIslanders and helps them gain the one precious thing deemed essential to success in the BVI—"support" from other people. One woman from Santo Domingo of BVI ancestry put it to me quite explicitly.

> The most important things here are a *name* and *support*. Some may have name, but without support . . . ! People meet me and I say my name, people say, "So, you *marry* a Smith?" and I always say, "No, I was *born* a Smith." Then the attitude changes! If you got the last name by marrying, you get a harder time. If people give me a hard time, I make sure they know I am not married to a Smith, and then I mention my cousins—it's a matter of who your people are, not who you

are. But you need support from your people. To get my job I
had to use my family—if you don't have family here you won't
get nothing. It's a matter of who around you, who you know,
not who you are. If you have family and no support, then nothing can help you.

Name helps, but support is the key to success. The great majority
of immigrants do not have BVIslander names, so for them support
is everything.

On two separate occasions, apart from my teaching, I was
called upon to perform in front of an audience. Once was during
a "BVI Nice Taxi Driver" competition, in which taxi drivers com-
peted for the "BVI Nice" title as part of a tourism promotional
activity. The competition was based on questions directed at the
drivers from a panel of persons involved in the tourist industry,
and it ended in a series of role-playing exercises. One of the organizers of this event was responsible for coming up with actors to
play the part of tourists in these role-plays and was short one actor.
A friend coerced me into participating. I was nervous—how would
an audience of BVIslanders receive my performance?—but she
assured me, "People know you, man! You have support!" And they
did support me, laughing at the hapless taxi driver forced to deal
with a difficult passenger instead of laughing at the fool trying to
play the part of the tourist who had lost his passport.

On another occasion, among Guyanese immigrants, I was told
it would be a nice "gift" for an old woman who was leaving the territory for me to sing a "Haray Rama" song at a Hindu religious
function. Again, I was nervous: here I was, a white guy and a non-
believer—how would I be received? My friends assured me, "People will support you, Bill. People will join in and help. You'll see!"
And they did, joining in almost as soon as I began singing so I
would not have to do it alone.

Preference and Identity, Labor and Law

The idea of support tends to individualize immigrants' relationships with BVIslanders. Immigrants are granted access to
BVIslander society not through collective action and certainly not
as a group. There is no one group of immigrants that BVIslanders

accept more than other groups. Furthermore, people grant support to individuals, not groups. The surest method of not winning support from BVIslanders is to act as if one's allegiances lie with one's immigrant group and not with one's own self: to greedily and clannishly work for the success of the group is to act out of self-interest and to demonstrate one's neediness and failure at being independent. However, most immigrants, by virtue of their status as immigrants, are always-already defined as acting on greedy motives. Their greedy natures help explain their low socioeconomic status, since if they had virtue, they would "naturally" be successful.

Standing as an individual and not as a member of an immigrant group helps one gain support and eases entry into BVI society. Immigrants who have acquired status as members of BVI society deny any group connection when they are challenged by BVIslanders. They tend to cast their "difference" from BVIslanders as one of preference or choice, not as "natural" or derived from ranked statuses such as "citizen" versus "immigrant." One Guyanese immigrant explained to me that the stereotype of Indians as clannish was based on BVIslander misunderstandings of her Hindu "preferences": "People here think we stick to ourselves; they ask why we don't go to restaurant. Well, I tell you why—we don't eat pork or beef! And in restaurant, you know how it is, they use the same spoon to mix the one thing and the beef, and so we can't eat it! We think is just nasty. That's it!"

In many ways, it is as simple as that. For this woman, religion is a matter of individual preference. Not eating pork or beef is simply a (religious) choice. The perception of Guyanese Indians as different "racially" and therefore as having motivations for action that stem from "bad natures" hinders easy acceptance of this preference as a "mere" preference and not a "racial" or "clan" attribute.

For nonracially marked immigrants, however, the emphasis on preference and individualism is equally important. Members of immigrant clubs and associations, for example, have a difficult time being accepted by BVIslanders, because they are held to have group allegiances and hence be more clannish than immigrants who do not belong to such organizations. In a rather significant incident, an African-Guyanese immigrant was being teased by a group of people about a well-publicized meeting of the Guyanese Association immediately prior to elections in Guyana. In her defense, she stated, "I don't know no thing about those meetings." But she continued to be ribbed. The atmosphere, for the BVIslanders, was one of innocent revelry and jest, but the woman—who had been living in the British Virgin Islands for years and who was universally well-regarded by BVIslanders—exploded, saying "I am *me!!* That's *all.* I have no business with these names [i.e., 'Guyanese']!" She stormed off, and a BVIslander commented, "That's just what Luís [a Dominican immigrant] does say—he is he and that is it." Those who had been teasing the woman later apologized.

In standing as individuals, as "me"s, immigrants demonstrate that they have no prior commitments and are willing to "contribute" as individuals to the wider social scene. This stance garners them respect and status in the community. Culture and identity are cast as preferences, as individual attributes and nothing more. In asserting that they are choice-making individuals, not members of "ethnic" groups, immigrants render themselves as similar and equal to BVIslanders and reject or deny inequalities (Laclau and Mouffe 1985:164). As they attempt to "get in" to BVI society, immigrants do not explicitly challenge that sutured "society" that depends for its closure on their exclusion. While the recognition of their presence momentarily challenges the autonomy and solidity of "society" constituted as a collection of similar and equal individuals by highlighting the antagonisms that are closed off from it, their attempt to fit into society as choice-making individuals "just like everyone else" helps sustain the fiction of the BVI as a sutured totality. In speaking of their choices and preferences, immigrants "are actively trying to influence the distribution of social rewards" and its institutional verification in the form of citizenship rights (Collier 1988:208; Bourdieu 1977:195–96). That explains why immigrants do not challenge the system that ensures their subordination, for that very system offers the promise of "choice" and through it, the "equality" of persons as choice makers.

But the logic of preference comes up against the logic of race and heritability for immigrants who are not "racially" similar to BVIslanders, and citizenship law's emphasis on "blood" contrives to cast all immigrants as "racially" different from BVIslanders (see Maurer 1995a). The logic of choice and the logic of nature depend upon each other to create a distinction between differences that are supposedly the result of individual choices and differences that are supposedly the result of natural capabilities or incapacities. Each logic is overdetermined by ideas about immigrant labor and the law. Immigrants are deemed hard workers because they are selfishly trying to get ahead in life without regard for others. Their choices get the better of them and "prove" that they have bad natures. And immigrant natures are legally defined as heritable. So no matter what you choose, you are born someone who does not quite "belong."

Chapter 6

Making Family, Making Genealogy: One Hundred Years of Family Land

On April 13, 1927, the Virgin Islands Commissioner's Office received a lengthy letter from a troubled woman, begging for the commissioner's assistance in settling a land dispute that had arisen between her brother and her other kin. The woman, resident in St. Thomas, wrote on behalf of her illiterate relatives in Tortola, who in the past few months had been subjected to all manner of injury from her brother. After a thirteen-year absence from Tortola, he had returned recently, following the death of his mother, claiming he was entitled to the entire family estate and telling all he fully intended to pass it on to the children he had fathered during his time abroad. While he was away, five of his eight siblings had been living on the land. One of them, Rebecca,[1] had been living there with her husband and two sons. She had also been looking after the upbringing of the four siblings who remained with her, all of whom the letter describes as "children." The remaining three siblings were abroad. Two of the sisters had been living and working in Santo Domingo, and the third—Ginny-Ann, our petitioner—in St. Thomas. These three sisters together earned the only steady income in the family, sending remittances back in order to pay the land tax and, at their mother's death, her funeral costs. Rebecca and her husband, meanwhile, eked out a living making charcoal and baking bread, which it seems they sold or traded locally.

The land on which they lived, and which the prodigal brother,

Joshua, had returned to claim, had been part of an estate originally purchased by their paternal grandfather, Shadrick. He left
this land to his four children, "to be divided among them."
Shadrick's two daughters sold their shares of the land to others.
One of his sons died and left his share to his daughter. The other
son was Ginny's father. He had had ten children, but his first-born
son had died young. His son Joshua and three of his daughters
were already abroad when he died. He left no will but, according
to Ginny, said before his death "that all that want to come home
must live in peace." He was survived by his wife, who stayed on the
land raising her four children and living with her daughter
Rebecca, Rebecca's husband, and their two sons. When the
mother died, it was Ginny's sisters in Santo Domingo who paid for
the funeral.

Three days after the mother's death, Joshua returned. As
Ginny tells the story, peace was far from his mind. First, he
demanded all the receipts showing the cash transactions that his
father and mother had made during their life. "Then he started a
rumpus with my Brother cultivation then he ordered him to leave
the Estate." He took the young brother's cultivation and rented it
out to people to grow potatoes; the income this generated, Ginny
tells us, would have more than covered the costs of the funeral and
the land tax that her sisters had so generously paid. Meanwhile,
"Daphne [one of the children] and Rebecca stood there after he
drove away my brother Tim. he got mad on Daphne and she had
to run, now only Rebecca remain she have two son and they had to
run, now Rebecca is there and now he have orderd her to leave
with some terreble trats saying he is the only ear to what my Father
left." As for Rebecca's husband, Ginny writes, "my brother fell on
them and beate him speachless;" so he ran off, leaving Rebecca
with the children.

Joshua's intentions were clear: "he married a woman just one
year [;] she and her children will become ear to the land." To
Ginny, that was the crux of the matter (beating people speechless
notwithstanding): "My brothers Woman family is to have the
power and not my father Children." She wrote to the Commissioner asking "if the Law Book give him that power over what my
father left."

Ginny concludes her letter with a plea:

13 year now neather hereing from him not even to send them bread and he would not permit the children to remain on the land for they to make a bread and he is ordering them to leave with such Volgar Langue, Now I am asking you My Honor where must she go to make a living I await an answer from you and if you need my present you can call me, I am not goin to run any suit with him for I have no money but I will meet with him face to face.

no more to say
But remain your Obedent Servant

Ginny Ann Jenkins
address   St. Thomas
Dronningin Gade No.13

I came across Ginny's petition to the commissioner of the Virgin Islands in the British Virgin Islands Government Archives. From the late 1800s to the present day, all BVI government correspondence has been filed in folders and stored (or tossed) in the archives. Documents pertinent to a particular petition or piece of correspondence are filed along with the originals. Most files have been damaged, partially destroyed, discombobulated, eaten by termites, molded, or burned, and many are incomplete and in disarray.[2] The file in which I found Ginny's petition contained no record of the commissioner's response or decision. The only other piece of paper in the file was a handwritten note from one clerk to another, stating:

This is very involved. Is there any record of the will. Is G.-A. Jenkins a Tortolian? Shadrick Dawson appear[s] to have left his land to four children but GA Jenkins does not say whether they hold it in common. If it was held in common I believe the survivor [i.e., Shadrick's only surviving child] inherits all the land. Is this so? If each had a part of the land left to them, then the heir of each of those deed[s] would inherit. Can you follow Jenkins's [illegible word] statement?"

My contention is that the data available from such documents, fragmentary though they may be, can tell us much about the relationship between land law and custom in the British Virgin Islands and in the Caribbean more generally. This chapter provides an account of land disputes and their meanings in the twentieth-century British Virgin Islands, relying on archival evidence coupled with interviews on these and similar cases and on other information gleaned during fieldwork. It also incorporates some insights from previous work on the so-called family land phenomenon in the Caribbean.

Ever since Herskovits, scholars of Caribbean peoples have recorded instances of an apparent pattern of land tenure and transmission known throughout the region by such terms as *generation land, generation property, children's property*, or, most commonly in the literature and most widely used in the region itself, *family land*.³ While this chapter aims to demonstrate the complexity of this supposed "system" of land tenure and to unpack the assumptions anthropologists and Caribbean peoples have put into the notions of "system" and "tenure" themselves, for now, and simply put, *family land* refers to a pattern of landholding and transmission characterized by the inheritance of land by children of both sexes, from an original estate held by a supposedly common and often male ancestor, continuing over several generations, and held under some form of common tenure.

Twin notions of equality and hierarchy have played themselves out in local definitions of family and genealogy. In family land practices, notions of paternity have served to differentiate groups of otherwise "biologically" connected persons into separate "families," and in the process the idea of a "genealogy" or a "genealogical grid" that includes all persons presumed to be biologically related is conjured up and imagined as a given and natural ground. This natural ground is the stuff upon which people build "social" relations, specifically familial relations envisioned in terms of connections to presumed male ancestors. Notions of biogenetic relatedness can imply a hierarchical ordering of society, because every individual has a "place" on the kin diagram, just as in hierarchical models of society everyone has a place in a system of ranked statuses.

It is difficult to imagine how an individual could "fall out" into the realm of the nonhuman if everyone is included on the great genealogical grid of the human species. Yet this same vision of biology also construes every individual as the unique product of recombinations of biological substance, and so implies that every individual is equal to every other insofar as each is unique and not an embodiment of a specific social group or socially constituted type of person. Holding individuals as unique and equal, however, opens new room for inequality, since unique people can make uniquely "bad" choices and fail to live up to their potential, or can start off with "faulty" natures as a result of their particular articulation to the grand genealogical grid. In the logic I seek to make explicit, and thereby to deconstruct, hierarchy and equality come together with nature and choice to rationalize the given "facts" of nature and the inequalities that seemingly spring from those facts. The task here is to show how those facts take on the power to act as facts, to demonstrate their objectification and telos.

This chapter records early-twentieth-century land disputes among British Virgin Islanders. Focusing on land disputes among kin, it builds an argument about the construction of "family" and "genealogy" in the British Virgin Islands and the role of law in defining "family" and "land." Changes in the law encouraged people to think of kinship as an objective genealogical grid of biogenetic relatedness, and not as a system of relationships and obligations among persons. This shift accompanied a change in legal and popular notions of land ownership. At the beginning of the twentieth century, land law encouraged people to think about land in terms of abstract "estates," or rights to use land for a certain specified period of time. What one "owned" was a temporal construct. By the 1940s, however, changes in the law encouraged people to think about land in terms of ownership of physical property in perpetuity. What one "owned" was now the land itself, construed as an objective entity.

The chapter also considers the common-law foundations of land tenancy in the Caribbean. An analysis of the history of land law shows that the very categories of "family," "relative," and even "land" cannot be taken for granted—as they have been in much scholarship surrounding family land in the Caribbean—for the development of land law in the twentieth century charts in many ways the development of these very concepts. The history of land law is one in which abstractions built up after "nature" eventually dissolve back into nature (Strathern 1992a). The nature conjured up in land law and practices is also significant in explaining ideas about race and heritable identities in the Caribbean. Land law and the conceptions of kin it suggests support a logic that renders identity an attribute of descent and that places emphasis on biological ancestry in figuring identity (see Austin-Broos 1994). This logic is in contrast, for example, to Spanish colonial policies in Latin America, which, by settling groups of indigenous people on land held by the Crown, encouraged indigenous peoples to think and act in terms of "ethnic group" rights, group responsibilities, and group identities (see Vogt 1990, Borah 1983). The British common law in the Caribbean supported exactly the opposite logic, leading people to think and act as if individual attributes derived from descent are more important in figuring identity than corporate group membership.

When the common law deals with land, it echoes social constructionist thinking: people are not deemed to own "land," construed in the law as an objective and natural entity, but instead are deemed to own an "estate," an entity the law defines as a "temporal abstraction" involving sets of social—not natural—relations built up over the land itself. The resonance here with the idea that "families" are constructions built upon "natural" facts of "genealogy" has worked to naturalize both the land and the genealogical grid.

Inequality and Hierarchy

British Virgin Islanders say that hard work and education lead to economic and social success. If people have not "made it" in life, it is said, it is usually because of their own individual failings and shortcomings, their laziness, their lack of motivation, or their desire to have things done for them rather than doing things themselves. The belief in individual perseverance leading to success is an attitude shared by many people in the Caribbean. The ideology of advancement through education, for instance, runs so deep in Jamaican society that even class and race distinctions can become muted—or so people say—in the face of this bootstrap mentality (Austin 1984).

The idea that people get to where they are in life through their own individual effort—or failings—is of course central to the tenets of both liberalism and capitalism. Yet experience shows people that, even when they put their best effort into their work, they still don't come out ahead. A fundamental contradiction in liberalism and capitalism is that an ideology of equality and achievement through individual effort continues to exist and have force even as people realize inequality in their day-to-day lives. Attending to the ways this contradiction is played out in particular contexts can shed light on how this tension reproduces and transforms itself.

Verena Stolcke's work on marriage in nineteenth-century Cuba demonstrates one historical way of working through this tension. As people went about "choosing" marriage partners because of "love," they ended up recapitulating racial hierarchies because of the way gender was constructed and controlled through race and class (cf. Douglass 1992). Stolcke shows how "the liberal ethos of individual achievement and freedom" worked in concert—not in contradiction—with "imperatives of racial purity" (Stolcke 1993:33). Doctrines of race worked to naturalize social inequality and reconcile an ideology of equality with increasing inequality. If people are not successful, it must be because they have something wrong with them. Since an ethos of individualism provides no explanation of personal failings evidenced consistently within specific social groups, the tendencies for members of a group to fail gets written in biological terms. As Stolcke writes:

> If the self-determining individual, through persistent social inferiority, seemed to be incapable of making the most of the opportunities societies offered to him, this then had to be due to some essential, innate and therefore hereditary deficiency. The person, or better even, his or her biological endowment, rather than the socio-economic order was to be blamed for this. (1993:33)

The idea that one's failings can be due to biogenetic factors brings procreation into the picture. If biogenetic substance is inherited through the genealogical grid, and if some biogenetic substances are better than others, then people who have "succeeded" in life had better be careful about whose substances they allow to mingle with their own. They had better start worrying about "family."

There is a seeming contradiction between the ideas that people are self-determining and that biological substance determines peoples' "natural" abilities. But both poles depend on the unique individual as the point of departure, and both encourage a work ethic—you never know your biological endowment, so you never know if it is to blame for your failures; hence, you should always "keep trying" (Stolcke 1989:xvii). That this is so suggests a further tension between the idea that people are unique combinations of biological substance, and thus uniquely "new" persons, and the idea that people are members of groups like families that determine their social standing. This tension is neatly resolved, however, through a continual movement between "biological" heredity and inheritable social statuses like "family names" (Stolcke 1989:xiii).

It is this movement between the "genealogical grid" and the "family" that is at work in the family land phenomenon. In the British Virgin Islands, the tension between the two principles hinges on a notion of paternity as more important than maternity in determining both social and biological status, and on the ability of certain individuals to negotiate their way through their blood ties as they go about "choosing" family ones. Paternity sets the *family* of the family land in motion; in the land law and in people's conceptions, family land has to begin with one person, one (male) ancestor. Paternity also infuses the genealogical grid, for we shall see that in law, inmarrying women are legally defined as "not of the body" of their husbands unless they bear children. They do not truly share the substance of their husbands unless their own substance mingles with their husbands' in the body of offspring. In practice, the picture gets messy: we will see men asserting their legitimacy and connections to fathers—invoking "family" through "genealogy"—in an effort to deny inmarrying women's genealogical connection to the family tree, while these women claim allegiance to family in memory of their husbands—and in an effort to get the land for themselves. When we look at the ways in which "blood" is called upon to "speak"—through notions of legitimacy, legal marriage, class, race, and gender—we begin to see the refiguring of hierarchy and the retrenchment of the contradictions at the heart of Caribbean liberalism and capitalism.[4]

The Landers Lands, Mayfly Estate, and Little Bay Case

Elihu Kendall was married to Lydia and lived with her and three of their four children in a house on his family land in Mayfly Estate. Their firstborn, a son named Eustace, had left in 1917 to cut cane on the sugar estates in San Pedro de Macoris in the Dominican Republic. Eustace never returned, and, as the family received no news of him from other Tortolian men who went over on the sloops, they presumed him dead; it was not unheard of for Virgin Islander men to meet their maker en route to the fields, in the fields themselves, or in the factories.

From a mother's relative, Elihu acquired a sizable estate in Landers, and from another relative he inherited a couple of acres at Little Bay. It seems that he and his family did nothing with these inherited lands and maintained a provision ground and their home on the Mayfly land. There Elihu lived with his wife, his secondborn son, Andreas, and his daughters, Elizabeth and Alexandra, until his death in 1924.

Elizabeth married shortly before Elihu's death and moved off the family land to live with her husband. Andreas took over the affairs of the family's lands. In order to do so, however, he needed to establish himself as the heir-at-law of his father. Before 1945, intestates' estates passed to their heirs-at-law, often the firstborn son. Since his father had died before 1945 intestate, the firstborn son, Eustace, would have been the sole inheritor. But no one knew where Eustace was. In 1942, then, Andreas obtained from the court an "Order for the Presumption of Death" for Eustace as well as a "grant of Letters of Administration" for the estate of Elihu.

Alexandra, meanwhile, married Steven Charles, and the couple continued to live in the Mayfly house with Lydia. Andreas Kendall passed his time between this house and another he had built for himself on the Landers lands. Building a house required capital. So, in 1943 or so, Andreas sold all of the family land at Mayfly to his brother-in-law, Steven Charles. He then parceled out the lands at Little Bay to Steven and one of Steven's brothers. He also sold some of the Landers lands to two other men and another small piece to a third man. Another small plot went to someone whose name has been forgotten—"he sell it to a next young fellow." Steven sold a small piece of the Mayfly Estate to his second brother, he sold a piece of the Little Bay Estate to his third brother, and another piece to an unrelated man. By 1945, then, the Kendall family land at Mayfly had become Charles family land; Lydia Kendall still lived on it, however, and with her daughter became the center of social activity on the lands. The lands at Little Bay had passed over entirely to the Charleses (except for the small piece sold to an unrelated man). And the Landers lands became a patchwork, with Andreas retaining the bulk of it.

Life went on. Andreas built his house. Lydia continued to be the grande dame of the family land—even though in name it was now Charles land—and most certainly maintained a position as the head of her daughter's husband's household. But then, in 1960, to everyone's astonishment, Eustace returned from Santo Domingo. When he saw that the family land had been sold out, he demanded the titles to all of the lands ever held by his father Elihu and brought his case to court in order to establish his rights as the sole heir-at-law of his father. From a legal standpoint, the case was clear-cut: since Elihu had died before 1945 (the date of legal changes discussed subsequently), the firstborn son was indeed entitled to his entire holdings as the heir-at-law of the intestate. Of course, nearly all the lands had been sold! And nearly twenty years before, at that. Under the Real Property Limitation Act (Cap. 18, sect. 2 and 5), the statute of limitations for contesting the conveyances to members of the Charles family had expired. All the conveyances were let stand, then, and Andreas was forced to relinquish the portion of Elihu's estate that was still in his possession— the portion of the Landers lands on which he had built his house. The prodigal son won his case but, I am told, lost the respect of his mother and sister—after all, where had he been all those years?— and was not welcome on the old Kendall family land, on which his "navelstring" was buried, which had become in any case the new Charles family land. I do not know what happened to poor Andreas.

The case centered around the return of relative. Eustace was able to use the logic of paternity and primogeniture to gain possession of the family land. He did so for his own advancement, not that of his "family," but he needed to assert genealogical connection to family and father in order to be successful. Staking his claim on the genealogical grid, but also crucially on Elihu, his father, he attempted to fight off the counterclaim of his sister and her husband, and even his own mother, to family lands that had changed "families," but not individuals. Family had changed; the genealogical grid had not, and Eustace's assertion of genealogy worked to reverse the change in "family" from Kendall to Charles. The statute of limitations saved Lydia and Alexandra from giving up the Charles land, but it could not save Andreas.

The Sugar Apple Bay Case

This and the next case show how apparently contradictory ways of dealing with fractional interests turn on notions of paternity. Samuel Manley died in the early 1940s. He owned an estate of "35 acres more or less," which he willed to his seven children. In his will, he stated that the estate was "to be divided equally, share and share alike." A land case that came before the courts in the early 1960s hinged upon this phrase in the will—what exactly did it mean?

After Samuel died, the children marked off boundaries and, as far as they were concerned, considered the estate divided into separate holdings. His eldest son, Daniel, sold his "one-seventh share" to a man named Wilbur Randolph in 1950. One of the daughters, Trisha, also sold her "one-seventh share" to Wilbur in 1956. As far as Wilbur and the Manleys were concerned, both sales were final and valid. Six years went by, when Wilbur decided to sell his estate to another person. In drawing up the necessary paperwork, he discovered that the court would not accept the original conveyances from Daniel and Trisha as lawful, because the "share and share alike" clause indicated that it was Samuel's intent that his heirs should be seized of the land as "tenants-in-common." To make a valid transfer, Daniel and Trisha would have needed the consent of all the cotenants. Furthermore, since the will stated they were to be tenants in common, the original boundary markings the siblings had made were also invalid. Wilbur went about gathering the signatures of six of the seven siblings, agreeing to the transfer of the "shares" to him. He presented this document, written by his own hand and without the advice of a solicitor, together with a written statement and the statements of several witnesses, in 1962:

> On the 4th day of July 1950 I purchased the lands aforesaid from Daniel Manley. [. . .] [T]he said Daniel Manley was owner in common with six of his brothers and sisters of the lands aforesaid and I have now been advised that the signatures of the seven co-owners are necessary to convey a legal estate. [. . .] Trisha Joshua Jenkins one of the co-owners similarly sold her 1/7th share to me on the 12th day of December 1956 but she has now refused to sign any further document conveying the legal state [*sic*] to me. [. . .] [a]ll the other owners have singned [*sic*] a conveyance of the lands aforesaid to me in a document designed to regularise this previous transaction but [. . .] this document is rendered useless by the refusal of Trisha Joshua Jenkins to sign this further documenet [*sic*] [. . .].

Trisha, it appears, had felt that her hands were clean of the matter. She had married, had moved off the land to live with her husband on his family's land, and had no desire to "get mess up with the law."

The court still refused to declare the conveyances valid, but not because of Trisha's refusal to sign. The case turned on the "share and share alike" clause: the judge reasoned that the original will did not devise fractional interests to any of the siblings, but rather conveyed the estate to the siblings "to be divided equally, share and share alike." "Divided equally" did not mean "divided in sevenths"; this, the judge stated, was most clear: the will indicates that the land in question measures "35 acres *more or less*." It therefore could never be partitioned into neat sevenths since the whole is forever an unknown; more precisely, the whole is not defined in terms that make it possible to divide it into equal parts. Samuel had unknowingly created the equivalent of a "family settlement," a legal device described later in this chapter that keeps land in a "family" in perpetuity. Wilbur never was able to sell "his" land, since it was never legally declared his. However, Daniel and Trisha kept the money he had paid them, and the siblings made no fuss about the presence of Wilbur and his wife and children (and now, in the 1990s, his children's children) on what became, quite literally against the will of the Manley siblings, the Manley "family land."

The Windy Hill Case

In 1927, just months before his death, Richard Morgan made a gift of an estate to his wife and their four children. The lands at Windy Hill consisted of forty-one acres "or thereabouts" and were given by Richard to his wife Joanna, his children Edgar, Wesley, Connie, and Molly, and "their heirs and assigns forever [. . .] without any manner of condition whatsoever." With this clause in his will, Richard had granted Joanna and the children the fee simple; the estate was theirs to enjoy "forever."

The family lived on the land. Molly died in 1933, without leaving a will. From 1933 to 1950, Joanna, Edgar, Wesley, and Connie each paid one-fourth of the land tax each year. In 1951, Joanna died intestate, and the three surviving children began each paying one-third of the land tax. In 1952, the siblings mortgaged the entire estate in order to get money to build cow paddocks and to develop the pasture areas of the estate. The indenture of the mortgage considers the three siblings to be one unit—they three are listed as "The Borrower," not as "borrowers." All three enjoyed the pleasures and profits of the new pasture lands "equally."

In 1962, they changed their system for paying the tax: from that time on, they alternated in their payments. Edgar paid all the land tax for 1962; Connie paid it all in 1963; Wesley paid it all in 1964. But in 1965, the three siblings decided to "divide the estate equally." In the British Virgin Islands, however, nothing divides a family like the partitioning of property.

They ended up in court in 1966. The main dispute was between Edgar and Wesley, but Connie sided with Wesley. He and Connie thought that the estate should be divided into thirds. He testified that they had been paying off the mortgage "equally" and had "used the paddocks equally" and "agreed to divide the lands into three equal portions and each of us would take one of the three portions as his or her interest in the lands." For him, the concept "equal" had a mathematical referent; it signified "thirds" and did not imply the same kind of relationship among the cotenants as the phrase "in common" would have done. Edgar, on the other hand, felt that, as the eldest son, he should be entitled to a greater share. He was not contesting that the idea of partition contains within it mathematical referents; he just thought he deserved more.

The judge declared that the original conveyance from Richard gave the estate to five people "in equal shares." This is quite an interesting statement, especially in light of the Sugar Apple Bay Case. In that case, the original deed also defined the estate as a number of acres "more or less," or "thereabouts," and the judge decided that this indeterminate quantification of the estate made it impossible for the estate to be fractionally divided. In the case at hand, however, the judge took it as a given that the estate *was* able to be partitioned. The question was exactly how it should it be done.

This case is somewhat unique in that the court documents contain detailed notes on the solicitors' arguments. Wesley and Connie's lawyer made his case as follows: At the initial gift from Richard, his wife, Joanna, and his children, Edgar, Wesley, Connie, and Molly, were each entitled to one-fifth of the estate. When Molly died, her one-fifth should have been divided among the four survivors; at this point, each surviving family member would have had $\frac{1}{5} + (\frac{1}{4} \times \frac{1}{5})$, or one-fourth of the original estate. At Joanna's death, her one-fourth should have been divided among the surviving three; so each then should have had $\frac{1}{4} + (\frac{1}{3} \times \frac{1}{4})$, or one-third. Hence, each was now entitled to one-third of the estate.

Edgar's lawyer agreed that, at the initial conveyance of gift, each of the five persons was entitled to one-fifth of the estate. Molly died intestate; her one-fifth, this solicitor claimed, should have "reverted" back into Richard's estate—in spite of the fact that Richard had died. This is because Richard never alienated his fee simple; her portion of it appears to be, in this argument, an estate that reverts back to the fee simple holder at her death. Since Richard died before 1945, when inheritance laws were changed to provide for the equal division of intestates' estates among all surviving heirs, his estate should go to the heir-at-law, or the firstborn son—Edgar. Richard had already granted the estate in fifths to each of his descendants and to his wife. But, with Molly's death, Richard would be granted her one-fifth share—even though he was dead—and so that one-fifth should have devolved to Edgar as heir-at-law. Hence, at Molly's death, Edgar should have had his own one-fifth plus Molly's one-fifth; his mother and his two remaining siblings each would have their original fifth. Joanna died intestate in 1951; under the new laws, her estate should have been divided equally among all the heirs. Edgar thus should have $\frac{2}{5} + (\frac{1}{3} \times \frac{1}{5})$, Wesley should have his original $\frac{1}{5}$, plus $(\frac{1}{3} \times \frac{1}{5})$, and Connie the same. So, Edgar should have $\frac{7}{15}$, and Connie and Wesley each $\frac{4}{15}$.

Edgar won his case, but with two little wrinkles introduced by the judge. The whole estate was divided up according to $\frac{7}{15}$–$\frac{4}{15}$–$\frac{4}{15}$ fractions, except for two special parts of the estate. One part consisted of the best pasture lands. These were set aside from the whole of the estate and divided up independently into $\frac{7}{15}$–$\frac{4}{15}$–$\frac{4}{15}$ shares. The other part was the house plot, which was deemed to belong to all three as "tenants-in-common" in the fee simple. Edgar, Connie, and Wesley continued to live on the land, unhappily ever after, until their deaths. Their heirs sold it in the 1980s.

Neither the Kendalls nor the Charleses in the Sugar Apple Bay case had any interest in "family land" per se. People wanted to sell off their shares and have done with it. But because the "land itself" was of indeterminate area, "family land" was forced upon them. The resolution of the Sugar Apple Bay case reinforced paternal wishes and solidified "family" even as the people on the grid denied that the land ought to be in any way "familial." It was the land itself, in its indeterminacy, that created "family" and family land in common tenure. The "land," not the "abstract estate" presumed to be constructed out of it, did *not* relate here to its "natural" equivalent, the "grid," but instead pulled "family" together.

The situation was the converse in the Windy Hill case. The "land" was indeterminate here, as well. But it was the "estate" that became the focus. No one cared that the land was of indeterminate area; all parties to the case, including the judge, agreed that fractional interests were possible. So, what was important in this case was establishing the precise fractional "relation" among the three people. The ensuing fractional interests were necessarily abstractions, since the area of the land was never known. It was for this reason that the fractions could be applied, arbitrarily, to distinct and specifiable bits of the land itself. Competing logics of the "natural" genealogical grid thus map the abstract "estate." The dead father inherited his daughter's share, and the firstborn son acquired that share from the dead father—paternity was inscribed, but coexisted with fractional bloods figured on a genealogy. When the mother died, her share was divided "equally." The net result, however, was the success of the firstborn son over his siblings. Genealogy and family worked together both because of, and to reinforce, paternity. In contrast to the Sugar Apple Bay case, the Windy Hill case turned on a relationship between "estates" ("constructed") and "genealogies" ("natural"), not "land" ("natural") and "families" ("constructed").

The Good Hope Estate Case

Older Virgin Islanders I spoke with described the Good Hope Estate Case as one of the longest-standing, most complicated, and most amusing bits of trouble in the whole history of the British Virgin Islands. Arguments about this estate have been particularly rancorous, for the case accomplished no less than the multiple fracturing of family sentiments both between and within generations upon generations of people. And the fires are still burning. A new case is put forth regularly, every third year or so. An elderly woman laughed when I brought up the case, and joked, "Them people *still* fighting! Blood is thick, but when it comes to land, money thicker!" An old man told me, "That case there so confusing . . . and they be going on until Judgment Day itself, for true!"

In 1910, a group of six brothers decided to purchase an estate together and to share it as common tenants. They were the sons of John and Anne Yates. For £100, these men purchased title to lands measuring "215 acres or thereabouts," according to the original deed, "to have and to hold the said Heriditaments unto and to the use of the above named parties and to there [*sic*] heirs and assigns forever:"

> Witnesseth, that for and in consideration of the sum of one
> hundred pounds (£100) paid to Oswald Spottiswoode Beodie

grant to Peter Yates, Michael Yates, Derrick Yates, Jason Yates, Simon Yates, and Warren Yates and to there hiers [*sic*] and assigns, forever, that [hole in deed] of land called and kn[hole in deed] the Good Hope Estate, with all [hole], fences, woods, waters, watercourses, [hole] and singular the premises, and [illegible] Peter Yates have paid the amount, £20, twenty pounds. on purchase of said Estate, £80, [illegible] paid by Michael Yates, Derrick Yates, Jason Yates, Simon Yates, and Warren Yates [. . .]

One of the points fueling the dispute that arose was the fact that Peter put in slightly more than the others; but still, according to one who remembers the case well, "all of them considered that the land was equally shared." The trouble came when the brothers started dying off. "The children and grandchildren of the man who put in the larger part thought they should get more of the land," he said. "And then, there was the question of succession."

By 1950, all the brothers except Simon were dead. Simon had rented out pieces of the land to five people. In addition, he had allowed four people to build houses on the land. To three of them, he had sold the house plots outright; the fourth he simply allowed to build and live on the land. Simon himself lived on the land, as did Rodney and Ernest Yates, two of the sons of Jason, and Andrew Yates, one of the grandsons of Jason. Octavia, one of Michael's daughters, lived in a house on the land with her husband, Michael Hopkins. In all, then, there were nine houses on the estate and five tenants paying rent to Simon for the use of some parts of the estate lands (mostly for grazing).

In addition, seven people considered themselves "tenants in common," with usufruct rights to the estate lands and free access to all profits and privileges associated with them. These were Simon, Rodney, and Ernest, as well as Ira, the first son of Jason; Gillian and Audrey Yates, the daughters of Michael; and Julie Yates, the widow of Peter Yates. A number of the Yates clan had been living abroad when the disputes first began. These included Timothy, the eldest son of Julie and Peter, who was living in the Bronx, and all of the other children of Julie and Peter except for Juliette; and also Clive, the eldest son of Derrick (himself the eldest son of John and Anne), in St. Thomas.

The axis of the first major dispute was between Julie, Peter's widow, and Simon. Julie believed she was entitled to more of the land than any of the others, because her husband had been the one to contribute the greatest sum toward the original purchase of the estate. She objected to all the tenancies and sales Simon had made—all of which he did after 1924, the year of Peter's death—and in general felt that the money Simon and the children of Jason had made off the land was wealth unfairly gotten. After all, she was the widow of the man who had made the original purchase possible. She was entitled to more. A document was presented to the court as "Exhibit A": this was a piece of parchment on which Julie had written "Julie Yates" and, quite simply, "land belong to me."

The widow of Warren, Carlotta, joined Julie. She, too, felt that Simon and the sons of Jason had made too much money off the land and had let too many "strangers" on it. Who were these tenants Simon was allowing to graze their cattle on the family land? And who were all these new neighbors, who had been allowed to build houses on plots that Simon had sold to them without consulting the others?

Julie and Carlotta wrote to Clive, in St. Thomas. They convinced him to join their cause, and he and the two widows brought a suit in 1954 against Simon, Ira, and Rodney. They also brought suit against Julie's own children, Timothy and Juliette, who thought that they, and not their mother, were entitled to the estate as heirs of their father. And they brought suit against a distant relation to whom Simon had sold a piece of land in 1925, and another person to whom Simon had sold a house plot sometime after 1924.

The sole basis of their legal claim was that Peter had paid a larger amount for the original purchase. But things were such a mess on the Yates land—with multiple tenants and so many possible conflicting claims on the horizon whenever and whether the people abroad might decide to return—that the court, in 1956, attempted to put forth a partitioning decision based on legal principles, which the clerk and the judge thought would stand and which would, they had hoped, preclude future problems. Their hope couldn't have been more wasted, for further suits emerged (and continue to do so). But here is what they decided to do.

The court decided that the six brothers were tenants-in-common, since the deed of conveyance stated that they were "to have and to hold the said Heriditaments" and so were "there hiers and assigns forever." This clause legally established the estate as a fee simple. Since no one holder of the fee simple was named, the court took the deed to mean that all six brothers were to hold the fee simple in common. That Peter paid more makes no difference. The fee simple was not divided into differential fractional shares in the original deed. Hence, the court, in forcing a partition, divided the estate into equal fractional parts—each of the six brothers was entitled to one-sixth of the whole estate.

Now, Peter, Michael, Derrick, and Jason had all died before 1945, when inheritance laws still mandated that the estate of an intestate pass entirely to the heir-at-law, or firstborn son. Hence, the court determined that the eldest son of Michael would inherit his father's one-sixth. But this man had himself died in 1932, so his eldest son got his sixth. Jason's sixth went to his eldest son, Ira. Simon was entitled to a sixth. Warren and Carlotta had no children; the court determined that Carlotta had no right of dower to his sixth because she was not "of the body" of Warren since she had not "given him issue." So his sixth reverted back to his dead father, John. This sixth would have passed on to Derrick, the eldest of the brothers, who was also dead and who also had claim to a sixth of his own. These two sixths, then, passed on to the heir of Derrick, Clive in St. Thomas. Peter's sixth should pass to Timothy. But as Julie was still living, and as "she had given Peter issue" and was therefore "of his body," she maintained her right of dower and was entitled to her dead husband's sixth.

The lands sold by Simon after 1924 were considered by the court to be alienated from the estate because the statute of limitations had passed. The court, after determining that the lands should be divided into sixths, made no effort to delineate these sixths but left it to the claimants. This was probably a mistake, but it is interesting because it shows that, as far as the court was concerned in this round of the disputing, the estate was an abstract entity that could be partitioned without reference to the "actual ground" that the parties to the argument were really fighting over.

In 1960, Timothy, the son of Julie and Peter who had been living in the Bronx, initiated two suits during a visit to Tortola. One was against a woman whose house was on the land but who had never been asked to pay Simon anything for it. The other was against Rodney and Ernest. Timothy claimed that he was entitled to the land on which these three persons' houses were built. The woman settled out of court, paying Timothy $122 and paying the costs of the suit. People say she was a "sensible" person who "just wanted to stay out of trouble." Timothy, all seem to agree, was basically greedy. He didn't really want the land and had no intention of returning permanently to live on it. He just wanted to see what he could get during his short holiday in Tortola. The motive was money. The axis of the dispute was again between Peter's "line" and Jason's. But the fight represented something more—it was an argument between someone who had gone "off-island," made some money, and was returning craving more, and people who had "stayed on the land," "earning" money from the land, and maintaining "local" roots. Timothy lost his case against Rodney and Ernest. He went back to New York and never returned.

In 1966 there was another dispute between members of Peter's "line" and members of Jason's. This time, Ernest took Juliette to court, claiming she had trespassed on his land and had damaged his fences. He lost his case, too. All subsequent disputes over the Good Hope lands take this general shape, with people arguing over fences and boundaries and crying trespass.

The main line of conflict throughout has been between people connecting themselves to Peter and people connecting themselves to Jason. Initially, Julie thought she was entitled to the land—"land belong to me"—as the widow of the man who had contributed the most to purchase it. The reasoning behind her sense of entitlement was an interesting mix of a "family" mentality with the idea of individual contribution. Yet Julie objected to Simon's and Jason's sons' dividing and selling off of pieces of land to make profit. In the first dispute, she and the other widow in the picture, Carlotta, the wife of Warren, were able to enlist the support of the firstborn son of the firstborn son. Inmarrying wives appealed to the center of the paternal line to help them muster familial authority. But their logic hinges on an idea of fractional interests not conceived through blood, but through initial individual monetary contribution. The court "settlement" disproportionately benefits the absent Clive and leaves Carlotta with nothing. Julie, however, being deemed "of the body" of Peter because she "gave" him a child (the Tortolian expression would be "had a child *for* him"), received the right of dower over Timothy's interest in the estate.

In the second dispute, the lines of conflict were the same, but the motives were quite different. This was a "local" versus "off-islander" conflict where ideas about work and wealth came into play. Timothy's motives were purely monetary. His appeal invoked the genealogical grid, and he was cast on the local front as a greedy, bad relative. Julie wanted the land, and Timothy wanted the money. His logic mirrored that of Simon and the sons of Jason in the previous dispute.

The third and subsequent disputes all involved boundaries and trespass. At issue here were the boundaries of "family," but the motivation was purely monetary, and the enabling device for new claims and counterclaims was the genealogical grid. On the one hand, one could read these cases as following a progression, from ideas about family and land to ideas about money and fractional interests based on fractions of "blood." Julie's initial dispute, however, was also based on fractional interests, whose referent was cash.

People like Julie Yates thought about family land in particular ways. The land, by virtue of its being "family land," ought to be theirs if they have some genealogical connection to the people who bought or inherited it. Legal principles, unfortunately, sometimes came down against them; for women who marry into a family are not legally connected to the genealogy unless they bear a child "for" the family. Here the law intersects with British Virgin Islander practices and ideas about paternity and, from paternity, notions of family lines. People like Julie's son Timothy, and Edgar from the Windy Hill case, thought about family land in other ways. They had a clear sense that, if they could prove a claim, the land was theirs to sell. Firstborn sons are at a distinct advantage if one of their parents has died before 1945, for they can exploit the heir-at-law provision in pre-1945 law.

Law has paradoxical effects. On the one hand, it can force "family" land upon a group of people who just want to alienate and have done with it. On the other hand, it can fragment family land into multiple holdings, figured in terms of fractional interests determined by degrees of biogenetic relatedness. Sometimes these effects are consonant with what people want out of their land—as in the case of Windy Hill, where everyone essentially agreed that the land should be partitioned. Other times, they are not—as in the case of the Landers lands, which became "family" land almost in spite of the wishes of the "family" itself. Here, however, "family land" is forced not because of some attachment on the part of the courts to "family," but because of a kind of "objectivity": the uncertainty of land boundaries prevents divisibility. The concept of the "estate" as an abstraction built up from the natural facts of land handily resolves this problem.

These various manifestations of "family land" have coexisted and played off one another in the British Virgin Islands since at least the turn of the century. Next, I turn to the literature on the family land phenomenon to throw more light on these land cases.

Family Land: Besson's Contribution

Jean Besson has deftly summarized the sizable body of literature on the family land phenomenon (see Besson 1979, 1984). Her germinal contribution to the family land literature was published in 1979 and has since remained the most significant analysis of the phenomenon to date. Besson begins by locating the discussion of Caribbean land tenures squarely within broader movements in twentieth-century anthropology over "cognatic" or "nonunilineal descent groups."

Prior to Goodenough's (1955) essay on Malayo-Polynesian descent, anthropologists were in agreement that unilinear descent—which they had "identified" or "discovered" in sub-Saharan Africa—provided a means for guaranteeing social order in societies without states, sovereigns, or formal, written laws. Descent provided a handy concept for anthropologists and colonial officials who sought out the "leaders" of the societies they inscribed in their texts and empires. Unilineal descent provided a model that made sense to Europeans and seemed to reflect the ways people in African societies formed themselves into solidary groups for support in subsistence and in conflict situations (Evans-Pritchard 1940; Fortes 1953). Without such a descent system, the thinking went, one would be hard put to delineate a functioning social order (Radcliffe-Brown 1950:43). For instance, in a "cognatic" system, as opposed to a unilinear one, every person could trace descent and group membership from any ascendant, and so each individual would "belong to as many such descent groups as he has ancestors" (Solein 1959:578). This seemingly nonsensical proposition led anthropologists to use the "African" model to search out the "social structures" of societies around the world, while nonunilinear or bilateral kin groupings were "allowed to remain an unstudied residual category" (Davenport 1959:557). As Murdock wrote, "ethnographers rarely notice[ed] their presence and almost never report[ed] their absence" (1949:57).

This view had changed by the 1950s. World War II brought military and academic experience in the Pacific and Austronesia to many U.S. anthropologists. Here anthropologists found the unilineal descent model wanting, especially when they tried to understand the connections between descent and rights to land. Emphasis here seemed to be on "kindreds," groups of consanguines tracing their connections laterally to a common relative ("all the blood relatives connected to a living individual") or lineally through both male and female lines to a common ancestor ("all the blood relatives connected to a common ancestor"). Goodenough's "A Problem of Malayo-Polynesian Social Organization" (1955) was a first attempt at distinguishing these two "types" from African models.[5]

The "problem" of Malayo-Polynesian nonunilineal descent was the question of how to limit the number of descent groups to which an individual might belong in order to achieve some degree of social order. There had to be some "restricting" mechanisms, since otherwise every person would belong to multiple overlapping descent groups and there would be no way to figure out who was entitled to what rights in which pieces of land, let alone who was "related" to whom. A completely unrestricted system would by definition be cognatic in the purest form, for it would map exactly onto the entire genealogical grid without remainder. What a nightmare for structural-functionalists trying to find the "rules" by which people form themselves into kin-based groups![6]

In her contribution to the family land scholarship, Besson put forth the proposition that Caribbean family land is transmitted from generation to generation by exactly that which previous anthropologists deemed impossible (or, at least, improbable; see

Firth 1963:25): an *unrestricted* cognatic descent system. Several people had conceded that if a descent system existed that functioned with respect to only one resource, such as property, unrestricted descent might be possible (see Besson 1979:92–93).[7] Besson proposed "that the cognatic descent group throughout the Caribbean is, (and always has been) an unrestricted, dispersed, nonresidential group functioning in relation to a specific resource only (family land)—such as some anthropologists have conceded is theoretically possible, but ethnographically rare; and that this system of unrestricted cognatic descent has developed among Caribbean peasantries in response to the plantation system and its connotations" (1979:104). Her contention hinges on the idea that family land has a "crucial symbolic role: for it enables the retention of numerous co-heirs of inalienable rights to freehold land" (105). Such rights are "crucial in the Caribbean to the definition of free personhood [. . .]. In addition to symbolising freedom and prestige, freehold land rights also provide a symbol of security and independence in the face of the plantation regime" (105).

Besson's story about family land is roughly this: The symbolic value of land is that it represents individual freedom and, specifically, freedom from the plantation regime. Having your own land means having your own person and no longer being the chattel of another. To "possess" is to be "free" (cf. Macpherson 1962). Yet Caribbean peoples have had to contend with overall land scarcity: the islands are small, the plantations held most of the land, and so having one's own land could be a difficult goal to attain. Hence the emergence of family land, whereby each individual through various cognatic ties can make a claim to a piece of property, and "the smallest plot of family land can fulfill its role to an ever-increasing number of generations" (Besson 1979:107). Family land is thus a *symbolic* resource, not an economic one (106–7). The descent groups are flexible, fungible, and "corporate in a minimal sense only" (106–7). And thus the tension between people who thought Caribbean kin groups were "shallow" or ego-focused and those who saw descent groups is resolved by the ad hoc nature of Besson's unrestricted group: the "groups" only really exist as "groups" when land transmission is at issue, when one wishes to stake a claim, to assert one's freedom; otherwise, there are just associations of kin that may be construed as ego-focused.

Besson has been remarkably consistent in her approach to family land (Besson 1984, 1987a, 1988). And Caribbeanists have, in the main, agreed with her analysis (but see Berleant-Schiller 1987; Carnegie 1987; Crichlow 1994). Her argument has had great explanatory power for a wide variety of cases throughout the Caribbean (see her reviews in Besson 1984, 1987a, 1988). I would like to dwell on the critique put forward by Charles Carnegie, however, for it raises issues not so much with Besson's contribution as with thinking on land and kin in anthropology, and, more centrally, in Western cultures transfigured by the liberal polities and capitalist markets.

Carnegie's Critique

The title of Carnegie's (1987) article about family land perhaps best sums up his position. He asks, "Is family land an institution?" In essence, his answer is no, it is not. Family land is characterized by "ambiguity" and "inexactness" (1987:83). It is incorrect to assume that family land stands in relation to legal tenures as a form of "customary law," that it is an "institution" in itself, perhaps existing in contradictory or conflictual relations with state law, but nonetheless an institution with a degree of autonomy. Rather, he argues, family land exists as a kind of "intersystem," or "continuum" from legal forms to customary forms of tenure, with continual movement along the continuum between the poles. "[T]here are transformations taking place all the time, and not in one direction only, between the various types and this dynamic quality cannot be treated as an anomalous aspect of the system" (92). Previous research on family land, he argued, assumed too rigid a distinction between legal and customary tenures; and furthermore, it posited custom as a normative order. But, in the Caribbean, "we have individuals practising different forms of tenure simultaneously [. . .]. This begins to look suspiciously like the situation with which Creole linguistics has had to come to terms," namely, "a speech community whose members understand and routinely shift between utterances governed by very different sets of rules" (93). He refers to Lee Drummond's (1980) work on Guyanese ethnic categories, interacting within a similar "intersystem" or "continuum" of values and practices.[8] In his own research in Jamaica, Carnegie found that the marketability of pimento had a great impact on the division of family land into often minuscule fractional interests and sparked a "lively market in real estate" (Carnegie 1987:88–89). At the same time, people placed a heavy importance on maintaining family burial plots, and plots seem to be named after some presumed common ancestor of the people making claims on the land. Carnegie concludes, "family land is various in its manifestations" (91).[9]

Tenurial Traditions: "Customary" and Common Law

Besson explicitly contrasts "legal freehold" to "customary freehold" or family land. In doing so, she posits "custom" to be a separate domain from "law." At the root of the Besson-Carnegie debate (and other critiques of Besson, e.g., Crichlow 1994), is the question of whether family land is an institution opposed to the formal legal system. My data would suggest that perhaps this is the wrong question. Carnegie argues convincingly, and my data would support, that family land is too various and too ill-defined in Caribbean practices and ideologies to constitute a singular custom. However, Besson's argument about the symbolic value of family land is persuasive, but perhaps because it revolves around notions of property and personhood linked to liberalism and its reformulations in the Caribbean (Maurer 1996:362). By my reading, "custom" and "law" are not so distinct here, but mutually constitutive. Indeed, British Virgin Islanders' (and anthropologists') reiterations of law and custom lend force to these terms. Mediating them, their practices empower them and grant them a new, creole, reality.

Where Carnegie assembles counterexamples to criticize Besson's dichotomization of custom and law, I would rather begin by examining the legal status of land ownership in England and places influenced by the British common law. I do not wish to be misunderstood: I am not claiming that English common law gave rise to family land in the Caribbean, as Greenfield proposed in his book somewhat unfortunately titled *English Rustics in Black Skin*

(1966, see also Greenfield 1960). However, the common law might shed more light on "customary" tenures in the Caribbean than the review of examples and counterexamples provided by Carnegie and Besson. In other words, we need to be clear about what we're contrasting "customary" tenure to if we intend to claim that "custom" is any different from "law." Problematizing custom in this way helps show how a "nature" is concocted in family land and land law that takes on the character of a real, objective, and determining force in Caribbean family land and academic debates about it.

The Common Law

The family land literature and people I encountered in the British Virgin Islands with some knowledge of the law make casual reference from time to time to something called *freehold*. In the BVI, people who know the term generally contrast it to *Crown land*. But just what is the distinction in the common law between the two, and how did it arise?

Legal historians trace the distinction between freehold and Crown land back to William the Conqueror, who deemed all land in the kingdom to be "held of the Crown" (see Simpson 1961:1, 44–45). This is not to say that the Crown "owns" all the land in the kingdom. Rather, the Crown exists in relationships with other "lords" who "hold" land through, ultimately, the grace of the Crown. Lords, in turn, may grant the land to other tenants. People claiming right to the land did so by virtue of *seisin*, or their being in possession of it. The idea was (and is) that all land is held of the king (or queen), but one can be "seized" of the land for "estate" or an "interest" in an "estate" for a specified time. One thus does not "own" the land itself, but "holds" it in seisin. Hence the term *tenure*. Tenure thus does not refer to a relationship between a person and the land, but to relations among several people: "The person whom we may call the owner, the person who has the right to use and abuse the land, to cultivate it or leave it uncultivated, to keep all others off it, holds the land of the King either immediately or mediately" (Pollock and Maitland 1898:ii, 232).

The distinction between the land itself and an estate is crucial to the common law, although its significance has declined drastically in this century. Land is not something that can be bought and sold like any other good. One owns a good, and merely being in possession of a good is generally enough to establish ownership; as the saying goes, "possession is nine-tenths of the law." But one does not truly own the land, even if one is in possession of it. That is because, as Cheshire put it, "[l]and and goods must ever be on a different plane. Land is fixed, permanent and vital to the needs of society, and a subject-matter in which rights may be granted to persons other than the ostensible owner" (Cheshire 1982:5). Someone might be in possession, or "seized," of the land, but may hold it under a lease for a great number of years; or a person may hold a "life interest" in it, holding it until their death; or one may hold the "fee simple"—"the largest interest known to the law and the one that approximates to the absolute ownership of goods"—in which one holds the estate "forever" (5). Still, however, the land in which a person is seized is not something the person can be said to own. Rather, the person owns an "estate":

> What [. . .] emerges [. . .] is that land cannot be the subject-matter of ownership, though the person in whom its seisin is vested is entitled to exercise proprietary rights in respect of it. [. . .] [W]hat is the nature of the interest held by the person seised? Is there nothing that he can be said to own? The answer made by English law is unique. The person entitled to seisin owns an abstract entity, call[ed] an *estate,* which is interposed between him and the land. 'The English lawyer . . . first detaches the ownership from the land itself, and then attaches it to an imaginary thing which he calls an estate.' (Cheshire 1982:29–30; quoting Markby 1889)

There have been several types of estates in common law, which fall into two main categories: freehold estates and those that are "less than freehold." One of the most interesting—and counterintuitive—facts about estates is that they are not spatial entities. Rather, an estate is conceived as a *temporal* entity: "the main classification of estates depends on their quantification and their quantification depends on their *duration*" (Cheshire 1982:30, emphasis added). "Proprietary rights in land are, we may say, projected upon the plane of time" (Pollock and Maitland 1898:ii, 10). The difference between estates, then, is always a temporal difference. A freehold estate is an estate of indeterminate duration; the time during which one is entitled to be seized of the land is never certain. A "life interest" in an estate makes the estate a freehold estate, since one never knows when one will die (at least not at present levels of technology). An estate of less than freehold is one whose time is fixed or certain; leasehold is the most common kind of estate less than freehold. A 999-year lease, even though it is of longer duration than a life interest, is considered less than freehold because it is of a determinate duration.

There are two types of freehold estates: freeholds of inheritance and freeholds not of inheritance (which do not concern us here). Of the former, there are two types: estates in *fee simple* and those in *fee tail*. Estates in fee simple are longer than estates in fee tail. They are granted "to a man and his heirs" forever—or so long as the man has heirs—either ascending, descending, lineal, or collateral. In theory, then, they may never revert to the Crown and will exist in perpetuity. Estates in fee tail are inheritable only to specified descendants (and never ascendants) of the man (or, recently, woman) so seized. They are also descendable only to lineal descendants, not collaterals. "Thus [the fee tail] is inferior to the fee simple in the sense that it has not as great a capacity for perpetual existence" (Cheshire 1982:32). "[F]or he who has a fee simple in land has a time in the land without end or the land for time without end" (30, quoting Walsingham's Case, 1579). After the time of an estate is over, the estate reverts "back" to the Crown. Hence, Crown land is land in which no one is seized of the land for an estate.

Fee simple estates are alienable. One can sell them, or sell parts of them. These are parts in time: what is being transferred is a time during which the transferee will be entitled to be seized of the land. Let us suppose that Alfred is seized of a piece of land for an estate in fee simple. At his death, it descends to his heirs, Brian and Charles. Unless Alfred specifies otherwise, the entire fee simple passes on to the heirs. From the point of his death, Brian and Charles have the fee simple. If Brian and Charles agree to sell the estate to a fourth party, David, it passes in toto to him at the moment of sale. In effect, they sell David their "infinity."

Fee simple estates can be apportioned and the portions alienated as well. Cheshire writes that "the fee simple is regarded as an aggregate out of which any number of smaller *and simultaneous* estates may be carved, to be enjoyed by a number of persons, each of whom is the owner of his own individual portion," even if his portion is in the future (1982:32). Ownership is always in the present; it is seisin, or the condition of being in possession or holding the land, that is in the future.

Suppose Alfred does not wish Brian or Charles to be able to alienate the entire fee simple so easily. He could specify in his will that, upon his death, Brian is entitled to a *life estate,* and that, upon Brian's death, Charles is entitled to a life estate. In this situation, technically, Alfred maintains ownership of the fee simple. Brian and Charles only own estates in it for the duration of their lives after Alfred's death. If they want to sell their estates, they can do so—they can even do so before they become seized of them, that is, for Brian, before Alfred's death and for Charles, before either Alfred's or Brian's death. They own the estates in the present; their seisin is in the future. If Brian sells his life estate to David, then upon Alfred's death, David is seized of the life estate of Brian. But when Brian dies, David's life estate is over, since is was actually pegged to Brian's life, and Charles's life estate begins. The *entire* fee simple is inalienable in this situation; neither Brian nor Charles can alienate the whole infinity, since each only has a life estate. But when, at Charles's death, no one is remaining seized of it, for all purposes it reverts to the Crown (whence it came in the first place).

The system is supremely flexible since it is not connected to the soil itself; one can devise complex ways of dealing with the infinite number of estates possible in a fee simple. There were even ways, before legal changes in 1925–26 (and 1945 in the Caribbean), to ensure ownership and seisin within a family in perpetuity. This was effected through a device called a *settlement,* and this device is what Greenfield found evidence for in his study of Barbadian land tenures. He claimed that family land is essentially a "settlement" under common law.

The Family Settlement

The idea is straightforward, and the motivation equally so. Cheshire wrote, and Greenfield (1960:172) quoted:

The desire of the upper classes to order the future destiny of their land and to prevent it from being sold out of the family, which has been a feature of English social life for many centuries, requires attention. [. . .] The inclination of a fee simple owner [. . .], is to make what is called a settlement by which he retains the beneficial ownership during his own life, but withholds the entire ownership in the shape of the fee simple from his descendants for as long as possible by reducing them, one after another, to the position of mere limited owners. (Cheshire 1958:69)

The thirteenth edition of Cheshire's *Modern Law of Real Property* continues: "The English doctrine of estates is ideally adapted to the achievement of this object. The fee simple of infinite duration is divisible into shorter periods of time each of which may be allotted successively to a number of persons, with the result that while these periods are running there is no person able to dispose of the entire ownership" (Cheshire 1982:69).

The principle behind family settlements is simple. The fee simple owner merely sets up his will such that his heirs are seized in fee tail or through successive life estates (much as in the third aforementioned example), forever. Since ownership is always in the present, "future persons," then, are owners of parts of the fee simple estate in the present, even before their birth.

Greenfield reports that founders of family settlements in Enterprise Hall, Barbados, would *entail* (i.e., place in fee tail) the interests of "all their descendants" by the use in wills of the clause "I . . . (name of testator) . . . bequeath to . . . (names of all children) . . . *and their seed forever* . . . ," the piece of property in question (1960:173, original emphasis). He writes that "land became factually and legally inalienable and perpetually retained within the family as long as there was issue. Each generation also inherited no more than a life interest in the estate. Each member of the family obtained the rights and privileges associated with ownership but never actual ownership" (173). The so-called "seed-to-seed" clause skirted "legitimacy" of issue, since, he claims, the use of the word *seed* restricts the class of heirs entailed in the estate to those "of the man's body": all the "seed," all the "biological" descendants, are entitled to fee tail, not just the ones recognized by law as legitimate heirs, and not just the male ones, either (173). The man making the family settlement, in effect, created even as he presupposed a cognatic descent group, extending "down" from himself in perpetuity. This group is potentially restricted, however, since limiting inheritance to the "heirs of his body" precludes passing an entailed interest in the estate to, for example, the spouse of an heir—something not necessarily precluded in a "purely" unrestricted descent group, which is by definition the "genealogical grid" itself and everyone represented through it. As we have seen, this fact was quite significant in BVI land cases. It reasserts as it concocts a particular meaning for paternity, and it grants an almost divine power to men's "seed" as it denies inmarrying women rights to land (cf. Delaney 1986, 1991).

Changes in the Land Laws

The laws pertaining to land and estate ownership changed during 1922–26 and were phased in over a period of time in England and the colonies. They came fully into effect in the BVI in 1945 (Intestates Estates Act, Cap. 35). These changes would appear to have had the potential to disrupt the settlement system Greenfield describes for Enterprise Hall.

The legislation passed by Parliament in 1922–26 had one main goal: "to render the sale of land as rapid and simple a matter as the sale of goods or of stocks shares" (Cheshire 1982:4). First, the concept of tenure all but lost its meaning and was made to have "little practical effect" (85). Tenure today places no restrictions on the privileges and pleasures of the "tenant" of a piece of land, as might have been the case earlier. What had been conceived as a relation between people—the lord and the tenant or the king and the tenant—is now, in effect, a relation between a person and the land.

The concept of an "estate" was weakened as well. Before 1925, there were any number of legal estates—fee simple estates, life estates, entailed estates, and so forth.[10] After 1925, all possible legal estates were reduced, for freehold, to the "fee simple absolute" (fee simple with no restrictions or entailments) and, for leasehold, to the "term of years absolute" (leasehold only and absolutely for the stated term of years) (Cheshire 1982:92—93).

The person who holds an estate is now known as the "estate *owner*."[11]

This change was not really so radical, though, since even at the end of the nineteenth century the doctrine of tenures and estates was coming to lose much of its meaning. Maitland wrote, in 1880:

> "The first thing the student has to do is to get rid of the idea of absolute ownership." So says Mr. Williams;[12] but we may add, with equal truth, that the second thing he has to do is to learn how, by slow degrees, the statement that there is no absolute ownership of land has been deprived of most of its important consequences. (Maitland quoted in Cheshire 1982:86)

One truly significant change, however, was the elimination of future and entailed interests—drastically limiting the ability of estate owners to set up settlements. Rules thus came into effect against legal perpetuities (see Greenfield 1960:175; Maudsley 1979).

Another significant change was in the rules for transfer at death intestate, or without a will. Previously, estates were inherited by male heirs before female heirs and by rules of primogeniture, with lineal ancestors inheriting only after descendants. Wives were entitled by way of "dower" to "a life estate in one third of the land" (Cheshire 1982:811). A husband surviving his wife was entitled by "courtesy" to all the wife's freehold (under most circumstances; see Cheshire 1982:242ff, 810). After 1926, however, the surviving spouse (male or female) takes a life interest in half the estate, the other half being held in trust for the heirs (either the "issue" or brothers, sisters, and parents if there is no issue; Cheshire 1982:813). Where there is no surviving spouse, the estate descends to the heirs according to their share of the substance, as it were, of the parent: "If, for instance, the intestate is survived by two children and by four grandchildren, the offspring of a daughter who predeceased him, the children each take one-third of the estate and the remaining third is divisible equally between the four grandchildren" (Cheshire 1982:815).

This form of inheritance is called "taking *per stirpes*"—accord-

ing to the roots. " 'All the branches inherit the same share that
their root, whom they represent, would have done' " (Cheshire
1982:815, quoting Blackstone). *Per stirpes* reasoning entered BVI
law in 1945 and created the notions of fractional interests based
on fractions of "blood" we observed earlier in this chapter. It also
invigorated paternity. An estate depends upon its initial creation
by a male person. The ability of the fee simple owner to create a
perpetuity mirrors the monotheistic God's ability to create Adam
and, from him, a perpetual "line" of humans (see Delaney
1986:502). At the same time, the logic of *per stirpes,* to each according to their fraction of "blood," while mapping the genealogical
grid, also presupposes a notion of paternity, for the fractions imagined are fractions conceived from an initial ancestor, and this
ancestor is always male. Remember, too, that wives are not really
on the genealogy at all, unless and until they "give" their husbands
offspring.[13]

"Customary" Law?

Greenfield writes that changes to land law in the early twentieth
century effectively "end[ed] the legal status of family land." Yet
family land continued and continues, he writes, because "[m]ost
villages . . . knew little of the statutory changes," and "[f]or many
years they believed that the old rules were still binding" (1960:
175). Hence, they followed "pattern[s] established by their ancestors" (175). If there is "customary law" in Enterprise Hall, Barbados, and, Greenfield implies, the wider Caribbean, it is customary
only insofar as the past laws of the United Kingdom and its
colonies are, for today's West Indians, "customary."

To what extent does Greenfield's proposition erode the distinctions made by Besson between "legal freehold" and "family
land," between custom and law? It is true that most of the characteristics of family land are also features of pre-1945 "family settlements." In Enterprise Hall, at least, there seems to be compelling
documentary evidence that indeed "family settlements" were
being created. Besson's combing of the literature, however, easily
provides examples that would not support Greenfield's extrapola-
tion of the Enterprise Hall data to the whole Caribbean. This lack
of support is most evident when one looks for the legal documents

necessary to make a settlement. In many places there are no such documents supporting people's claims to family land, and there probably never have been. But in many cases, there are.

Another discrepancy between Besson's customary tenure and Greenfield's settlement is the inclusion or exclusion of "outside" children from inheritance. Under a family settlement with a "seed-to-seed" clause, "outside" children (either illegitimate, or not of the father's household) would indeed be entitled to an interest in the estate. Besson says they are not necessarily so entitled, and that is also a point of disagreement between Carnegie and Besson. One can find examples for either position.

That family land is inalienable would support Greenfield's settlement theory, for under a family settlement land is also inalienable. Here, however, history intervenes—family settlements of the kind Greenfield describes have not been around since the late 1940s. The idea that today's customary tenure is yesterday's law, however, might resolve this issue. So would the idea that it is through everyday practices regarding land that "custom" and "law" are continually reinvented by Caribbean people. Such practices matter so importantly because it is also through them that "family" and "genealogy" come to power.

Family and the Genealogical Grid: Inequality and Hierarchy Revisited

The distinction between "family" and the "genealogical grid" is muddled in most discussions about family and kinship in the Caribbean. Since many anthropologists and Western subjects assume, both in scholarship and in everyday life, that there is a thing called biogenetic relatedness—expressed with words such as *blood, flesh,* and *seed* in the British Virgin Islands and in other Western societies—we tend not to pay much attention to it when it's right before our noses. As David Schneider (1984) pointed out, Westerners are people who tend to "think kinship": we assume that there are genealogical "ties" which "connect" us to one another. "Families" are the units we construct, in various ways, out of these ties; they are the social "recognition" we accord them. The individuals on a kin diagram form the basis of these familial units. Each of these individuals is unique; all they share with those to whom they are linked is genealogical substance. It is up to these unique and all essentially different individuals to group themselves into families. How they do so is fodder for anthropological—and legal—discussion. Schneider pointed out that such discussion takes for granted what it should be investigating—how and why people think kinship in the first place.

Schneider had at his disposal ethnographic material from his time among the Yap with which to contrast our "thinking kinship." Marilyn Strathern, similarly, has recently put forth a contrast between the way we "think kinship" with the way some Melanesians "think relationships." She writes that "Melanesians take relationships for granted, as vital supports for all living persons, and work to differentiate persons from one another. Euro-Americans take individuality as basic to a natural condition, so that 'relating' persons to one another is itself a kind of cultural enterprise, even when one is looking for natural relations" (1992b:11).

The problem for Caribbeanist anthropologists, of course, is that Caribbeans are not Melanesians; they are people who think kinship in much the same way other Western folks do. Caribbean peoples and anthropologists thus become complicitous, as it were, in keeping silent the unspoken ground of the "genealogical grid." Making "thinking kinship" explicit (Strathern 1992a) is central to understanding family land in the Caribbean and to understanding the organization of inequalities in the region.

In a 1992 book, Lisa Douglass makes a distinction between "family" and "kin" that I find quite suggestive. She notes that "although [Jamaican elites] believe in the intrinsic meaning of blood ties," they often pick and choose from among the people biologically related to them, "selectively exclud[ing]" some of them from what they consider to be "family" (Douglass 1992:21–22). The processes by which they do this further the continual recreation of hierarchy and distinction. Hierarchy and distinction are built up, in part, through the selection and choice that go into determinations of "family." Intrinsic to these determinations are principles of "legitimacy," male heterosexual dominance, and "preferences" for legal marriages (21–22). The distinctions that produce "family" are built up from a ground of biogenetic relatedness taken for granted by the Jamaicans with whom Douglass worked. This ground Douglass calls "kin." "Family defines itself in part in contrast to kin. Kin is not a term Jamaicans use in the same specific and meaningful way they use family" (21–22). For Douglass, kin "denote[s] individuals who would appear on *an objective genealogy* based on consanguineal or affinal relations" (21–22, my emphasis). Family is constructed after the taken-for-granted, and indeed relatively undiscussed, network of kin. Family is the subject of negotiation and contest; kin essentially goes and comes without saying.

I would like to dwell on the "objective genealogy" Douglass identifies as the undiscussed but strategically manipulated basis of family construction among Jamaican elites. Research on Caribbean families would seem to demonstrate the same kind of family-kin distinction with variations across class and race lines throughout the region (Alexander 1976, 1977, 1984; Austin 1979, 1983, 1984; R. Smith 1988). Caribbean people seem generally to take for granted a notion of biogenetic relatedness; at the same time, they work out ways of "activating" these "relations" for specific ends: for the construction of family, for the mobilization of resources, and so on. An assumption guiding much feminist research in the region has been that women in times of need draw on a network of kin that always objectively exists, which is always there to be used (e.g., Anderson 1986). It is an analytical assumption, but it is also Caribbean good sense. "Blood speaks"—when it is strategically appropriate for it to do so (Berleant-Schiller and Maurer 1993, Bourdieu 1977).

Yet analysts of Caribbean societies tend unwittingly to come down on one side of the "family"-versus-"genealogical grid" divide, putting forth one as explanatory for Caribbean "kinship" and either assuming or discounting the other. For instance, Jean Besson's discussion of family land turns on a conception of Caribbean societies as composed of loosely organized descent groups, each of which is imagined as spreading down from a supposedly common ancestor; the argument depends thus on a weak notion of "family." Charles Carnegie, in contrast, emphasizes the "ambiguity" and "inexactness" in Caribbean definitions of the family entitled to the family land; his argument hinges on genealogy and the complex ways Caribbean peoples make use of "it." A marriage of their perspectives gives us a quite accurate representation of how Caribbean peoples talk and think about Caribbean family land. But we have not moved from description to explanation.

There are important parallels among the family/genealogy distinction and discussions of ethnicity in the Caribbean and discussions in the legal history of land tenure.[14] In each case, a similar narrative is constructed that contrasts certain "natural" or "objective" facts with the "constructions" built up "after" them, and that posits a progression toward increasing "nature." The effect of such narratives is to empower nature through recurring, creolizing iterations.

The family/genealogy distinction maps almost too neatly onto the so-called plural society debate. M. G. Smith's (1965) position, that Caribbean societies consist of relatively discrete groups with clearly delineated boundaries which interact on a social plane, has been identified as precisely the ruling ideology of some sectors of Caribbean elite classes (Robotham 1980). The thinking is essentialist and provides handy justification for class, color, and gender hierarchies. Yet its ideological character makes the pluralism model "false" only as an explanatory device; for, as many Caribbean people will recognize, it is rather descriptive of the ways some Caribbean peoples imagine "ethnicity," at least some of the time. For many Caribbean people, "ethnicity" is sometimes about "groups," which they take to be bounded units continually bumping into each other and causing conflicts. British Virgin Islanders make a clear and sharp distinction between, on the one hand, themselves and other Caribbean peoples and, on the other hand, Guyanese Indians. Indians are just "different"; differences in observed behavior are emphasized to the point of caricature; it must be becau[se of their "race" that they are so different. There is no question of a blurred boundary between East Indians and "real" West Indians, BVIslanders would say.

The counterargument to M. G. Smith has come from those advocating a "creole continuum" or "intersystem" approach, borrowed from linguistics (Drummond 1980). Here, ethnic, racial, and linguistic distinctions are seen as arranged along something of a spectrum. Caribbean societies are constituted through the movements of people along various continua. In a sense, the continuum is like the genealogical grid—it just "is." There is nothing too solid and immutable constructed on top of it, like "groups" or "families." People continually engage differences along the continuum, activating first one bit and then another, first in one context and then in others, and so forth, as they go about meeting their needs and fulfilling their desires. This perspective, too, rings quite true to Caribbean talk about ethnic and racial identities. Such identities seem to be about continual negotiation—by individuals—along various vectors of power and lines of hierarchy (Williams 1991). Such is certainly the case, for example, when British Virgin Islanders interact with people they call "Spanish." To take just one example, people might look askance at the marriage of a BVIslander and a "Spanish" person, but such marriages are within the realm of possibility and do happen. And there are "Spanish" people with "British Virgin Islander" surnames. But the idea of a BVIslander-Indian marriage is downright unthinkable—although one such marriage has occurred—and an Indian claiming the last name "Rhymer" would probably be considered a lunatic.

A division parallel to family/genealogy surfaces in the historiography of land tenure. This history is a narrative of how relations among people became relations between a person and the land. First, tenure referred to the relationship between a lord and a tenant, thought of in terms of land. Then, tenure became a relationship between a tenant and the land itself. There was nothing constructed on top of the "man-land relationship." Like the creole continuum or the genealogical grid, it is thought to exist objectively. In the historiography of English land law, the distinction between "relations among persons" and "relations between persons and land" does not take the shape of an either-or proposition the way that the family-grid distinction or pluralism-intersystem positions seem to do. Rather, histories of land law portray the contrast as an evolutionary change. Once, legal scholars suggest, we thought that land tenure was really a relationship among people; now, we think (or, we "recognize") it is "simply" a relationship between an individual and a piece of land.

It might be quite tempting to tell the same story about the family/genealogy or pluralism/intersystem dichotomies. One could start either from the premise that the Caribbean has gone through an objective change, or the premise that anthropological thinking on the Caribbean has gone through a paradigm shift. But the extrapolations from both premises are essentially the same. Once, Caribbean peoples thought of themselves (or "we" anthropologists thought of "them") as belonging to agnatic descent groups, to lineages—just like their African forebears!—along which relations of mutual obligation and support flowed. Now, after ("our" recognition of) the debilitating effects of slavery, the fool's gold of emancipation, continuing exploitative labor exaction, colonialism, capitalism, and structural adjustment, Caribbean peoples think of themselves (or "we" think of them) in terms of negotiation and strategy through kin networks, sometimes invoking family, to make ends meet and fulfill basic necessities. Similarly, once, there were distinct ethnic and racial groups—the Africans, the Indians, the Portuguese, the Caribs and Arawaks, the Chinese, the Jews, the French, the English, the Syrians, the Spanish, and the Scots, either in Caribbean people's minds or in the anthropologist's; now, after a century of intermarriage and nation building, reformulated inequalities, and the retrenchment of old class distinctions, the boundaries are changeable. Identity is about the deployment of fragmentary and contradictory allegiances. The Caribbean has gone from being pluralistic to being fully creole. Or, perhaps, anthropological awareness of the Caribbean has.

This kind of narrative comes too easily, and it is not the story I wish to put forth here. While there have been both paradigm shifts in anthropology and objective changes in Caribbean societies in the past century, we cannot claim with confidence that there has been such a tidy historical progression in the Caribbean, from pluralistic to creole, from family lines to kinship networks. The twin dichotomies of family/genealogy, pluralism/intersystem—and their transmutations, such as agnatic/cognatic, group identity/ negotiable identities, even society/individual and system/individual action—are structuring principles that continually play off one another, in people's discourses and in their practices. It is no surprise that they play off one another in scholarship on the region as well.

The poles of these dichotomies do not represent "earlier" or "later" stages in the development of Caribbean societies. Rather, they are moments of one larger ordering system of inequality. It is a system that attempts to suggest a resolution of the contradiction between the belief in equality and the perpetuation of existing inequalities, even as it entrenches that contradiction. It permits equality of individuals—"all are produced by the same kinds of ('blood') relations"—while it perpetuates inequality—"some individuals are simply better than others because made of better bloods or combinations of bloods"—and hierarchy—"some individuals are entirely different classes of persons from others." And it relies on two seemingly unalterable "facts" that people realize and reiterate as they go through their daily lives, facts that in becoming facts are made objectively real for people having to deal with them: the fact that individuals make "choices" and the fact that "nature" provides conditions for and places constraints upon those choices.

Chapter 7

The Cadastral Survey: A Modern Reordering of the Territory

The character of land disputes in the British Virgin Islands fundamentally changed in the 1970s. The loose system of written deeds and agreements between neighbors for usufruct rights and rights of way came to a rather abrupt end after the completion of the Cadastral Survey, and this survey is now a talking point for people in the islands when they discuss land and land disputes. The survey broke with the old methods of titling lands and put in place administrative and scientific structures for the accurate mapping and systematic recording of property titles. For most if not all BVIslanders, the Cadastral Survey represented a step forward in the development of the territory. As the current registrar of lands put it in her report on the survey, the "new system offered to the general public simpler, cheaper and safer land titles" (J. Penn 1986: n.p.).

Using aerial photography and scientific surveying techniques, the survey team—led by members of the British Technical Assistance team of the British Overseas Development Administration—produced maps of the entire territory of the British Virgin Islands and established an objective grid of "sections" and "blocks" according to which landowners could mark out their claims. The BVI government invited this project and paid for it. The British "experts" who visited the BVI from 1970 to 1975 to conduct the survey acted as technical advisers, not policymakers. One of the purposes of this chapter is to explore what difference it made to have land and land disputes treated as "technical issues," rather than family issues, legal issues, or political issues. What are the politics of the "technical," the "rational," the "systematic?" How do they contribute to modern orderings and understandings of both the British Virgin Islands as a territorial-political entity and British Virgin Islanders as the people living there?

More than any other aspect of the Cadastral Survey, its "scientific" basis and its "accuracy" had deep consequences for understandings of the land and the people living on it. That is a strong claim. Some might object and argue instead that the most lasting impact of the survey was that it facilitated house building and property development, on the one hand, and revenue collection, on the other. With systematic and accurate recording of titles, banks could more readily offer building loans to landowners who put up their title as collateral; with systematic and accurate measuring of land parcels, the government could more readily assess the value of an individual's land for taxation purposes.

Rational land titling has been and continues to be a prime force in bringing capitalist forms of property and debt to the developing world, and whole development schemes are built on the mortgaging of landholdings to establish agricultural credit (see Goheen and Shipton 1992, Shipton 1992). In the British Virgin Islands, rational land titling and the mortgaging it encouraged in part fostered the character of the tourist industry today— instead of corporations owning big condo-style hotels, as in St. Thomas and other Caribbean islands, individual BVIslanders have small guest houses and rental units they were able to build with the help of bank loans. My goal in this chapter, however, is to avoid adding my voice to the chorus that cheers on the "development" and "progress" achieved because of the Cadastral Survey. But it is also not to simply condemn the survey as an instrument of capitalist penetration and domination. It is hard to see domination, except in the abstract, when bank loans have contributed to one of the highest standards of living in the Caribbean and when the term is perhaps best reserved for the development of underdevelopment in places like Haiti and Dominica. BVIslanders are successful. There is no denying it.

However, the technique of land surveying itself had practical effects for landowners and redefined "the land." The Cadastral Survey was not simply a means for capital and people to use the land and land ownership in a novel way. Rather, the Cadastral Survey created "the land" itself such that it could be put to those novel uses. The Cadastral Survey created the land's objectivity, made the land an object needing ordering and owning, at the same time that the survey itself was this ordering and a means for owning. The "land" conjured up by the Cadastral Survey then took on a dynamic all its own. It became an object with power to determine lives and life chances, an object against which to measure what the BVI is to become and who is to become a "BVIslander."[1]

The Cadastral Survey as Exhibitionary Mode of Power

In modern mapping, "accuracy [is] a new talisman of authority" (Harley 1988:300). The Cadastral Survey was the first systematic mapping of the British Virgin Islands. And it resulted in the first "accurate" map of the territory ever to be produced. The survey relied primarily on aerial photography. Represented as a picture of an objectively real space, the map of the territory provides a means of determining titles and arbitrating disputes that will last as long as the land itself continues to peak above the Caribbean sea.

The BVI Legislative Council enacted several laws to facilitate the system of land registration envisioned by the survey team. The central pieces of legislation were the Land Adjudication Ordinance (No. 5 of 1970), the Registered Lands Ordinance (No. 8 of 1970), and the Land Surveyors Ordinance (No. 20 of 1970). Together, these laws set forth a new system of surveying, titling land, adjudicating disputes, and keeping records of land transactions. Most important, they set up the Land Registry and the Surveyor's Office as separate offices under the Ministry of Natural Resources and Labour. For the first time, the judiciary and the legal profession—crucial, as was evident in the previous chapter, to the drawing up of deeds and the arbitration of arguments—had no guaranteed role in land titling or dispute resolution. For this reason, some lawyers opposed the idea of the Cadastral Survey, especially given how lucrative the old system had been for them and, it should be added, for the courts. The change in responsibility for handling disputes is reflected in the archives: all documents dealing with land disputes prior to the Cadastral Survey are housed in the Vault of the Registry of the High Court. Most docu-

ments dealing with postsurvey disputes are in the Land Registry;
records for disputes that made it to court are in the vault, but most
were cut off at the Land Registry level before they became cases.

After the survey was conducted and the registered land acts
took effect, people could still take their disputes to court, but
before they got there they would have to visit the Land Registry,
where often the dispute would be resolved by reference to the
maps and registers kept there (cf. Yngvesson 1988). The registrar
of lands, meanwhile, together with her staff, enjoys powers very
much like a judge—she can admit or refuse evidence brought
before her to make a claim or argue in a dispute, and she can hold
hearings on disputes and demand oaths of the people who come
before her. She and her staff also enjoy immunity from any legal
action directed against them that is connected with their official
duties. In other words, you can't sue the Land Registry. It is not,
according to the ordinances that brought it into being, a political
entity or legal subject. It is a records room applying objective and
rational criteria to lands issues, backed up by the authority of the
maps it houses and the accuracy of the surveying conducted by its
sister office, the Survey Department.

The registrar of lands of the BVI summarized the new land
registration system: "All lands are divided into Registration Sections and within these sections are blocks. For each registration
block, there is a Registry Map [index map] drawn to the scale of
1:2500 which covers a particular area. [. . .] Under the system
properties claimed are numbered consecutively upward e.g. Parcel
No. 1, 2, 3 etc." (J. Penn 1986:8–9). Corresponding to each index
map is a set of pages in a ledger book, a "register" manufactured
for the Land Registry by an English company called Moore's Modern Methods, Ltd. (fig. 6). Each titled parcel in each section block
occupies a page of the register, on which is recorded the name of
the titleholder and a record of the encumbrances and changes in
title for that parcel. This register page is the sole legal record of
property title. Whereas before the innovation of the Land Registry,
one's deed was one's record of title, and whereas each property
owner possessed the deed itself, today one's proof of ownership
resides in the ledger book alone. After registering one's property
title in the Land Registry, the proprietor of a parcel receives from
the registrar an official Land Certificate documenting one's pro-

prietorship. Along with the certificate, a proprietor receives a sheet of "Information Notes" about the certificate and about the register. This sheet informs the certificate holder that, first of all, the legality of his or her title "is vested in the Land Registers kept by" the Land Registry, and that, "the attached [Land] Certificate is for your information only and confers no right. It is not to be used for any transactions, except with the Registrar of Lands." It is not a deed.

Land claimants come to the Land Registry to register their claim. They no longer need to possess written deeds they would have worked out with their family, friends, adjoining neighbors, and sometimes their lawyers. Rather:

> In the process of registration the first thing that should be done is a search [to ensure there are no competing claims to a parcel of land]. This is done by going to the Registry, paying a fee of $2.00 and requesting to see the necessary map and register for e.g. Map—3139B EAST CENTRAL—on that map the searcher would identify his parcel as 54; the register for 3139B EAST CENTRAL, PARCEL 54 would then be produced by the counter clerk. (J. Penn 1986:9)

In his book on law in Yemen, Brinkley Messick (1993) demonstrates the importance of attending to such seemingly insignificant details as methods of arranging text on the page for understanding new configurations of power and knowledge. Messick charts a connection from the spatial arrangement of words on a page to the spatial ordering of a colonized society and to a generalized "space of knowledge." The codification of Islamic principles into an "Islamic law," as Yemeni elites became bent on modernization and maintaining autonomy from Ottoman and English colonizers, went together with the codification of the text itself, as a notation and recording device: the spiral of older documents gave way to the straight-ruled text. Following Foucault, Weber, and Goody, Messick stresses that "these small techniques of notation, of registration, or constituting files, of arranging facts in columns and tables that are so familiar to us now, were of decisive importance" in forging the new epistemologies of the modern order (Foucault 1977, quoted in Messick 1993:237). As Messick observes, the new

BRITISH VIRGIN ISLANDS

LAND REGISTER

A — PROPERTY SECTION

Edition _____

Opened _____

Registration
Section _____

Block _____   Parcel No. _____

Approx. Area _____

APPURTENANCES	Description of land	CROWN/PRIVATE
	Nature of title	ABSOLUTE/PROVISIONAL
	Particulars recorded in para. 7 of adjudication record (provisional titles only)	
	Origin of title	
	FIRST REGISTRATION _____	
	MUTATION No. _____	

B — PROPRIETORSHIP SECTION

ENTRY No.	DATE	INSTRUMENT No.	NAME AND ADDRESS OF PROPRIETOR(S)	SIGNATURE OF REGISTRAR

Moore's Modern Methods Ltd., London
To repeat order state No. 55284 1-2-L.

Fig. 6. A Page from the Land Register

technique suggested a new relation to the text and to knowledge. "In the new, straight documents, form is separate from, prior to, and more determinate of the shape of the textual contents. In the old spiral texts, by contrast, form and content are not clearly separable, and it appears that, if anything, it is textual contents that determine form" (Messick 1993:237).

The new system of land registration brought about in the British Virgin Islands by the Cadastral Survey parallels the case described by Messick. Prior to the Cadastral Survey, a deed to land was bound to a particular textual form. Most deeds were handwritten; most mentioned boundary markers put in place by the person drawing up the deed or agreed upon by deed holders for adjoining lands. Deeds spoke to each other; one deed might refer to another in the course of detailing the extent of the parcel of land for which it had been drawn up. In contrast, the Cadastral Survey, like the straight-ruled text, provided a rigid, predetermined, and determining form. The form "reflected" a "reality"—that of the land itself, an object for all to see—and demanded that people fit themselves and their claims into that reality, into that objective and objectifying form. The Cadastral Survey altered the "space of knowledge" of the British Virgin Islands. The territory of the BVI existed in a new form, as did the people living on it.

A short etymology of the term *cadastral* is in order. The word is derived from the Latin *capitastrum,* the register of poll tax, "the register of *capita* . . . or units of territorial taxation into which the Roman provinces were divided for the purposes of *capitatio terrena* or land tax" (OED, on-line). The Latin root is the same from which English gets the term *capital.* In English, *cadastral survey* is related to *ordnance survey,* an official survey of a territory for *ordnance,* or military supply and storage. Today, the terms *ordnance survey* and *cadastral survey* are relatively interchangeable. *Ordnance* is a variant of *ordinance,* "the action of ordaining, ordering, or arranging; the fact or condition of being ordered or arranged." *Cadastral* came into English through the French *cadastre,* which, in English, refers to "a register of property, . . . a Domesday Book." And a *Domesday Book* is a record of lands and land ownership. This term is derived from the original Domesday Books, the "record of the Great Inquisition or Survey of the lands of England, their extent, value, ownership, and liabilities, made by order of William the

Conqueror in 1086" (OED, on-line). The term *Domesday* "appears to have been derived directly from Domesday"—an early spelling of *doomsday*—"the Day of the Last Judgment, and Domesday book, the book by which all men would be judged." *Domesday Book* came to be popularly applied to William's survey because of its status as "a final and conclusive authority on all matters on which it had to be referred to."

Unlike the world of William the Conqueror, the modern world need not appeal to Judgment Day for its authority to order people and places for purposes military or monetary. Cadastral surveys are still orderings, but rational and scientific ones. Their referents are not otherworldly, but very much of this world. They call into being the world itself, a reality on which an order can be imposed or from which an order can be discerned, already in the nature of the thing. They make a reality that can be represented as a picture or map, a reality whose representation is transparent, always-already given and discernible without the distorting or magnifying lenses of politics, power, or interest (Mitchell 1992, 1988), a reality that simply "is," as doomsday once, perhaps, was— an inevitability. Science gives a God's-eye view without God.

It also gives an eminently democratic, almost Protestant, view. "Seeing is believing" (Harley 1988:285). Everyone and anyone can "see" the world represented as a map, and they can see it for what it is. There need be no mediators between the facts on the map and the people using those facts, once the map has been drawn and if the map has been drawn with standards of accuracy firmly in place. The registrar of lands reports that one of the great advantages of the Cadastral Survey system of land registration is "more identification with the land; not only is it referred to in documents *it can also be seen* on [the] Index Map" (J. Penn 1986:12, emphasis added).

As a scientific endeavor, the BVI Cadastral Survey would not be a mapping of the territory in the interests of any one person or group. It would not reproduce social hierarchies in a spatial idiom. It would not, for instance, make politically powerful or important places—Road Town on Tortola, for instance—look any bigger or any more central than they "actually," "spatially" are. The land is just there, and the map represents it as it is. The registers and index maps are the ultimate arbiter, like the Domesday Books.

Timothy Mitchell has traced the division between an "objective" reality and its "accurate" representation to the particularity of Western colonization and to "a method of order and truth essential to the peculiar nature of the modern world" (1992:314, 1988). He notes that "modern means of colonizing a country [. . .] represented the techniques of ordering up an object-world to create the novel effect of a world divided in two: on the one hand a material dimension of things themselves, and on the other a seemingly separate dimension of their order or meaning" (1992:302). Colonial agents rendered the colonized world as an "exhibition," imposing a particular ordering upon it so that it could be objectively represented by such technical devices as ordnance surveys (see also Edney 1993). Relaying Arab reports of their experience of the great European exhibitions of the nineteenth century, Mitchell argues that what these writers witnessed were not merely "exhibitions and representations of the world, but the world itself being ordered up as an endless exhibition," a world that existed as a given reality of essence and that could be rendered up into objective representations of "it" (1992:290). The BVI Cadastral Survey exemplifies this process of exhibitionary ordering, here along spatial lines.

The fourth and fifth paragraphs of the 1974 Report of the Regional Cadastral Survey and Registration Project in the Caribbean illustrate the exhibitionary character of the new disciplines of space:

1.4 The Cadastral Survey and Registration process transfers the main emphasis in land recording from documentary evidence and people, who may temporarily have interests in land, to the pieces (or parcels) of land themselves. [. . .]

1.5 Unlike the old system of documents, the land is a better basis of record, because it is not easily destroyed, lost, or stolen [. . .]. (British Development Division 1974)

This ordering of a spatial reality is a mode of power, a kind of "space discipline" grounded in the authority of accuracy, which "create[s] an ethic and virtue of ever more precise definition" (Harley 1988:285). Space discipline encourages people to refer

the spatial dimensions of their lives—land disputes, territorial bor-
derings, and so forth—to the thing-ness of space itself, represented apparently unproblematically on the objective map. As
Harley writes, maps "tend to 'desocialise' the territory they represent." He adds that "[t]he abstract quality of the map [. . .] lessens
the burden of conscience about people in the landscape. Decisions about the exercise of power are removed from the realm of
immediate face-to-face contacts" (1988:303).

Harley is concerned with the exercise of power on a grand
scale—invasion, rebordering, districting, and so forth—yet his
insight that maps encourage ways of dealing with spatial problems
in terms of space itself and space alone holds true for arguments
over land among individuals. Boundary disputes can be settled by
referring to the scientifically produced, objective "truth." One-on-
one haggling takes a backseat to the consultation of an ultimate
authority—a reality, represented on the map. Competing individuals can refer to the map to settle their disputes. The object of
ownership is completely separated from the owner, and the owner
is invested with the power to *consult* the objective facts, not to create or contest them (Pashukanis 1929).

Land Disputing After the Survey

The form of the Cadastral Survey and the records registration system that came along with it determined in many instances the content and character of land disputes and the character of the disputing parties. Here I will concern myself only with disputes that
came about during the period of transition from the old system of
land titling to the registered lands system. The registrar of lands
was not the adjudicator in these cases, for her post had not yet
come fully into operation. Rather, these disputes were handled by
the land adjudication officer attached to the Cadastral Survey
team. It was his job to settle disputes as they arose during the
implementation of the new registration and titling process. The
disputes here fall into three types: (1) arguments about the objectivity of the land and the survey system; (2) arguments that result
in an enforcement of a new moral order on disputing parties; and
(3) arguments that reflect a reshaping of family and personhood.

These are transitional events; together they exemplify the instantiation of a modern episteme.

The Land's Object Status. Two men came to the adjudication officer with the following problem. Their deeds indicated that they together had a piece of land they were to "hold jointly," as common tenants. "They had free access over it all." One of the men's deeds indicated he was entitled to "a 2//3rds share," and the other a one-third share. Remember from the previous chapter that shares are not the same as divisible pieces of land, but rather *interests* in the land. One does not "own" land, but rather an interest in it. Interests, like "estates," are supposed to be temporal abstractions with implications for usufruct and other rights. Under the old system, a "two-thirds share" was not the same thing as two-thirds of a "physical" area. But that is precisely how the adjudication officer read the case.

He noted that "the land has never been surveyed, there is no plan and it is impossible to ascertain how the whole parcel was apportioned on a 2/3rds—1/3rds basis." The officer assumed that the two-thirds/one-third share division ought to be reflective of a physical division of the land parcel itself. Such was not the case, and he went about making it so. There are of course other ways of figuring fractional shares. But the officer followed a method of mapping abstract shares directly onto "real" property. "Estates" fell "back" into the "land itself," in the progressive move from abstractions built up out of the land back into the land itself as an objective entity. The Cadastral Survey sealed off this conception of the land as a thing in itself, as a quantifiable entity that can be measured and cut up.

This is the dynamic of another dispute, this time between a titleholder and the Cadastral Survey and lands registration system. The landowner petitioned the adjudication officer:

> I have inspected the Adjudication Records together with the Demarcation Map at your office and have found that my land . . . has been recorded as 0.55 acres. Before the demarcation of the land, I gave your office a copy of my survey map which shows that the land is 0.578 acres. I would like your record to be corrected, and to read 0.578 acres.

The adjudication officer's telling reply:

> I refer to your letter of —th September, 197–.
> Project personnel neither add to nor subtract from, a
> claimant's parcel of land—they merely measure what exists
> and the measurement is final.

Accuracy has become the talisman of authority. The accuracy does
not derive from power or interest, but from the "fact" of the land
itself. The survey team "measures what exists," and there can be no
argument with the fact of an area.

Moral Order. But the adjudication officer did settle arguments with facts beyond those of the land itself. Sometimes he
referred to a level of common sense that the fact of the land would
naturally suggest to any reasonable person.[2] One case involved
three brothers who, upon their mother's death, decided to partition the family land into physical shares, following the logic of the
new order of land and estate. They divided the land themselves
and set up boundaries, but Oscar, who ended up with the largest
piece of land, disagreed with his brothers George and John over
the boundary separating his land from theirs. He claimed sixteen
feet farther into their parcels and argued that it was necessary for
him to have this extra sixteen feet so that he would have a right-of-
way to the main road to the south of John's and George's lands. In
considering the dispute, the officer noted that "there has been a
long standing antipathy between Oscar and his brothers. Oscar
has the largest piece of property and a perfectly good right of way
to his land and his houses from the main road."

Based on this commonsense position, the officer ruled in
favor of the existing boundaries, that is, in favor of George and
John. This decision may seem reasonable and fair, just as it seemed
reasonable and fair to the adjudication officer. Yet in this case what
the adjudication officer adjudicates is really nothing more than an
assessment of the parties' character and reasonableness and the
moral worth of their claims. The facts on the map are the most
damaging piece of evidence against Oscar. He has the biggest
piece of land; he already has a right-of-way to the road. We can see
it. We know nothing about the circumstances that led him to this
disagreement with his brothers. He may have been a truly dis-

agreeable fellow, greedy and nitpicky. The determination of his character, however, comes as much from the map, the objective representation of an incontestable reality, as from anything else. That is the morality of the Cadastral Survey. It is a morality that is "natural" and commonsensical because it comes through the speaking of the facts of the land itself, facts we can all see on the map of the territory, facts with a force all their own.

Reshaping Family and Personhood.   Statements about the reasonableness or moral worth of parties to disputes were common in the records from the transitional days of land adjudication, especially when the disputes involved family members. In one case, the officer noted, "neither party is willing to compromise and there is ill-feeling of long standing between Florette and her sister-in-law Ramona." One man involved in a dispute "forced his mother and sister to trespass and seems a strange character altogether." And of another dispute, the officer wrote, "There is considerable ill-will between Rachel and Filomena which has bubbled over in other disputes as well. In this one the anticipated slinging match soon materialized and the family skeletons came tumbling from the security of their cupboards."

These asides are funny, and I found myself laughing out loud as I read them for the first time. One reason they are so funny is that they speak to everyday understandings of family and family relationships that people in the United States share with people in the British Virgin Islands. "You can't chose your relatives," the saying goes, and so interactions with relatives are highly charged, rife with disagreement and conflict, and yet long-standing because the ties that bind are "blood" ties. What we see in other disputes, just as in pre–Cadastral Survey cases, is a configuration of the blood tie and a creation of family after facts that, like the fact of land, are supposedly "natural" and given. The joke makes no sense without that given ground of natural relatedness.

With the rationalization of land titling that came about through the land registration system, and with the demise of "family land" as a system of undivided shares, came many more "family quarrels" over land. For instance, of the sixteen disputes adjudicated for the East End Section of the Cadastral Survey between 1972 and 1974, eight involved family members. The family became the zone of contest over land. There is a critical difference between these disputes and earlier ones, however. Previously, disputes involved who "counted" as a "real" family member and thus was entitled to a claim or share of an estate. Do in-marrying women count? Do people who have gone abroad count? Now, however, the question of who counts as family rarely arises. Everybody "knows" who is family. A family quarrel is not a quarrel over the boundaries of family; it is a quarrel between members of an already-understood collection of "blood" relatives.

Only one dispute from the early 1970s involved determinations of "family." A man wanted to bury his brother's wife on "family burial grounds" but was prevented from doing so by another member of the family with claim to the grounds. This second man claimed that the east side of the grounds belonged to his side of the family, and the west to the other man's side of the family. The dead woman, he argued, therefore should be buried on the west side. The adjudication officer decided to honor the second man's claim, since it provided a means of neatly partitioning the land into two parts. He even went so far as to write the division between the two parts of the plot—and thus the two "sides" of the "family"—into the registration records themselves: he gave the east and west sides of the plot each a different parcel number. What had been one family burial ground—and one family—became two, and became two objectively different, separate, and measurable entities, each recorded in a separate page of the register.

Alienability, Aliens, and the National Community

As I mentioned at the beginning of this chapter, the Cadastral Survey facilitated people's applications for bank loans. Individual titles, duly recorded in the Land Registry, provided the kind of guarantee of proprietorship that banking institutions need in order to determine collateral and the ability to back up debts with real property. The Cadastral Survey helped people who wanted loans for development projects get them and begin building on their property. Today, people with land routinely submit applications to the British Virgin Islands Development Bank for such loans. People also figure out ways of recording as much land as possible in the registry so that they can get bigger loans. During my stay in the British Virgin Islands, several people I knew were in the process of dredging land from the sea and from mangrove swamps in order to add fractions of acres to their property titles, specifically for the purpose of applying for a larger bank loan and better terms for a mortgage. Haggling also goes on regularly at the Land Registry, where people try to squeeze out more land from their plot demarcation in the registers. The Cadastral Survey report of 1974 noted, somewhat offhandedly, that "materialism seems to corrupt land owners to the state of contesting every last inch" (British Development Division 1974:25). Putting the situation in a more positive light, the registrar of lands writes, "Land registration has gained not only the trust and confidence of the property owners but also that of the Financial Institutions, foreign investors and the legal profession. More and more land owners are becoming aware that their new land titles can offer them the security of owning their own homes" (J. Penn 1986:16).

Land registration has also helped settle some long-standing boundary disputes, with the result that the government can now go about implementing one of its back-burner projects: the creation of a systematic street naming and numbering system. In the not-too-distant future, people's addresses will not consist of just a place name, but also a street name and number. Truly modern localities will come into being—easily identifiable, easily found on a map or diagram.

Of course, individual titling and rampant mortgaging bring with them land alienation. People can more easily sell their land to other individuals when their title is secure and their land is registered in an objective record. And naming of streets begs the question of which names to choose—ones given by old owners of land or by new ones? Already, BVIslander leaders have begun renaming schools, for instance, with the names of prominent local persons. It is an open question whether street names will follow local family names.

Meanwhile, however, land alienation throws into question the stability of already existing local place names. The Cadastral Survey team tended to map out first those areas that they and the government thought were ripe for commercial and residential development. The small bay on the southeast coast of Tortola, today called Maya Cove or Hodge's Creek, was one such area. When the area was registered, the owners chose to subdivide it into house plots and to sell these to foreigners and well-to-do BVIslanders. Within twenty years, the region has become, as one informant put it, "a nest of white people." Many of its residents winter there; others keep their yachts in its well-sheltered small harbor protected by the surf from outlying mangroves. One of these residents had a boat he called the *Maya*, and, the story goes, soon everyone started calling the place "Maya's Cove," and eventually, "Maya Cove." Hodge is a local family name, and the locale has gone by the appellation Hodge's Creek for at least one hundred years. Many youngsters, however, know the place only by its new title, Maya Cove. Even many older residents of the BVI call it that. Immigrants and expatriates know it only as Maya Cove. I was able to score points with many BVIslanders by consciously using the name Hodge's Creek.

The alienation of land to foreigners, especially whites, has been a topic of discussion and debate in the British Virgin Islands at least since the time of local self-government in 1950. Several scandals involving government lease or sale of large tracts of land to unscrupulous developers and shady characters have heightened people's concern with land alienation.[3] But the Maya Cove/Hodge's Creek place-name debate—insignificant economically, unlike the lease of major portions of the island of Anegada, for instance—is the one people concerned with the integrity of "BVI culture" and the BVI national community invoke in public forums and in interviews with anthropologists.

Naming is the central issue. Who shall have the power to name? What name shall be given to a place? There are very old associations of particular places with specific family names, usually deriving from old plantations and estates under slavery. The Cadastral Survey, by allowing land's easy alienability, brings naming to the front of people's minds when they think about the presence of immigrants and expatriates in their midst. At the same time that it shifts the emphasis in land disputes from the demarcation of family members to arguments within already assumed families—and thus appears to diminish family's importance in favor of individual disputants—the Cadastral Survey brings family back into the picture. Now, however, it is the *name* of a family that is important. Now, that name stands for something other than the people who share it. It stands for the *place*, the land itself in the case of place names, and the land's special national character.

Recently, prominent local people and politicians, fearful of alienation of land and a subsequent "alien-nation," have proposed the idea of establishing a Land Bank. The government would set aside parcels of land in the Land Bank for BVIslanders who can prove citizenship but who have no land. This development is connected to a particular imagining of community: when all people have individual relationships with the land itself (represented in a register) instead of with each other (represented in deeds), a horizontal community of equals-as-property-owners can be envisioned. It also reinvigorates the myth that all BVIslanders are property owners and, as several informants put it, "each and all owns a piece of the rock." It is especially important that this myth become reality now, as children leave and immigrants arrive.

In her speech commemorating the twenty-fifth anniversary of the ministerial system of local government, a prominent intellectual and leader voiced concerns about guaranteeing the "patrimony" of the British Virgin Islands, forcefully arguing for that patrimony to remain the preserve of BVIslanders alone (Varlack 1992). In her speech, she warned against land alienation, stating, "at all costs we [must] refrain from alienating the land: as one president reminded the governor when he was bewailing the absence of English settlers more than a century ago, permanent prosperity is in great measure identified with that of the owners of the soil. On land that belongs to foreigners our children can only be servants" (Varlack 1992:5).

While it is changing place names—like Hodge's Creek into Maya Cove—that give these statements their power to reflect and to shape BVIslander sentiment, it is the presence of immigrants from other parts of the Caribbean, not whites from England or the United States, and the fears of BVIslanders that immigrants will spoil their beautiful land and their peaceful way of life, that bring the issues home. In the breath immediately before the statement quoted in the previous paragraph, Varlack warned that "we [must] control immigration. A more than 70 percent increase in the population of Virgin Gorda alone over a ten-year period does not bode well for stability and threatens control of the local patrimony by the people to whom these islands belong" (1992:5).

The concern over place names brought on by the Cadastral Survey contributes to the consolidation of BVIslander national

identity and of the sense of BVIslanders as a people. The Cadastral
Survey, by rendering the world as an objective reality that could be
represented as a picture, demanded a correspondence between
the places indicated on the picture—place names—and the "reality" of the places so named. The British Virgin Islands, named on
the map and drawn to scale, point for point, place name for place,
was created as a solid, real entity. As in the pre–Cadastral Survey
world, land here is central to identity and definitions of community. When land was untethered from its more "genealogical"
definitions in favor of "individual" holdings and titles, people in
the BVI devised new means of understanding community equally
tied to land, but to a different conception of what land ontologi-
cally is and what it is about. The community so defined differed in
quality from earlier notions. There needs to be a Hodge's Creek
for BVIslanders like never before. There also needs to be a certainty of family, since "we shall know our compatriots by their
name." Presurvey disputes were about just who made up those
families. Postsurvey disputes begin from the certainty of those families themselves. This certainty, together with the certainty of the
land, makes for definable, incontestable, objectively real "British
Virgin Islands" and "British Virgin Islanders."

Chapter 8

Making a History for the Nation

"British Virgin Islander" identity was consolidated through the institutions and apparati of statecraft. Discourse about immigrants marks the boundaries between those who "belong" and those who do not. Can there be said to be a British Virgin Islander "nationalist" discourse? How do British Virgin Islanders themselves articulate their "history" as a "nation"? British Virgin Islander conceptions of their "national history" place *law* in the center of narratives of territorial development. This chapter considers how law and the legislature became vital components of BVI "nationalism." It illuminates a central paradox: the discourse that emphasizes law as central to British Virgin Islander identity also fosters continued colonial rule and the consolidation of large-scale legal arenas and capital flows. For BVIslanders, writing their "own" laws became key to envisioning a nationalist project and a national identity. But the first truly self-authored law was the law that created tax haven services in the BVI and subjected the territory to the scrutiny of British and U.S. regulators and the vicissitudes of the global finance markets.

This chapter intertwines two themes.[1] The first is the place of law and the legislature in making the "history" of the nation told as a history of law and making BVI "culture" in terms of "law and order." How does the British Virgin Islands achieve its "cultural" and "historical" "distinctiveness," its "national identity," through law? The second theme, drawing from the first, is how that distinctive BVI national identity becomes just the thing to enable the movement of capital across international borders and the consolidation of large-scale legal arenas—specifically, the jurisdictional spaces of the United States of America and the United Kingdom.

To weave these strands a little more closely, I rely on a notion of "jurisdictional spaces"—legally defined spaces demarcating zones of legislative, executive, and judicial power and authority. Jurisdictional spaces only sometimes correspond with "physical" spaces; when they do, they naturalize "physical" space and hide their own constructed and contingent character. It is a correspondence of jurisdictional space with some definition of physical space that naturalizes a "national" space. The idea of jurisdictional spaces clarifies how a national identity is built upon a legislature through the arrangement of these spaces in a "physical order," and also how the actions of the legislature to ensure its and its "nation's" distinctiveness further the merging of jurisdictional spaces and thereby further global integration.

History, Law, and the Nation in Modernity

The ways BVIslanders have used "law" to construct a distinctive "national" history reflects Western nationalist discourse more generally. Ever since Rousseau, European and American nationalist thinkers have drawn connections between the laws of a people and a people's "character": "The same laws cannot be suitable to so many different provinces, which have different customs and different climates, and cannot tolerate the same form of government" (Rousseau 1967:50). Sketching a "history" of BVI nationalism in the terms used by BVIslanders demonstrates the connections between "history" and "law" as complementary modes of knowledge production within modern narratives about the "nation-state."

Critics of colonial discourses have demonstrated that History, as an academic discipline and a general mode of knowledge, tends to apply purportedly universal categories—"development," "progress," and even "capital," "bourgeois"—to the particularities of peoples outside Europe. Such categories derive their force and persuasiveness because of their place in modern discourse about modernity itself, about what characterizes "modern" societies from "traditional" ones. In creating non-European, nonmodern others through knowledges about those others, "modernity" and "Europe" create themselves. "Other" histories, by tacitly accepting the grounds of "historical knowledge," thus end up recapitulating

"European" terms, even when they attempt to subvert them (Spivak 1988). Non-European peoples attempting to articulate anti-colonial positions through such concepts as "nationalism" find themselves doing so in terms already set by colonial discourses (Chatterjee 1988) because nationalist histories have as their referent an imaginary "Europe" that has already reached the "ends of history" toward which nationalists aspire: the telos of liberal political philosophy and industrial capitalism embodied by the independent nation-state and its citizens (Chakrabarty 1992). We will see that, for the British Virgin Islands, the only "history" it has is the history of its steady—but endlessly deferred—march toward becoming an independent nation-state. This is a tale told as a story of law.

The work of postcolonial critics usefully supplements recent sociolegal studies of law and modernity. Because they chronicle the "development" of "self-rule" through "law" over both anarchy and subordination to despots or gods (Fitzpatrick 1992), "histories" are legal legends. Their characters are rational citizens: people with clearly delimited public and private lives, people with true selves who know their desires and rationally go about fulfilling them. Modernity effects a split between this true self, the speaking "I," and its objectified self, the "me," the subject of (self-)scrutiny, (self-)consciousness, "(self-)restraint or indulgence," and self-improvement (Comaroff 1989:665; after Foucault 1975:197). Modern subjects regulate their selves primarily through language, rendering their objective selves up for self-examination and self-analysis. Unlike their premodern predecessors, so the story goes, moderns, when they write, indulge in self-expression; they are not, for instance, merely mediums for divine knowledge, transcribing what is revealed to them. They write, and their writings give them insight to their true selves (Foucault 1979; Gagnier 1991).

For BVIslanders, their "distinctive culture" of "law and order" depends on a conception of "culture" as something that is part of one's true self, or one's identity, and, as such, is *owned*. "Culture," like "history," has as its referent "Europe," because "culture"—conceived in *proprietary* terms—is inseparable from the constellation of modern imaginings of possessive individualism, the nation-state, and the law (cf. Macpherson 1962, Coombe 1993, Handler 1991). Culture as something owned lends a distinctive character to the nation's history. It is central to understandings of difference as essential (Williams 1993). In a world where nations are the players in international politics and capitalism, anticolonial and postcolonial peoples struggle to found nations for themselves, and their struggles become culture-building projects. Such projects are part and parcel of the need to be modern and to demonstrate modernity in order to be self-governing.

When modern peoples imagine themselves as essentially different from others, and especially the others who may be ruling over them, they can make a forceful case for "self-rule." Their "heritage" and "culture," which make them unique, make them uniquely ungovernable by others not partaking in their distinct essence, others who could not possibly understand their ways or motivations, and thereby write laws for them to follow without expecting dissent. Law, as one genre of writing, and one self-consciously keyed to self-regulation and discipline, expresses modern selves within a collectivity. Hence, "the nation's law is one of the key components of a unifying nationalism": it helps us define— and then regulate—our "national" selves. For modern subjects, the "ability to make law is the mark and preserve of independent political society," and, by implication, of the rational, modern individuals making it up (Fitzpatrick 1992:115, 117).

Ideas about (national) difference as essential also serve capital, since distinctions conceived in proprietary terms presuppose alienability and marketability. In the British Virgin Islands, the self-authoring of law, heralded as historic for the nation, has encouraged the marketing of the BVI as a unique and distinctive jurisdiction in the worlds of tourism and transnational finance. The fact of authorship of the laws, often without regard for their content, has been crucial to the articulation of a BVI national identity.

The evident contradiction with which any British Virgin Islands "nationalism" must deal is the fact that the "territory"—the term itself is used by BVIslanders to describe the land in which they live—is a *colony.* That the BVI is a colony becomes significant in trying to come to grips with its claims to a national identity. Although it is not independent and, by most accounts, its people and government do not wish it to be so, the BVI as a political entity—like perhaps all things founded in the furnace of European colonialism and its overarching discourse of "modernity"—

gains its meaning within a teleological narrative of "development" and "progress" toward the "nation-state." While the end of the narrative—political "independence" and "self-rule"—may forever be deferred in the case of the BVI, still the teleological narrative of nationhood retains its currency, shaping how people think about themselves and the place in which they live. Since central to BVI conversations about nationalism and identity are the law and the legislature, they will be central to my account as well.

A less obvious contradiction within any British Virgin Islands claim to "national" identity has to do with the territory's place in the world economy, as one of a network of tax havens through which a truly significant proportion of global capital passes each year.[2] Transnational financial transactions take place through financial institutions or other investment entities having a legal existence—if not always physical presence—in the BVI. The BVI, as a legal jurisdiction, is thus not in any sense marginal in the world economy. With the coming integration of Hong Kong into China, for example, Asian capitalists are increasingly coming to rely on the services the BVI and other Caribbean tax havens have to offer, in order to "protect" themselves from perceived threats of Chinese economic nationalization (Friedland 1992, Burton 1992).

One of the apparent paradoxes of the current moment in the history of capitalism is that, despite the ever increasing integration of the world economy, and with it, the invention of supranational polities and legal fields, like those envisioned in the North American Free Trade Agreement and the European Community (Harvey 1989, Trubek et al. 1993, Cappelletti 1986), nationalist feelings and ethnic tensions are on the rise (Harvey 1993, Stolcke 1995). How and why are "nations" gaining their power to shape sentiment with their claims to be special, unique, and distinctively "different" entities from other such units during this supposedly "unprecedented" era of globalization, rapid communication, and transnational integration? Is there any way to account for the simultaneous production of difference (of national and ethnic identities) and integration (of capital, of legal fields, or polities)?

Looking at multinational legal consultancy firms, Yves Dezalay has recently shown how a new class of legal "experts" specialized in negotiating among multiple regulatory regimes "are led to 'recreate the State' so as to structure a transnational market which is

their raison d'etre" (Dezalay 1993:91). Dezalay is mostly interested
in the production of commercial law, the restructuring of economic power, and, with it, new international divisions of legal
labor and rationale. Yet his insight that the legal practices surrounding market regulation reinvigorate "states" as they fabricate
suprastate legal orders will be helpful in understanding how the
British Virgin Islands has established for itself a distinct "national"
identity even as it gets incorporated into the global finance capital
circuit. A multinational consultancy firm had a small part to play
in this process, too.

Everyday Political Vocabularies

At present, the British Virgin Islands government consists of a Legislative Council and an Executive Council. The territory is divided
into nine electoral districts; each district elects one representative
to serve on the Legislative Council. In addition, as of 1994, the
entire electorate selects four representatives to serve the territory
"at large," bringing the total number of representatives in the Legislative Council to thirteen. The political party winning a majority
of seats in the Legislative Council, or the first seven individuals
elected who organize themselves as a voting block, form the "government" members. The Crown-appointed governor selects the
government member most capable of securing the loyalties of the
majority to be the chief minister. The chief minister, in consultation with the other government members, selects from among the
government members persons to serve as the other three ministers
of government—minister of natural resources and labor, minister
of communications and works, and minister of education and
social services (sometimes called the minister for health, education, and welfare). The chief minister also serves as the minister of
finance. Ministerial portfolios—the lists of administrative duties
and offices for which each minister is responsible—vary little from
election to election. The nongovernment members form an
"opposition" and recommend to the governor one of their number to be selected as leader of the opposition. The whole Legislative Council together nominates a speaker, a nonvoting presiding
officer responsible for maintaining proper parliamentary proce-
dure. The whole council also nominates one of their number to be

a deputy speaker, in case of the absence of the speaker, and a deputy chief minister. An attorney general, appointed by the governor, serves ex officio on the Legislative Council. The governor formally opens each session of the Legislative Council, with a "Speech from the Throne," but has no other official role in that body. The ministers of government, the attorney general, and the governor form the Executive Council, whose duties include providing for internal defense and security (through the Royal Virgin Islands Police Force, or RVIPF), drafting new legislation, and writing executive orders on matters that do not come under the jurisdiction of the legislature (generally, matters having to do with international law and which directly involve the United Kingdom, e.g., deportation orders, international treaties).

How do British Virgin Islanders think and talk about their government in the 1990s? There is a vocabulary for political life in the BVI that sheds some light on the importance granted to the legislature in people's sense of the British Virgin Islands as a distinct national entity and their view of themselves as "British Virgin Islanders."

When British Virgin Islanders use the term *government,* they are usually understood to be referring to the Legislative Council—not the other structures of governance and statecraft. Only occasionally—as when a member of the opposition speaks out against "government" decisions—does the term *government* signify the ministers, that is, the "government members" of the Legislative Council who also serve in the Executive Council.

The abbreviation for the Legislative Council—LEGCO or LegCo—has entered into common parlance as a synonym for "government." (*LegCo* is pronounced "Ledge-co.") There is no common agreement on an abbreviation for the Executive Council—the press sometimes uses "EXCO" and sometimes "ExecCo"—but there is agreement that the abbreviation, however it might be spelled, is pronounced "Edge-Co." I have been unable to come up with any contraction of the words *Executive Council* that would yield an acronym pronounced "Edge-Co," and neither could BVIslanders I asked. It would appear that *EXCO* or *ExecCo* is pronounced "Edge-Co" because *LegCo* is pronounced "Ledge-Co." In other words, and to be a bit linguistically reductive, "Edge-Co" obtains its linguistic identity from LegCo; it is derivative in peo-

ple's conceptions of "government." It rarely enters discussions of
politics, the law, or current events.

The vocabulary of government and politics in the British Virgin Islands also includes words to refer to the chief minister: he is
often called "the chief" or "Chiefie." The role of the chief minister
is equated with that of the president of the United States. Like the
president, people say, the chief minister truly is "the chief"; "hail to
the chief!" The deputy chief minister is similarly styled "the deputy
chief," the "second-in-command." Such nicknames elevate these
two legislative, elected positions and tend to downplay or even
deny one of the underlying political "realities" of the British Virgin
Islands: it is a dependent territory of the United Kingdom and is
subject to the authority of the Crown, embodied for practical purposes in the governor and the Foreign and Commonwealth Office
(FCO) of Her Majesty's Government.

Jurisdictional Spaces and the Organization of Power

This history of colonial administration resulted in a particular spatial organization of power for the British Virgin Islands. Santos has
written that laws and maps, "in order to fulfill their function . . .
inevitably distort reality" (1987:282). The relationship between
laws and maps, within an official discourse of modern legality, is
more than metaphorical. In establishing jurisdictions, laws make
maps. These maps are not distortions of reality; they themselves
are the reality: the maps do not reflect spaces of power; rather,
they constitute these spaces. The colonial governance of the BVI
today implies three sets of jurisdictional spaces: a legislative space,
an executive space, and a judicial space. Each space is a field of
power; the powers are set out in the documents and practices from
which "the British Virgin Islands" as a legal entity comes into
being. These jurisdictional spaces, furthermore, map onto "real"
spaces. Significantly, the executive and judicial spaces do not map
onto the "real" territory of the BVI without remainder. But the legislative space does. For the BVI, the correspondence between legislative jurisdictional space and "real" space, in part, lends the former its power to define the "BVI" as a unique, "national" space.

The Executive Space.   The executive functions of governance are carried out by the Executive Council, and the jurisdiction of ExecCo is coterminous with the territory of the British Virgin Islands. But it is not autonomous: the executive is empowered by the Foreign and Commonwealth Office, and on matters of constitutional reform, international affairs, and citizenship policy, ExecCo can act only under authority of the FCO. The executive jurisdictional space thus coincides with the territory of the British Virgin Islands but is perforated by the figures of the governor, attorney general, and RVIPF, who are under the jurisdiction of the FCO. The executive space encompasses both the territory of the BVI and, through the FCO, the United Kingdom.

The Judicial Space. The judiciary of the British Virgin Islands is one with the judicial apparatus of the former British colonies in the Caribbean. Formerly called the West Indies Associated States Supreme Court, the Eastern Caribbean States Supreme Court has jurisdiction over all the former and present colonies of the United Kingdom in the Caribbean. Local magistrates sit in each of these territories or countries. The Eastern Caribbean States Supreme Court is composed of two units: the High Court and the Court of Appeals. Justices in the Supreme Court are nominated by their peers—not by the citizens of the states in which they will serve—and come from all over the Commonwealth (not just the Commonwealth Caribbean). A High Court justice sits in the BVI six months out of the year. High Court decisions can be appealed to the Court of Appeals. Further appeals can be made to the Privy Council in London. The judicial jurisdictional space thus includes the former and present British colonies in the Caribbean, the British Commonwealth, and the United Kingdom.

The Legislative Space. The Legislative Council enacts all laws for the British Virgin Islands. Its sole jurisdiction is the BVI, and it is not within the jurisdiction of any other body. The legislative jurisdictional space is the only jurisdictional space that is coterminous with the territory of the BVI and is autonomous. It is the center of the map of "the BVI" as this entity is legally constructed. From its position at the center of the jurisdictional map, the Legislative Council gains its potency and salience as the center of national sentiment. The correspondence of legislative jurisdiction with the "physical" space of the BVI naturalizes that space and imbues it with a power "of its own." This power comes to appear autochthonous: it seems to spring forth from the soil of the national territory itself.

Histories of Nation and Legislature

In his history of the British Virgin Islands, Isaac Dookhan writes the "national history" as the "legislative history"—reflecting BVIslander popular conceptions and unintentionally illuminating the basis of much BVI nationalist discourse. He echoes popular sentiment that "progress" came to the BVI when it got its "own government"—its own *legislature*—when he states in the concluding paragraph of his study:

> The history of the British Virgin Islands in the twentieth century has demonstrated the importance of legislative government in achieving progress. When the islands were more or less under external control before 1950, economic growth was negligible; thereafter, the restoration of a legislature enabling greater local participation in directing local affairs has been followed by rapid economic expansion. (Dookhan 1975:234)

Note how Dookhan ties economic prosperity to local participation in government. Such stories of progress and self-determination hinge on the idea that control of economic resources must be placed in the hands of local people through "indigenization" and other protectionist policies in order to demonstrate the "rationality" of self-governing peoples. Self-government goes hand in hand with capitalism when colonized individuals make a case for self-rule by asserting their ability to "rationally" manage their own economic affairs.

Dookhan's national history is a particular version of legislative history. It is also an expression of popular BVIslander sentiment that the history of the territory is the history of its legislature. The tale told by Dookhan is about the slow and steady march toward BVI "self-"governance through an autonomous legislature. It is a powerful expression of the teleology of modern, Western historical metanarrative. We always-already "know" how the story will "end"—with the "triumph" of democracy, self-representation, self-rule, and the modern, national selves that make representation and rule possible.

The history of the legislature is an interrupted tale, for between 1902 and 1950, the British Virgin Islands possessed no legislative body. To understand the importance of the legislature today, it is necessary to recount the (national) history behind its reinstatement in 1950. An administrative unit of the British Leeward Islands Colony by 1773, the BVI legislature consisted of a lieutenant governor, a Council, and an Assembly. Both the lieutenant governor and the twelve members of the Council, which together shared executive duties, gained their positions through appointment by the governor of the Leeward Islands from his base on the island of Antigua. The Assembly, "the legislative body par excellence," consisted of fifteen members elected triennially (Dookhan 1975:195). But because the governor of the Leeward Islands maintained ultimate executive authority and had the power to convoke, prorogue, and dissolve the Assembly at will, real political control of the BVI sat firmly in Antigua. And because of this fact, "Lieutenant-Governors rarely assumed office in the Virgin Islands" (195), their post being filled by the president of the Council, to the great annoyance of the elected Assembly. As a consequence, late-eighteenth- and early-nineteenth-century political life in the BVI became characterized by incessant squabbles between the Council, made up of colonial officers with an eye on advancement within the British Caribbean colonial apparatus, and the Assembly, propertied men selected by a minuscule proportion of a tiny electorate of local planters and merchants.[3]

So many of these latter men foresaw financial disaster on the horizon with the eventual emancipation of the African slaves that "through . . . immigration and absenteeism the numbers of those capable and qualified to legislate were depleted" (Dookhan 1975:199). As a result of this situation, the Constitution Act of 1837 reduced from fifteen to nine the number of representatives elected to the Assembly; furthermore, "to ensure regular attendance" at Assembly meetings, "a fine was imposed on representatives who refused to serve, and no member could resign without the consent of the Assembly" (201). Although, in England, the Colonial Office recognized the problems of elected legislative governance in so small a piece of the British Empire with so few white

men of property (and even fewer with the coming of emancipation in 1834), it was reluctant to abrogate the Assembly and establish more direct, crown colony rule—officially, because of the
"constitutional precedent" such an act would establish (201). My
guess is that the British were more worried about the cost such a
measure would entail: crown colony government would mean
another high-salaried administrative position for what was considered a backwater of the greater Leeward Islands colony.

Nevertheless, in 1854, in the wake of mass antitax riots that
left parts of Road Town burned to the ground and that demonstrated to colonial lackeys the ability of the Methodist Church to
galvanize the majority black population, the Colonial Office
decided it could not "protect" the (white) population of the BVI
without direct Crown control. The fear of "disorder"—of newly
freed blacks—took precedence over cost or constitutionalism. But
the local government, in the face of metropolitan demands,
instead passed the Constitutional Amendment Act of 1854. This
act abolished the Council and Assembly and set up a "Legislative
Council," which consisted of ten members, including a president
appointed by the governor of the Leeward Islands as an ex officio
member; hence the Virgin Islands became a "presidency" within
the Leeward Islands colony. Three of the members were to be
nominated by the Crown and six elected. While persons elected to
the Legislative Council had only to be British subjects, voters had
to meet property qualifications designed to ensure a majority
white electorate even in the face of depreciating property values
associated with economic depression.

The British, however, viewed this act as a "renegade" action,
since it did not move in the direction of complete Crown governance, and retaliated in March 1855 by removing from the British
Virgin Islands a detachment of troops stationed in Tortola. Riots
again occurred in 1856 and 1858, and all requests for military assistance fell on the deaf ears of the governor of the Leeward Islands.
The Legislative Council capitulated to metropolitan calls for more
direct involvement in BVI affairs and adopted another constitutional amendment, providing this time for a Legislative Council of
eight members: four nominated by the Crown (including the president) and four elected. Furthermore, the president acquired a
deliberative and a casting vote. Thus, the Crown's representa-

tives—not "the people's" (the white, male, propertied people's)—would always be assured a majority. It was a small step from this constitutional change to, in 1867, complete crown colony status, or direct Crown control through the offices of the governor of the Leeward Islands in Antigua, with the assistance of an appointed Legislative Council made up of three colonial officers—a president, a colonial secretary, and a colonial treasurer—and three Virgin Islanders nominated by the president with the approval of the Crown. There is, of course, another side to this tale: direct Crown rule guaranteed that the British government would be able to maintain control over a territory peopled by former slaves and their descendants without having to extend to them the franchise, while it would "protect" the few white planters and merchants who chose to remain.

In 1871, facing financial problems in the administration of the Caribbean colonies, the British government created the Leeward Islands Federation. Local colonial legislatures had the option to defer legislative powers over certain subjects to the federal legislature in Antigua. The office of the president of the Virgin Islands was reorganized, overburdening his portfolio with new administrative duties—including those of magistrate, coroner, Crown prosecutor, treasurer, and some others besides—while drastically reducing his salary (from £800 a year to £300 by 1873). From being a representative of the Crown before federation, the president became an "organ of the Governor" of the Leeward Islands. "As an external symbol of the President's decreased status his official designation was changed to that of 'Commissioner' in 1889" (Dookhan 1975:209).

As a cost-cutting measure for the British colonial establishment in the Caribbean, federation was rather successful. By 1902, the Legislative Council of the Virgin Islands, always more interested in furthering the careers of its members than in actually doing any legislating, had deferred all of its legislative powers—"declar[ing] the constitution of the Presidency a subject within the legislative competence of the federal legislature" (Dookhan 1975:208)—to the federation legislature. In 1902, thus, the Legislative Council dissolved, and Virgin Islands governance became the task, locally, of the commissioner and his Executive Council—three (and, after 1937, four) appointed men who "met primarily for ceremonial reasons" (218). All legislation emanated from Antigua. The legislature was not reinstated until after the protests of the late 1940s, culminating in the Freedom March.

A major occurrence for British Virgin Islanders—and one now remembered with its own national holiday, Territory Day (July 1)—was the dissolution of the Leeward Islands Federation in 1956. "Defederation enhanced the political status and legislative power of the British Virgin Islands by making them *a colony in their own right* and by transferring to the local legislature subjects previously reserved for specific treatment by the federal legislature" (Dookhan 1975:222, emphasis added). The commissioner was renamed administrator, and now that the post of governor of the Leeward Islands had been abolished, the administrator "became the direct royal representative in the colony" (223). Refederation efforts were underway in the other West Indian territories, but, in 1958, the BVI Legislative Council opted to stay out of the new Federation of the West Indies, "principally because the legislature was jealous of its newly acquired powers and it did not want to transfer these again to an *external* body" (222, emphasis added). In characterizing the federal legislature as external, Dookhan affirms the legal creation of the "distinct" space of the "British Virgin Islands" that came with nominal "self-rule."

A few points about the role of "race" in this history need to be addressed. In the 1800s, the legislature was the ground fought over between local whites and the colonial apparatus in Antigua and London. As the primary site of struggle between colony and metropolis, the legislature came to stand for "the local," as the one place where people living in the British Virgin Islands—white people—could assert control over their own affairs without interference from either colonial lackeys or London. The majority African-descended population is absent from the "history" of this struggle, except as a riotous rabble mobilized by the Methodists and threatening the local white population.[4]

What is striking in Dookhan's text, however—so striking that, for me, his description of the transition from the legislatures of the nineteenth century to those of the twentieth demanded several rereadings—is the elision of the all-white Legislative Councils of the nineteenth century into the post-1950 racially mixed Legislative Councils. His story is of the "*re*constitution of the Legislative

Council"—not of the constitution of a new, "representative" council. The post-1950 Legislative Councils, for Dookhan, are part of a
clear line of Legislative Councils, a line only broken, for him,
between 1902 and 1950. Dookhan's story charts a line of progress
toward self-representation, beginning with the early Assembly.

For present-day BVIslanders, the post-1950 Legislative Councils are distinctively different from the nineteenth-century ones.
But this difference is not based on "race." Indeed, of the first four
elected members to the 1950 Legislative Council, one was "white,"
one was "Portuguese," one was "half-white and half-black," and
one was "half-black and half-Portuguese."[5] The defining character-
istic of the members of the Legislative Council elected in 1950,
and in all subsequent councils, is not that they are "not white," but
that they are "local." Early councils were composed of people who
could pack up and leave the Virgin Islands whenever they saw fit;
and many of the early representatives did just that. The defining
feature of the post-1950 councils is that the men serving on them
have bound themselves to the territory. They are men who "will
not leave." It is in this sense that they are "sons of the soil." Only
since the late 1960s have BVIslanders conflated "local" with
"black"; as a result, some of those first legislators are now coming
to be defined as "black."

In spite of the de facto control exerted over the reconstituted
Legislative Council by the Executive Council, and specifically the
nonelected members—British colonials and some elite local businessmen and others who had gained administrative experience as
clerks and officers in the colonial establishment—British Virgin
Islanders today look back to 1950 as the date when the British Virgin Islands won its "own" government. For many British Virgin
Islanders, the territory's true "history" as a "nation" begins with the
Legislative Council of 1950. Indeed, for all BVIslanders today, the
council established in 1950 was the "first" Legislative Council,
indeed, the "first government" of the BVI. The perception of the
1950 Legislative Council as the "first" council derives in part from
its perception as the first "local" legislature and in part from the
actions of the keeper of the minutes of Legislative Council meetings: in March 1957, the clerk titled her report of the minutes
"Twenty-Second Sitting, Fourth Session, *Second Legislative Council
of the British Virgin Islands*" (Minutes 3/13/57). As far as I can

determine from my extensive research with Legislative Council documents and from interviews, that was the first time a council was referred to by number. And from that point forward, it became standard practice for clerks (and later, the press and then the general populace) to label each consecutive Legislative Council by numbers, using the council of 1950 as the starting point. By contrast, Executive Councils—which were maintained from 1902 to 1950 despite their limited role—are not given numbers, distinct identities from one another, or pride of place in histories in books or in public discourses. Dookhan's book chronicles the "evolution" of the BVI up until the point of "local" legislative representation. The reinstitution of the legislature thus becomes for present-day BVIslanders the defining moment in the creation of a distinctively *"British Virgin Islands* history." And the Legislative Council assumed a position as the defining feature of British Virgin Islands "national" life and history.

The Law and Legislature as the Symbol of the Nation

In November 1992, the British Virgin Islands celebrated the twenty-fifth anniversary of the ministerial system of government. It was the first major celebration self-consciously styled by its organizers and participants as a *national* celebration. The ministerial system, of course, is a form of government and (colonial) administration in the BVI. Its major and lasting practical effect was to guarantee a majority of elected members on the Executive Council. On this level alone it is interesting that the anniversary of "ministerial government" would be cause for "national" celebrations. But what is more interesting is that the focus of the events commemorating the inception of the ministerial system was the legislature. Former legislators were honored in various public forums. One of these was a volume a group of people compiled to commemorate the event. Entitled *Challenge and Change: The Awakening of a People, British Virgin Islands,* this volume was devoted to the "progress" the BVI has experienced since 1967 under the ministerial system. Almost all of the instances of "progress" were discussed in terms of the *legislation* effecting or enabling them. The two main "overview" articles detail the development of the system of elected representation in the legislature (Romney 1992; Rhymer 1992); other articles tell the history of the territory as the history of various acts and ordinances, and still others chronicle the rise of the territory's economic mainstays—tourism and the offshore finance sector—in terms of the legislative acts which made them possible. In our coauthored contribution to the book, Michael O'Neal and I noted that the first ministerial government instituted new legislation that both reflected the socioeconomic changes caused by tourism and in turn generated other changes (O'Neal and Maurer 1992); but we, too, told a story which equated "legal developments" and "national developments" without questioning how and why the law became the key signifier for the nation. Instead, the law became, in our own and in others' contributions to this volume, both descriptive of and explanatory for "the nation." Why was it so simple for us all to conflate the nation and the law?

I will try to suggest an answer by way of anecdote. One day during my fieldwork, I happened to stop by the shop of one of the BVI's Arab population. Over Coca-Cola and thick Turkish coffee, I asked the proprietor of the shop why he thought BVIslanders had for the most part accepted Arab settlers into their society, granting them citizenship in many cases, and having come to see them as "fixtures" of BVI life. He didn't respond to this question; instead, he told me why he considered the British Virgin Islands a nice place to live. Before settling in Tortola, he'd visited the United States, Puerto Rico, Canada, and St. Thomas (in the U.S. Virgin Islands). But he liked the BVI best. "I have liked being in the West, [but] there is too much freedom! We [Muslims] are not used to that; that is not our way . . . I like the BVI because it is not like that; there is not as much freedom here. America is a good country, American money is the money for the world, but there is too much freedom in America." What, I asked, is "freedom"? "You know, with women going about . . . all dressed up with makeup and bikini, . . . and all the crimes, crime you see on the TV every day!"

I hurriedly ran off to the office of a BVIslander friend and fellow anthropologist to share with him how the shopkeeper had characterized life in the BVI and his ease blending in. Without blinking an eye, this native social scientist leaned back in his chair, smiled and said, confidently, "What did he say? 'Law and order'?!"

I cannot count the number of times BVIslanders characterized their society with the words *law and order*. "We are a law-and-order people"; "I am a law-and-order man"; "Without law and order, where would we be?"; "We need law and order"; "We aren't like people in St. Thomas; we have law and order"; "The immigrant population [or drugs, or guns, etc.] is a threat to law and order"; "I've always been for law and order." One hears the expression continually, and in all sorts of contexts. The BVI Tourist Board, meanwhile, markets the territory as "peaceful"—not in the sense of Club Med "serenity and tranquillity," but in the sense of "law and order." One tourist advertisement sports a member of the RVIPF in full regalia. Tourist brochures and people involved in the marketing of the British Virgin Islands contrast the BVI's "law and order" with "crime-ridden" Antigua or St. Thomas. And the offshore finance sector relies on an image of the BVI as a "stable, law and order society": "Our people are very strong on law and order," said the deputy chief minister in an interview with the international finance magazine *Euromoney* (1989:51).

But what does "law and order" mean? For one thing, it means "We will never separate from Britain"; "We have the best of both worlds—the American dollar, and British law and order"; "Why would we want independence? We have the security of Scotland Yard behind us!" People speak of their "British heritage of law and order." People also contrast the BVI's law-and-orderliness with the perceived disorder and criminality of other Caribbean peoples, especially those living and working in the British Virgin Islands. Such contrasts are as commonplace as the "law and order" catchphrase. When I asked BVIslanders, in the most general of terms, how they "feel about" different groups of immigrants, invariably I got stories about these groups' lack of "law and order." Let me give just two examples.

Immigrants from St. Lucia and Dominica, people say, are not at all lawlike. They try to subvert the legal process. It is well known, the story goes, that St. Lucians and Dominicans are all into obeah—a form of "witchcraft" and "voodoo," which, "you know, is illegal in the BVI." And "see what happens when one of them is in court—you look down the street and see one of them *sukuyas* [an obeah-woman] running up and down; Lord! And she puttin' on and carryin' on all kind of nonsense and obeah, and the men them in court never does get put in jail!"[6]

I once challenged my BVIslander students on their stereotype of Dominicans as prostitutes. I told them I knew many Dominican women, and none of them was a prostitute. One student replied: "Oh yeah? How you is so sure?" Another said, "Well, OK, that may be so; they is either prostitutes, or hairdressers!" A third interjected, "And you know them hairdressers is prostitutes just the same!" All Dominican men, meanwhile, are into drugs and crime (if they're not hairdressers and, therefore, homosexual and, therefore, prostitutes). Dominicans of BVI ancestry are the "children of whores," and "aren't [or shouldn't be] legitimate members of BVI society."

These kinds of stories about immigrants solidify a sense of BVIslander "law and order" by defining what is it not, and thereby defining what it is to be a "British Virgin Islander" within a narrative of nationhood (cf. Fitzpatrick 1992). But "law and order" is not only defined negatively. When one looks at the relative lack of crime in the British Virgin Islands, it appears that there is some truth to the claim that the BVI is a "law-and-order" society. To many BVIslanders, meanwhile, it is the mostly foreign-born police force that is responsible for what little crime occurs. "Them a bunch of down-island hooligans," one BVIslander described the police, more than half of whom are from other Caribbean islands. It should be noted, however, that what crime there is involves BVIslanders more often the immigrants or—at least directly— the police. The governor's recent appointment of a "native" BVIslander with a well-known and respected family name to the post of commissioner of police has served to bolster BVIslander confidence in the RVIPF and, perhaps, to further solidify the identification BVIslanders feel with "law and order," while resolving for them the contradiction between distrusting the police and being lawlike.

"Our Own Laws! Not Exotic Plants!"

Because BVIslanders constantly converse about "law and order," and because law both solidifies a sense of "national" identity and expresses the "national self," a recurrent concern of the legislatures has been "borrowed laws"—pieces of legislation drafted in the other colonies and states of the Caribbean and Commonwealth, and then brought in to the Legislative Council by the attorney general's office to be adapted and adopted for BVI use. The adoption of "foreign" laws has been unpopular and has been a continual sticking point between the attorney general's office and LegCo. At times, the debate has even turned toward recalling the attorney general of the day, and/or demanding a "local" attorney general be appointed by the governor.

In response to a situation in which the territory had an "Attorney General who had been so concerned with other countries, that he had written into a BVI law, what was done in Antigua," as one council member put it (Minutes 12/7/78), the Legislative Council passed a resolution calling on the governor to appoint "a qualified West Indian barrister or retired judge" to fill the post (Minutes 4/13/78). In a similar vein, during the introduction of a minor piece of legislation (Summary Jurisdiction Act [Amendment] Ordinance 1977) amending certain legal fees and giving the magistrate jurisdiction over suits brought for damages up to $2,000, the attorney general mentioned that it "followed the pattern in Antigua." A member of the Legislative Council replied that "what was good for Antigua was not relevant for us. . . . the 1st July 1956 was the day when the BVI broke away from the Associated States [the former Leeward Islands Federation] and that . . . day should always be a holiday" (Minutes 4/21/77).

In another incident, a piece of legislation designed to amend building and construction codes and fees (Land Development [Control] [Amendment] Ordinance 1978) was held up in LegCo because, as one member stated, "the time had come to look at what was good for the BVI, because what was good for Antigua and the Bahamas was not good for the BVI . . . they should stop bringing 'exotic plants' [Eric Williams's[7] term to describe "outside experts" and "outside legal draftsmen"] but should look within what was relevant to the needs of the Territory" (Minutes 1/26/78). Another bill, to provide for apprenticeship training (Apprenticeship Bill 1978), also brought out concerns over borrowed laws. One member remarked that the bill "seemed to be from St. Kitts" and added, "[We] needed legislation relevant to [our] own needs." Another member responded that "foreign" legislation such as this pointed up "matters of greater precedence"— that "this legislation had been brought here to keep the indigenous people in the saddle" and that "we were going into slavery."

"It is time," he added, "that the elected members run the country," and he called for the creation of a fourth ministerial post (Minutes 2/23/78). Such a post was, in fact, created in time for the 1979 elections.[8]

None of the laws disparaged as "foreign," as "exotic plants," however, has ever failed to pass the Legislative Council; in fact, usually they pass unanimously. Furthermore, concerns over foreign laws, or over the United Kingdom "forcing" laws upon the British Virgin Islands or attempting to "control" the BVI through such laws, have never crystallized into sustained criticism of colonial rule; they have not led to constitutional crises; they have not inspired public demonstrations; they have not produced boycotts of LegCo or ExecCo meetings; and they have not fomented calls for independence among council members or within the community.

What is important in cries against "exotic plants" is not the laws themselves, then, their contents, their intended or unintended effects. What is important, solely, is their origins: Where were they written, and by whom? Is a piece of legislation "our own law" or somebody else's? The fact of the law alone, its presence, and not its provisions, its "letters," are what matter to British Virgin Islanders and to "British Virgin Islands-ness." We need "our own" laws as emanations of, demonstrations for our "uniqueness." In authoring their "own" laws, British Virgin Islanders demonstrate to themselves their ability to be "authors," to write from a coherent, unified, and unique subject position, to authorize a "nation"—to be subjects of (legislative, national) history.

The International Business Companies Ordinance of 1984

In 1984, British Virgin Islanders became authors. The Legislative Council enacted what was perhaps the most significant piece of legislation in BVI history; and it was a piece of legislation they could claim as their "own." The International Business Companies Ordinance of 1984, in addition to being touted as the first "truly local" law of the BVI, heralded a new era in offshore financial services worldwide. The irony is compelling.

The International Business Companies Ordinance set up the provisions for the incorporation of a new kind of "investment entity"—the international business company, or IBC. Under the ordinance, an investor can set up an IBC in the BVI for an incorporation fee of $300 and an annual licensing fee of $300, if the IBC has share capital of $50,000 or less; or an incorporation fee of $1,000 and annual licensing fee of the same, if the IBC has share capital over $50,000. IBCs are subject to no other fees and are subject to no income tax.

Prior to the invention of the IBC, other jurisdictions marketing themselves to investors as tax havens (e.g., Jersey, Guernsey, Panama) charged minimal income tax on investment earnings or mandated that boards of directors meet once a year on tax-haven soil. The British Virgin Islands, by placing neither of these constraints on offshore investors, rapidly rose to prominence among the world's tax havens. The BVI legislators who drafted the IBC Ordinance had their ear to the international financial community and fashioned a law that provided exactly what the investors were looking for. As a result, in less then ten years the offshore financial services sector has overtaken tourism as the primary source of revenue for the BVI.

Members of the Legislative Council invoke the International Business Companies Ordinance almost as often as they used to gripe about "foreign" laws. Members proudly proclaim that now, other countries copy *their* laws. They have gone from being imitators to being the source; they have become originary. And the IBC Ordinance has become a benchmark against which to judge all new legislation that comes through LegCo. As one council member said of a mental health bill he was introducing, "This Bill which I am asking this Honourable House to pass into law constitutes one of the most far reaching pieces of social reform to be introduced into this Territory in recent times. It seeks to do on a social level what the International Business Companies Ordinance has sought to achieve in the financial sphere" (Minutes 6/28/85).

It bears emphasizing that the IBC Ordinance, while certainly one of the most important pieces of legislation for the economic prosperity of the territory, occupies a place in the national imagination because it is a "local" law, because "we" wrote it "ourselves" and didn't "borrow" it from anyone, and not necessarily because it had such a huge impact on the economy. Most BVIslanders have no idea what an IBC is or how it works, much less how it contributes to the government coffer through its system of fees. People refer to all aspects of the offshore financial services sector vaguely as "trust company business," or "the banks." What is important to the everyday thinking of BVIslanders is not what the IBC Ordinance says or does; what is important is that it is "ours," and "our own."

In the national imagination, the IBC Ordinance is something unique and special that demonstrates that "we" can make our "own" laws. It establishes a charter for a uniquely national subject, an author of laws. In the world of international finance, IBCs created under the ordinance are the BVI's "own" in a *proprietary* sense: they "own" the possibility of IBC creation, and it can be sold on the market to offshore investors. The logic undergirding these two notions of "own"-ership is the same: both are supported by ideas about the distinctiveness of the British Virgin Islands. The IBC Ordinance as law makes for BVIslanders a BVIslander author, a speaking subject, a unique national identity as law writer. The subject created is also an owner: it now possesses laws that can be copied by lawmakers in other countries, and through these laws, it possess a potentiality—of IBC incorporation—that can be sold to international investors. For these investors, the IBC Ordinance creates a BVI product, a distinctive entity into which they can put their profits, a specialized niche. For both local BVIslanders and international capitalists, the law has produced difference; this difference is proprietary in character and constitutive of a national subjectivity.

Local Difference and Global Integration

The IBC Ordinance made another difference for the BVI: in 1992 alone, just eight years after the introduction of the law bringing them about, IBCs contributed $21 million directly to government revenue, out of a total revenue of approximately $54 million—an increase of more than 30 percent over 1991 figures (Meyers 1993a; British Virgin Islands Legislative Council 1992). Slumps in the tourist sector led the chief minister to report, in 1993, that moneys from IBCs had "more than offset stagnating or declining revenues from just about all other areas of the economy," leading BVI newspaper headlines to proclaim, "Financial services driving economy" (Meyers 1993b).

Since 1984, more than sixty thousand IBCs have incorporated in this territory of eighteen thousand souls. The discovery of links between financial activities in the Cayman Islands and Oliver North's arms-for-hostages deals (Lohr 1992), as well as the BCCI scandal, took some of the financial winds out of the Caymans' sails; they now blow in the direction of the British Virgin Islands. After the fall of Noriega, the BVI turned out to be a godsend for Panamanian financiers. And just within the past year, capitalists in Asia have begun to set their sights on the BVI. The territory is now touted in leading Asian finance magazines as the best place to incorporate in preparation for Chinese integration of Hong Kong. The BVI has also become attractive to investors in the United States and the United Kingdom, who are looking for a secure and reputable jurisdiction relatively untainted by scandal and drug money, but also conducive to the free movement of capital (of course, from another perspective, the entire idea of moving funds offshore could be seen as scandalous!). As one New York lawyer said in an interview with the *Far Eastern Economic Review,* "Lawyers love the British Virgin Islands. You can do anything you want" (Burton 1992:43). The *Review* continues: "Obtaining tax-exempt status in the British Virgin Islands is as difficult as choosing a name and paying a registration fee" (43).

Although most people have no idea what goes on inside "the trust companies," they can not miss the public presence of the world of international finance in the British Virgin Islands. New buildings housing lawyers and consultants are springing up throughout the capital city of Road Town. The road coming from the east into town is flanked on both sides by these new "trust company" buildings, and the seaward facade of Main Street is dominated by two such structures. Each week, anywhere from one to three pages of each of the BVI's two twenty-page weekly newspapers are taken up by IBC incorporation and dissolution notices. High school students see "working for the trust companies" as lucrative, prestigious, and glamorous—even when the only available jobs are limited to front-end office management. Indeed, teachers bemoan the fact that the best and the brightest of the

BVI High School are looking toward "the banks" for careers instead of pursuing vocational training or college degrees. People who get "trust company" jobs, meanwhile, are highly paid and themselves make the best advertisement for the "trust company" career path.

While, for the general public, the offshore financial services sector might mean little more than "bank jobs" and their associated prestige, government and offshore investors are keenly aware of the instability of the investment market and the risks involved in depending heavily on revenue from financial services. Examples of failed tax havens—like Panama—put a damper on optimism. Many factors influencing the success of the British Virgin Islands as a tax haven are beyond the government's control; but the government has actively bolstered the one crucial intangible that seems to make or break a haven—reputation (Roberts 1994). In a *Euromoney* marketing brochure, BVI government officials and members of LegCo repeatedly stress that the BVI is a stable jurisdiction, free of drug money and shady dealings, and only for "legitimate" business enterprises, stating that

> while the Government strongly encourages some types of activities, it strongly discourages others, including certain types of banks. "We have not and will not be granting offshore banking licences to individuals, or unproven entities," says Financial Secretary Robert Macthavious. "They can go elsewhere and form their bank in a day or two. Be we do invite those banks with an established track record to consider the BVI. They can expedite their application through a local legal advocate or through one of the trust or service companies already established here. I should emphasise, however, that we will search into the bona fides of all applicants, and it may take some time . . . This is an offshore centre that is not for everyone. But it is for those who want to do legitimate business in a stable environment, a British dependency based on Anglo Saxon common laws. For those who want to do business from such a jurisdiction, we strongly believe that they can find no better place to do it. (*Euromoney* 1989:49)

The former chief minister stated, in the same brochure:

We always ask, does this go with our image, and whether or not it has the wherewithal to be a credit to those here and to the people who choose to come here. That's the recurring theme in everything we do. . . . We have been very conservative in our approach. We may have been too conservative at times for some people's taste. But, we want to make sure everything we do does justice to and enhances the reputation of the Territory. (*Euromoney* 1989:49)

The Gallagher Report

But how to maintain a good reputation in such a fickle and risky business as offshore finance? For the BVI and other Caribbean dependent territories who took the tax haven road, the answer was an in-depth study of the finance services of each of the territories, to determine what loopholes needed to be filled and what safeguards needed to be taken in order to lessen the chances that money laundering and other illegal activities would occur. The territorial governments and FCO invited Coopers and Lybrand, a well-respected financial management consulting firm, to conduct such a study; and, in 1990, the firm issued its *Report of Mr Rodney Gallagher of Coopers and Lybrand on the Survey of Offshore Financial Sectors in the Caribbean Dependent Territories,* published by Her Majesty's Stationery Office and "ordered by the House of Commons to be printed." This report became known in the BVI as "the Gallagher Report," and it reviewed, territory by territory, the operations of the financial services sector, the potential weaknesses, and possible remedies to enhance "supervision and regulation" (Gallagher 1990:3).

There were two main recommendations. One involved "legislative changes, including new legislation in a number of instances." For the British Virgin Islands, the report specifically recommended "new legislation in order to give legal strength to . . . proposed [new] regulatory procedures" (Gallagher 1990:3). The other recommendation was "the establishment of a Financial Secretaries Advisory Panel," which, "for consistent progress to be made," required, in Mr. Gallagher's opinion, "an on-going programme of technical assistance support" to be provided by "H[er] M[ajesty's] G[overnment]" (3).

The legislative recommendations in the Gallagher Report are

not general or vague suggestions. The report contains *actual drafts of proposed legislation* that Gallagher thought appropriate for each territory. These drafts, in fact, make up the bulk of the report. For instance, in the section on the British Virgin Islands, only thirteen pages deal with the prospects and problems of the financial services sector; the other thirty-one are pieces of proposed legislation: a "Draft Bank and Trust Law," a "Draft Insurance Law," and a "Draft Company Management Law." These drafts are detailed and complete, right down to the dotted line on which the Legislative Council has to sign. All the Legislative Council had to do to adopt Gallagher's "laws" was to fill in the appropriate date, change the word *Assembly* to *Council* and *President* to *Speaker,* pass the bill into law, have the speaker and clerk sign it, and send it off to the government printers. And that is exactly what it did. The Draft Bank and Trust Law became the Banks and Trust Companies Act (No. 9 of 1990); the Draft Insurance Law became the Insurance Business (Special Provisions) Act (No. 1 of 1991); and the Draft Company Law became the Company Management Act (No. 8 of 1990), each with only minor additions, deletions, and modifications.

The other recommendation of the Gallagher Report, the establishment of a dependent territories financial advisory panel, at first wholly supported by LegCo (Minutes 9/10/90), is perhaps bearing fruits LegCo did not expect. The FCO and dependent territories did not, outright, follow the recommendation. But late in 1992, the FCO announced the creation of a Board of Management for Dependent Territories (later named Ministerial Group of Dependent Territories). It was to be composed of the Crown-appointed governors of each territory, and it would be created to consider "aid allocation, [to] monitor drug trafficking activities, and [to] revise outdated laws in the dependent territories" (Meyers 1993c:3). One of the explicit purposes of the proposed board was to provide international investors some degree of confidence that Britain's dependent territories were "clean" of illegal offshore activities. The impetus for the proposal of the board grew from a variety of factors, but the BCCI scandal involving the Caymans was surely a great embarrassment to the FCO and a contributing element in this decision. There is probably, too, an implicit racism in the FCO's decision: investors would be assured that, as a BVIslander might say, "the English boys are looking over things."

The proposed board became a sore point and was the occasion for fiery words from the former chief minister, H. Lavity Stoutt, to the Foreign and Commonwealth Office. Stoutt maintained that such a board would be an insult and an affront to the "sovereignty" of the British Virgin Islands and other dependent territories. His arguments exemplify the teleology of BVI historical progress, of moving ever "forward" toward the nation-state—a goal jeopardized by the possibility of the board. The local paper reported, "The chief minister said he views the establishment of the board as a 'backward' step. 'We've had 25 years of ministerial government and now we've got to move on,' he said. 'Therefore I am still not happy that there is now a move to have certain intrusion on the present constitution'" (Meyers 1993c:3,12). But he made no calls against the continuing colonial relationship with the United Kingdom. Progress marches on but never gets to independence.

The Mutual Legal Assistance Act of 1990

The financial services sector and the possibilities it holds for criminal activities sparked another round of legislative action. In 1990, the BVI Legislative Council adopted the Mutual Legal Assistance (United States of America) Act (No. 5 of 1990). As Stoutt reported to the Legislative Council,

> the purpose of the Bill is to give effect to a Treaty providing the Governments of United States and the BVI to help each other in the investigation of a variety of serious crimes. That Treaty between the UK and the USA pertaining to Cayman Islands was executed in 1986 and will be extended to the BVI shortly after passage of this Bill. The extension will be done by an exchange of notes between the British Government and the State Department of the USA. (Minutes 8/31/90)

The treaty that the bill was to rubber-stamp provides for "mutual assistance" in investigation, enforcement, and prosecution in cases involving transnational crime—mainly drug trafficking and money laundering. In the BVI, the main official effect of the treaty was to provide legal means for U.S. federal investigators to scrutinize offshore financial records.

Cyril Romney, then the leader of the opposition, spoke, rather eloquently and with humor, against the bill:

> You know it's very difficult for me to take on a situation where unequal partners or incompatible partners go to bed together. There is in this community a wise old sage . . . who at one time found himself in a sort of partnership with the Government in an enterprise and he wanted to move ahead at his pace. The British Virgin Islands Government could only move at its pace; and his comment at the time was 'we are unevenly yoked; separate me, Banabas [*sic*] and Saul.' So he went his way . . . Here in this measure we find ourselves unequally yoked, not because it's something we want to do as a Legislative Council but because our metropolitan masters have deemed it fit to enter into a Treaty with a . . . friendly foreign power, a superpower if you please, and have entered into that Treaty with the object and intent and the power to ensure that it takes place, of us having to comply here in the British Virgin Islands. I don't have any problem with that; that's the Constitution under which we exist; that's our preferred association with Britain; and you can't have your cake and eat it too; but I just want to point it out for the benefit of those who will, ultimately, like myself, criticise this relationship. (Minutes 8/31/90)

Nevertheless, Romney, along with all the other members of the Legislative Council, voted in favor of the act.

The Reconfiguration of Jurisdictional Spaces

The Gallagher Report and the Mutual Legal Assistance Act restructured the jurisdictional spaces of the British Virgin Islands. In particular, the report and act broke the relationship between BVI legislative jurisdictional space and "real territory." Part of the resistance to the Dependent Territories Board and to the Mutual Legal Assistance Act stems from the erosion of this legal-spatial relationship.

When Rodney Gallagher's draft legislation became "real" legislation, the Legislative Council deferred its authorship to Coopers and Lybrand. That action, for the members of LegCo at least, and somewhat after the fact, represented a tragic abrogation of authority to another power and another space: the space of international finance capital. For Coopers and Lybrand, in contrast, the situation couldn't have been neater: the consultants got to design laws to benefit investors consulting them. Here lies a part of the reason for the turnabout on the issue of the Dependent Territories Board: when the legislative jurisdictional space effectively dissolved, LegCo had to take a stand against further "encroachment" into its domain. Of course, the encroachment was already complete. The Gallagher Report established a legislative precedent. The Legislative Council is no longer autonomous. Similarly, the Mutual Legal Assistance Act, as Romney argued, is an agreement between unequals. The United States has executive authority to intervene in BVI affairs in the pursuit of criminals. The Executive Council, never autonomous because of its links to the United Kingdom, now has to contend with a bigger executive and judicial space— one that includes the United States.

Law became the symbol of nationhood and the center of territorial development, in part because of the division of jurisdictional space and its charting and naturalizing of "real" territory. Indeed, the history of jurisdiction made the history of the British Virgin Islands appear to be a history of its legislature's creation, dissolution, and reinstatement as a "local" entity. In spite of continued colonial status, or perhaps in conjunction with it, law became a technology for crafting identity and distinctiveness. BVIslanders hungered for the distinctive national self promised by authors of law and got it by writing the International Business Companies Act. With this act, BVIslanders acquired a national self and a proprietary self. Yet law also mapped the BVI into a new terrain and recharted its legal spaces. As a site of offshore banking and international finance, as a site newly reconfigured by the law, the BVI is a quintessential example of the new spaces of postmodern capital, spaces whose autonomy and sovereignty are always in question.

Conclusion

The production of national difference is not in conflict with globalizing tendencies. Rather, the processes of globalization, including the creation of large-scale legal arenas, capital flows, and migrations, work to foster rather than mute ideas about national uniqueness and national difference. What does the future hold for a people who fiercely define their identity in opposition to Caribbean immigrants with whom they share a history of oppression, but who do not challenge—and indeed seem fearful of losing—their colonial relationship with Britain? If the British Virgin Islands lends insight into processes of creolization that produce the stable entities they claim to meld, then what does the "Caribbeanization" of the world bode for new imaginings of identity, personhood, and reiterations of "reality"?

In the British Virgin Islands, the way jurisdictional authority had been split among the branches of government created the conditions for the prominence of the Legislative Council. LegCo furthered the BVI's movement down the path of "modernity," as the "local" legislature became a primary site for inscribing national selfhood through law writing. As it worked toward "self-"rule, the BVI legislature engaged in a struggle for the authority to constitute a distinct national "self" that could write laws expressing and regulating its identity. This was a struggle over authorship. The stakes were modern identity and subjecthood. The struggle made a "history" for the BVI written as the history of "progress" toward legislative self-determination.

But the kind of national self created through law deeply entrenched continued colonial rule and at the same time fostered the integration of the British Virgin Islands into the world economy. With the authoring of the International Business Companies Ordinance, the BVI named an identity for itself as an author, a modern writer and subject of law, and also as a specialized niche in the world economy, an identity that is marketable. British Virgin Islands national identity and its identity on the global market are now inseparable, so long as the IBC Ordinance remains in effect and so long as current global conditions and inequalities require the movement of capital across legal regimes.

The BVI's emergence as a tax haven bolstered continued colonial rule around the idea of "reputation." To maintain reputability, the BVI has had to assert its "heritage" of "law and order." The national self envisioned in local lawmaking and popular discourse is a "law-and-order" self, a self-regulating and self-disciplining self. Being a "law-and-order" people has been founded in contrasts with immigrants' "lawlessness." But now, after the introduction of the IBC Ordinance, being a "law and order" people also entails assertions of the BVI's connection to the "Anglo Saxon common law" tradition. The national self is at once "distinct" and "British." As the leader of the opposition stated, local claims of autonomy, authority, and self-rule are founded in the territory's "preferred relationship with Britain," and the British Virgin Islands "can't have their cake and eat it too." That cake comes from a mix of "law" and "history" baked in the oven of "modernity" fueled by an imagined "Europe" and its historical ends in the "nation-state."

Yet the idea of "progress" toward "self-rule" carries force for current imaginings of the British Virgin Islands as a national entity, even though the authorship of the national self has been abrogated to extraterritorial legal realms, and despite the fact that maintaining its reputation is linked so closely to maintaining its colonial relationship with Britain. The sense of law and order that is the basis of claims to autonomy, authority, and self-rule has "Britain" as its referent; but at the same time, "law and order" keeps the BVI in the progressivist teleological narrative of "history," a story of getting ever closer to "self-rule" as a distinctive "nation-state," a story that paradoxically depends on the BVI never reaching that predetermined end point.

As I was completing the dissertation on which this book is based, the British Virgin Islands came to grips once again with the ambiguity of its colonial relationship with the United Kingdom.

Imperial legislation altered the BVI constitution and provided for an increase in the number of elected members of the Legislative Council from nine to thirteen. The additional four, furthermore, were to be elected "at large," by the people of the entire territory and not by district. The next Legislative Council therefore would be composed of nine people each representing a district and four people representing all the citizens of the BVI. In May 1995, the first Legislative Council under the new "mixed" system of representation was elected.

The chief minister at the time, the late H. Lavity Stoutt, expressed outrage at the action taken by the colonial power without proper consultation with local officials. The chief minister and several other legislators did attend a meeting in London to discuss the change before it went into effect, but whatever concerns they raised seem to have been dismissed by London. Opposition members Omar Hodge and Walwyn Brewley spoke in favor of the change, and Brewley even hinted that he might run as an at-large candidate in upcoming elections (*Island Sun* 1994a:1, 4, 25). Meanwhile, a poll conducted by the Eastern Caribbean Center of the University of the Virgin Islands (U.S. Virgin Islands) revealed that 49 percent of the people surveyed favored the change, with 16 percent opposed and 35 percent undecided. Sixty percent believed that the chief minister should be elected at large (*Island Sun* 1994b:2–3).

The chief minister's response to the imposition of the "mixed system" of representation highlighted the nature of the relationship between the United Kingdom and the British Virgin Islands as one between unequals. He viewed the imposition of the mixed system as an affront to the legislative autonomy of the BVI—an autonomy that may be largely ephemeral in light of the offshore finance business. In contrast, people in support of the mixed system seem to believe that it will encourage the formation of true political parties and will help unseat traditional political forces (such as the former chief minister himself, who as the representative for the First District [West End] was elected by a very small proportion of the total BVI electorate). They see this unilateral, colonial decision as furthering the interests of true "democracy." To win a seat on the Legislative Council, candidates for the at-large seats need to mobilize large segments of the population. Interest groups may form, and new "votes" might emerge—the "immigrant vote," the "women's vote," the "expatriate white vote," the "business vote," and the "intellectual vote." Previously silent voices will emerge, and candidates will be successful only if they are able to negotiate these "votes" and voices. Indeed, under the "mixed" system, women were elected to the Legislative Council for the first time in BVI history, perhaps because of just such a "vote."

Those who stand to win in the new system are in many cases the very people who would contest colonial rule—immigrants, intellectuals, and persons with a strong belief in democratic party politics. Those who stand to lose—the traditional politicians who run on the basis of their personality and their ties to their home districts—are in many cases the very people who benefited most from the colonial system that now threatens to unseat them. The future is uncertain, but the mixed system speaks volumes about the ironies of colonial rule in the late twentieth century and about the BVI's creolizing practices that work to mix, as they stabilize and entrench, colonial rule with national identity.

Constructions of "Place"

The British Virgin Islands story has much to tell us about the resurgence of ideas about place-based identities occurring during the current time of global capitalist integration. It is curious that, in his project of elucidating "why the elaboration of place-bound identities has become more rather than less important in a world of diminishing spatial barriers to exchange, movement and communication," David Harvey (1993:4) pays scant attention to law and the legal practices that may be enabling both the shrinking of "space" and the reinvigoration of "place." Harvey examines how uneven capitalist investment shifts the boundaries of places invested with meaning by those living in them. He notes that increasing mobility of capital allows capitalists "a much freer choice of location," which in turn allows capitalists "to take more rather than less advantage of small differences in resource qualities, quantities and costs between places" (1993:7). He continues that, at the same time that capitalists are seeking out the attractive qualities of different places, the people trying to attract capital investment to their particular place come to emphasize the qualities that make their place "different" in some significant, competitive way from other places vying for the same investments (1993:7–8).

Yet, Harvey neglects to interrogate how different places constitute their difference and whether encouraging capitalist integration is the intended effect of the elaboration of difference. Law is crucial to the BVI's construction (and subsequent marketing) of itself as different from other Caribbean islands and tax havens. There is a mutuality, as Harvey points out, between "cultural politics"—the creation of an identity founded in a particular place—and "political-economic end[s]"—increased capitalist investment and articulation to global capitalist regimes (1993:19). Law is important to both.

The case of the British Virgin Islands sheds light on the role of law in the contemporary internationalization of markets and the simultaneous resurgence of nationalisms. The apparent tension between nationalism and economic integration seems to hinge upon a particular understanding of law writing. For the BVI, writing laws for the "nation" does not imply writing laws against the colonial order. In other words, law writing does not center around claims to political sovereignty and independence—even if such claims are occasionally invoked—but, rather, claims to an essential "difference" that is not coincidentally marketable to investors. Modern law, with its rhetorics of progress, its formations of history, and its construction of national selves, is a key point of connection between the cultural politics that create differences and draw borders between peoples and places, and the processes of capitalist integration that demand such differences and at the same time appear to make borders redundant.

Constructions of "Race"

Changes in citizenship law came to the British Virgin Islands at a time when capitalists were developing new strategies of accumulation in response to the crisis of the 1970s. Some of these strategies came to depend on the financial services offered by places like the BVI. The 1981 British Nationality Act contributed to an ongoing proliferation of citizenship and other statuses and led BVIslanders and immigrants to new concerns over paternity, legitimacy, and family. BVIslanders' new naturalized identity and their "British heritage" of "law and order" contributed to their great success as a tax haven.

The BVI case illustrates contemporary global processes and the response of legal institutions and local practices to globalizing markets and labor movements. The unprecedented integration of markets and large-scale migrations that have accompanied it have led to new logics and rhetorics of exclusion (Stolcke 1995). In the British Virgin Islands, state policies stress citizenship by descent and not birth within state boundaries and hence create a whole stratum of long-term working residents who may have been born in the territory in which they work but nonetheless do not share the rights of citizens.

Locally constructed essentialized differences between immigrants and citizens become incredibly significant as global integration and competition force states to redirect their resources and position themselves in terms of the global, not national, marketplace. In the United States, political leaders have begun to consider limiting state resources and welfare benefits to citizens and denying protections to immigrant workers. The boundaries of the community of belonging are sharply drawn, and those left outside the circle are not entitled to state protection.

This resurgence of concern with the rights of immigrants in much of the West touches a contradiction in modern law between the ideal that all people enjoy certain basic human rights and the notion of sovereignty underlying the rights of states to create and enforce these rights. Globalization may appear to call sovereignty into question, thereby diminishing the importance of the state and requiring increased attention to universal human rights. In fact, however, the British Virgin Islands case demonstrates the reverse. The state is not withering away, and it need not even be "sovereign" to police its populations. Rather, it is redrawing its borders and the limits of the community of belonging in essentialist terms, reserving the spoils of capital movement for its citizens.

But the spoils themselves may turn out to be fleeting or altogether illusory. In the British Virgin Islands, the "stability" brought by the conjuncture of the offshore finance sector and new citizenship law depends on the labor of a disenfranchised stratum of exploited workers and on an inherently fickle and highly volatile industry. As the United States and other countries close their borders or consolidate racist and exclusionary policies within their borders, it may be only a matter of time before noncitizens in the BVI decide to stake a claim in the territory of their birth instead of using their ambiguous or multiple legal statuses as opportunities for mobility to the United States or other destinations. And as global free-trade agreements like NAFTA and GATT work to "harmonize" the laws of sovereign states in order to facilitate the needs of capital, the "islands" standing outside the emerging transnational network of legal regimes may soon find their access to global capital choked off by the very institutional practices that enabled offshore financial arrangements in the first place.

"Nature" and "Choice": Off the Charts

Consider the similarities among BVIslander nationalist discourse, BVIslander stereotypes of immigrants and immigrants' responses, and immigrants' efforts to get into BVI society. In no case is the overarching system of dominance challenged. BVI nationalist discourse is crucially dependent on the BVI's colonial status and its subordination in the world finance markets. Indeed, were either element lacking—British status or tax haven status—BVI nationalist discourse would come unraveled, for there would be no stakes in maintaining it. British status underwrites investors' confidence in the BVI's financial services; the BVI's financial services sector underwrites the maintenance of the territory as "British." In effect, British Virgin Islander nationalist discourse empties out "the BVI" as a signifier, leaving nothing "original" behind—much like the uninhabited islands of the tourist brochure. Immigrants share with BVIslanders a moral discourse of individual contribution that also animates notions of clannishness and greed. Similarly, immigrants approach the British Virgin Islands as "individuals" in order to gain acceptance. In effect, they empty out their "selves" of "original" attachments or "natures" in order to be accepted as simple individuals—"I am *me!!* That's *all!*"

Of course, there are traces of identity in the apparently empty space of the nation and the person. What is lacking is ground, and what is in its place is a network of technologies whose effect is to produce the fiction of a new stable ground—the ground of "choice" reduced to consumer preference at the "gut" level (Strathern 1992a:216). Choice at the "gut" level, a new materialization of discourse, works through other articulatory practices—practices I've termed *creolizing*—to produce momentary stabilizations of and sources for identity. These stabilizations include, at times, "ethnic" stereotypes; "races" and communities bound to "places"; "families" and "genealogies"; "land" and "country"; "classes" and "parties"; "states" and "societies"; "individuals" who owe nothing to society; and "nations."

The creolizing technologies map out a stable order for the world that at the same time seems always in flux. Like transition narratives, themselves creolizing technologies, they materialize certain objects and entities and give the illusion that such entities are separate and separable, and sometimes determining and determinate. The "Caribbeanization of the world" narrative is itself one such transition narrative, one that stabilizes "the Caribbean" and "the world" just at a moment when offshore finance (among other things) makes that separation more a fiction than ever.

The materialization of stable objects is effected in part through law and legal practices that are themselves effects of the stable objects they help produce. Liberal law, declaring with Hobbes that "Nature hath made all men equall," constitutes the Nature that will be both its bane, by creating inequalities it cannot redress, and its raison d'être, by constituting individuals with natural differences that the law must mitigate and mediate. The law and its nature leave little room for alternative ways of imagining the world (Olwig 1993:208), but themselves provide possibilities for the empty actors, networks of power and meaning, that they help crystallize. "Democratic consumer culture," after all, helped give rise to the new social movements of the latter half of this century (Laclau and Mouffe 1985:164) by interpellating individuals as equals in their capacity as consumers with "gut"-level preferences and predilections. Although the picture I have painted of the British Virgin Islands may appear gloomy—in sharp contrast to the sunny tourist brochure—the fact that immigrants and BVIslanders have not rearticulated themselves to directly confront their subordination (to citizens and to Britain and the world market, respectively) does not in itself close off that possibility. Indeed, liberal law and its nature, with their notions of "free choice" and the substantive, "natural" equality of all persons, provide the very language that could be used to form an oppositional consciousness.

The Caribbean experience presented in this book thus may suggest paradigms for identity in the contemporary world after all. Stuart Hall writes that "identity is like a bus! Not because it takes you to a fixed location, but because you can only get somewhere—anywhere—by climbing aboard" (Hall 1995:65). Perhaps identity is more like a ship in previously uncharted waters: As its cartographer fills in the blank spaces of the map, the condensation of its spray proves it has not sailed off the earth, but that new regions have just materialized to support it and that new journeys and new routes may lead to new eddies and undercurrents that may one day rechart the map entirely.

Notes

Introduction

1. At present, out of a working population of 10,096, 60 percent (6,099) were born outside the BVI. Of this number, 3,914, or 64 percent, have obtained neither the right to work without a permit nor citizenship. Most of the remaining 2,185 can work without permits but do not have citizenship rights. In 1990, the Labour Department granted work permits to 354 Europeans, 446 North Americans, 298 people from the Dominican Republic, 385 people from Dominica, 593 people from St. Vincent, 624 people from St. Kitts and Nevis, and 389 Guyanese. Preliminary census data report that there are 1,422 people born in St. Kitts/Nevis currently resident in the BVI; 954 from St. Vincent; 769 from Guyana; 681 from the Dominican Republic; 616 from the United States; 565 from Dominica; 518 from St. Thomas; 402 from the United Kingdom; 355 from Antigua; and 291 from Grenada. See British Virgin Islands Department of Labour 1990 and British Virgin Islands Development Planning Unit 1991, 1992.

2. In 1987, I conducted nine months of fieldwork on the island of Dominica, in the eastern Caribbean, as part of my undergraduate training in anthropology. There, I worked on issues of gender and development. When I arrived in the British Virgin Islands, I had Dominica very much in mind but found the differences between the two places striking. Dominica is a country whose economy is based on peasant and export agriculture and is a sending country for migrants. The BVI is a territory whose economy is based on tourism and offshore finance and is a receiving country for migrants. Dominica is poor, the BVI is rich. The BVI unsettled many of my comfortable assumptions about "Caribbean life."

3. For a review of some of this literature, see Kearney 1995 and Basch, Glick Schiller, and Szanton Blanc 1994. See also Grewal and Kaplan 1994.

4. And Caribbeanist anthropology has been dominated by the "village ethnography" genre; classic examples of this genre include Herskovits and Herskovits 1947, Herskovits 1937, Smith 1962, and Horowitz 1967.

5. This literature can be broken roughly into two categories. One includes anthropological and historical work concerned with social stratification,

notably the work of R. T. Smith (1996, 1995, 1988, 1970) and his students (e.g., Austin 1984; Alexander 1977, 1984; Douglass 1992); Stolcke (Martinez-Alier 1974, Stolcke 1989); Williams (1991); and Caribbean scholars like Braithwaite (1975). The other category concerns issues of gender, race, class, and economic development and includes Safa 1995, Anderson 1986, Bolles 1985, Mohammed and Shepherd 1988, Momsen 1991, Barrow 1988, and Yelvington 1995. Carol Smith's work in Guatemala makes similar arguments about class, race, and gender hierarchies (Smith 1995; see also Streicker 1995 and Mohanty 1991). My own thinking is deeply indebted to these bodies of literature.

6. I would like to thank Jane Collier for her assistance here. See Collier, Maurer, and Suárez-Navaz 1995.

7. In transcribing the speech of persons I spoke with in the BVI, I have tried to retain both the cadence and tone of their spoken language and the class distinctions evident in different people's speaking styles.

8. Paul Gilroy quotes Foucault in attempting to chart an "anti-anti-essentialism" to counter debates between constructionists and essentialists on the question of race. Constructionist positions that race is a cultural elaboration or cultural construction out of natural or social structural facts fall flat when they seem to deny the power of constructed racial categories that feel very real to people and appear to determine people's lives. They also fall flat when critics point out that the facts from which race is supposedly constructed are themselves constructions, from their moment of entry into language in the very phrase "constructions of natural facts." Foucault shifts the scene for Gilroy, allowing critics to look at the "technologies" that produce the *effect* of natural and essential races. As Gilroy puts it, this move "point[s] towards an anti-anti-essentialism that sees racialised subjectivity as the product of the social practices that supposedly derive from it" (1993:29). Focus shifts when we chart out the *techniques* and *practices* that make nature natural and culture constructed from it (cf. Bourdieu 1977).

9. Olwig suggests that emigration resolves this contradiction because through inclusive (hierarchical) ties of sociability and obligation, emigration provides a means of sending remittances back "home" so that family and friends there can achieve and display (egalitarian) respectability without appearing to have "got ahead" at their compatriots' expense. What this does, for Olwig, is call into question the very notion of "home"—of the Caribbean in the world and the world in the Caribbean.

Chapter 1

1. A passenger list for the sloop *Lilian,* recorded in 1931, contains entries for 21 Anegadians, 6 Tortolians, and 1 person from Santo Domingo. The 1911 Census of the British Virgin Islands divides the population into the color categories "white," "black," and "colored" and records, for Tortola, 33 whites, 3,402 blacks, and 787 coloreds; for Anegada, 0 whites, 123 blacks, and 336 coloreds; for Virgin Gorda, 1 white, 238 blacks, and 178 coloreds; and for Jost

Van Dyke, 1 white, 246 blacks, and 103 coloreds. Interestingly, the census also records the total population of several islands that are now, except for tourist facilities, depopulated: 52 for Salt Island, 42 for Peter Island, 15 for Thatch Island, and 5 for Sombrero.

2. This chapter retains persons' real names in an effort to preserve the historical memory of these events.

3. In this and in subsequent chapters, when quoting from archival sources, I have preserved all spelling and grammatical inconsistencies and errors that were in the originals. Material added by me to aid the clarity of a given extract is placed in square brackets.

4. In 1931, a James Smith of Anegada was accused of squeezing too many people on board his sloop the *Carmen Maria* (VICO 27 of 1931) headed for La Romana estate, Dominican Republic. The twenty-eight or twenty-nine people had been recruited by a foreman of the estate.

5. Indeed, two serious hurricanes had hit the British Virgin Islands in 1916 and 1924, and people without family abroad earning cash were hard-pressed to put their lives back together again.

6. Michael O'Neal suggests (personal communication, 1993) that the term *cocolo* is perhaps derived from the word *Tortola*.

7. At first there was some confusion whether it would be administered within each presidency or federally; the commissioner of the Virgin Islands thought it should be kept within each presidency (VICO 1929, no number).

8. According to J. R. O'Neal, in a 1993 interview with the author.

9. I found records about one Virgin Islander, James Stoutt, who had gone to Aruba to work for Lago Oil and Transport Company; he was killed in an accident, and his mother received compensation in florins, pounds, and dollars (VICO 647 of 1931).

10. Michael O'Neal has characterized the postemancipation period of BVI history as one dominated by "non-capitalist forms of production." He points out that, unlike in other parts of the Caribbean where peasantlike relations developed soon after the end of slavery, in the BVI people began producing goods for sale on markets early on and in general owned the means of their production. However, he argues, it would be incorrect to call the postemancipation period a time dominated by a "petty commodity mode of production," since the connections to markets were unstable and often intermittent. People made charcoal, grew root crops and vegetables, raised livestock, and trapped fish. They brought their goods to market in St. Thomas when they needed cash; otherwise, they used them for subsistence or for barter with their neighbors. Families and individuals participated in markets only occasionally and meanwhile provided for their own subsistence; they were therefore "not dependent on the wage for the full production and reproduction of familial labor power" (O'Neal 1983:90; quoting Deere 1979:145n). The linkage of these noncapitalist forms of production to market relations in St. Thomas, along with labor migrations to the Dominican Republic and other places, "subsume[d]" production in the BVI "under capital" (O'Neal 1983:90) but did not make them necessarily "capitalist" in character. The sub-

sumption of BVI labor and production under capital was also, in a sense, a step removed from the capitalist world system of the nineteenth century, as the BVI's contact points to the world system were themselves quite marginal to it (O'Neal 1983:90–91). Four factors differentiate Virgin Islanders engaged in seasonal labor in the Dominican Republic from those residing on a more-or-less permanent basis in the Virgin Islands, and which complicate somewhat O'Neal's analysis. The great majority of Virgin Islanders who worked in the Dominican Republic were men. Furthermore, they were wage workers, unlike those who sold their produce directly on the St. Thomas market. The migrating populations of places like Anegada, East End, and Virgin Gorda were larger, proportionally, than those of the hills and west of Tortola and Jost Van Dyke; they also tended on the whole to return during the off-season.

11. One such incident was the surprise success of a suit brought against Wailling by Godfrey de Castro, a public launch operator (see Harrigan and Varlack 1975:156).

12. The British Virgin Islands' remaining whites had by this time all but departed for England.

13. The original must be in the Government Archives somewhere, but I am not sure where. Copies exist in the Public Library, and the entire manifesto is reproduced in Harrigan and Varlack 1975:159.

Chapter 2

1. See Merry and Milner 1993 and Fitzpatrick 1993 for a critique of the assumptions behind legal scholars' discussions of "alternative dispute resolution" (ADR), many of which involved romantic constructions of the customs of so-called simple societies. ADR proponents would almost certainly view this conflict as having been resolved through "alternative" means and would hold it up as an example of how alternatives to the courts can help settle disputes.

2. On machine and organismic metaphors at midcentury and the techno-scientific imaginary from which they emerged after World War II, see Haraway 1989. Norbert Wiener's (1950) book *The Human Use of Human Beings* represents a midcentury voice for humanist cybernetic organizing principles for modernity but is also a product of this imaginary and shares many of its assumptions.

3. The British Virgin Islands Boundaries Commission also paid particular attention to Anegada, Jost Van Dyke, and Virgin Gorda, almost to the exclusion of the Tortola districts. As with Proudfoot, the concern was to tie the people from the outlying islands closer to "government" in Tortola, and the commission made special visits to these islands. The BVI Boundaries Commission report stated that Virgin Gordians from the North Sound region "were not even discussing" districting, such was the level of disinterestedness, but that people from the Valley were very interested in it and were "strongly opposed to any link with any part of the island of Tortola" (British Virgin Islands Boundaries Commission 1966:6). People from the Valley argued, furthermore, that people in the small islands south of Tortola—Salt, Peter, and

Cooper Islands—were, like them, "landowners" and would form a district with them based on that "community of interest." Anegadians, meanwhile, told the BVI Boundaries Commission that they "would prefer to be linked to Road Town, with which they had business contacts" (6) and a long history together forged in the period of migration to the Dominican Republic. People from Jost Van Dyke strongly opposed linkage with Road Town or the islands to the south and sought to remain part of the West End district—a community of interest formed in the period of smuggling and migration to St. Thomas and strengthened by the 1954 district boundary connecting them with West End.

4. Data were collected from the BVI Public Service Staff Lists for 1953, 1957, 1962, 1966, 1973, 1979, 1983, and 1988 and from the BVI telephone books from 1950 through 1994 to produce a count of civil servants from different regions of the British Virgin Islands.

5. I would like to acknowledge the work of Diane Nelson, Jane Collier, and Liliana Suárez-Navaz in helping this chapter materialize.

Chapter 3

1. For instance, Allen Ehrlich quotes a Jamaican cane worker as saying: "You will find few fair-minded Indians. They care only for themselves. They will help one another and step on someone else. Many of the Indians have plenty of money, but they don't show it. They have a humble, poor look; but they're tricking you to make you think they're poor—they have money in the bank. Indians have brains when it concerns money. . . ." (Ehrlich 1976:22). Another of Ehrlich's informants jokes, "Pay an Indian £1 a week and he'll save £1.10.0" (22). Elliott Skinner's work on race and ethnicity in Guyana similarly records African-Guyanese characterizations of Indian-Guyanese as "thrifty" and "cheap." According to his informants, "while the black man eats and drinks well, the East Indian saves his money" (Skinner [1955] 1971:119). Neither Skinner nor Ehrlich, however, go beyond the face value of these comments in order to account for them. Skinner, in fact, seems to treat these stereotypes as having a basis in fact. The "acquisitive trait" of Indians is crucial, he argues, in a market economy like colonial Guyana. Yet Skinner does not explain why Indians "have" this "trait," while blacks do not. Nor does he discuss why African-Caribbean people, who have been articulated to a market economy at least since the time of slavery, did not "develop" it.

2. For a recent analysis of the problem of Caribbean ethnic hierarchy and stereotypes and a sympathetic but important critique of Williams's thesis, see C. Smith 1995.

3. In the BVI, one of the most common aspirations of young men is to erect an apartment building on family land and become a landlord to immigrant families; being a landlord is seen as a good job because it leaves one a lot of free time.

4. By *crystallization* I mean essentially Laclau's and Hall's "condensation" (see Hall 1980). I prefer my term, however, because it highlights the "solidity" of the ideological terms that are made to "matter" as people live their lives.

5. A sixth group, which I will not deal with here, includes immigrants from Trinidad. These are very few in number and have few interactions with the other Indian immigrants in the BVI.

6. All spellings of Hindi terms were obtained from interviewees. According to the pandit, a *hawan* is a gathering of people to "make devotions to" the gods or the various manifestations of the One God involving the burning of offerings in a *kund,* or fire (in our case, a small hibachi covered in aluminum foil). A *pooja* is the more general term for a paying of devotions.

7. On the observance of these and other Hindu holidays in the Caribbean, see Jha 1976, Vertovec 1992.

8. In fact, obeah is illegal, by the Obeah Act (Cap. 53), originally passed in 1917 and never taken off the books. This law concerns some Hindus quite a bit, who worry that BVIslanders' "ignorance" will lead them to try to halt the practice of Hinduism in the territory. This concern is one reason why the pandit is eager to appear on radio whenever any political news reaches the BVI from Guyana or whenever there is a Hindu holiday, such as Diwali, to put in a good word about how "religious" and "devout" Hindus are, and how they worship "the One God" (Brahma). He is very careful, in other words, not to encourage the idea that Hinduism is polytheistic, instead repeating that the various *dewtas* and *devis* are "god-manifestations," that is, manifestations of the One God.

9. In all fairness, neither are many other religious groups invited. The Christian Council has representatives from the following only: Methodists, Anglicans, Seventh-Day Adventists, Baptists, and Roman Catholics. The other faiths represented in the BVI include Muslims (organized in the BVI Islamic Society), the Church of God of Holiness, the Church of God of Prophesy, the Jehovah's Witnesses, and several very small evangelical congregations. At least one representative on the Christian Council considers all of these other faiths, including Hinduism, "cults." Others are not so hostile; in fact, several members of the Methodist congregation have actively campaigned not only for a broadening of the Christian Council into a true interfaith organization, but also for immigrants' rights.

10. There are, however, two cooperative organizations (the Tortola Cooperative Credit Union and the Fishermen's Association), both of which got off to a shaky start and continue to founder, and both based not on the notion that the people making them up are members of a particular socially constituted group, but on the principle that individuals can come together, as "individuals" acting cooperatively, to help each other out in time of need.

11. That is, "The negroes [*deh* as plural marker] know about these things and they come and sit, too, right down on the ground."

12. One of the reasons for stressing this point is to interrupt the anthropological discourse that casts Indian-Caribbean people as "different" from African-Caribbean people. These writings of difference reproduce dubious orientalist assumptions: that Indians are "more religious," "more family oriented," "more collectivist," and so forth, than Africans. For a discussion, see Miller 1994.

13. *Creolize* is here taken in the sense discussed in the introduction, as a mediating and purifying practice that produces the objects it names.

Chapter 4

1. The masculine-gendered pronoun is probably the most appropriate here, given that Hobbes was concerned with "free men" and not other humans he deemed to be dependents on them, such as women, children, and slaves. See Pateman 1988.

2. The critique of the concept "race" put forth by Wade has been echoed in recent work by geographers on space and place. Edward Soja (1989) and Michael Keith and Steve Pile (1993) situate their work against the idea that meaningful places are constructed from natural spaces. Instead, they suggest that it is the belief in and material effects of constructed places which give force to the idea that there exists a separate object-domain of "natural" space out of which places get fabricated.

3. I truly believe this, and I believe it holds as well in the BVI as it does in small-town USA, where my own roots lie. Many people have told me that my sister's son looks just like me. He's adopted. The idea of family resemblances and their continual rediscovery, to me, point to a broader heterosexual matrix and its attendant conceptions of children as products and possessions of their parents. This is a logic I would like to see deconstructed (see Butler 1993, Wittig 1992).

4. This calypso is discussed further in Maurer 1996.

Chapter 5

1. Labour Code Ordinance (Act), 1975 (No. 7 of 1975).

2. British Nationality Act 1981 (U.K.) (Gazetted in the BVI at G.32/1988).

3. Anguilla, Bermuda, British Virgin Islands, Cayman Islands, Montserrat, and Turks and Caicos Islands.

4. Bahamas (independence in 1973), Grenada (1974), Dominica (1978), St. Lucia (1979), St. Vincent (1979), Belize (1980), Antigua and Barbuda (1982), and St. Kitts–Nevis (1983).

5. The motion picture *Malcolm X* was screened in the British Virgin Islands during my fieldwork. It generated a good deal of interest in Islam among many BVIslander and immigrant youths and educated adults, some of whom attended programs hosted by the BVI Islamic Society to learn more about the religion. During the screening of the film, put on as a special event by the Toastmasters Club, members of the audience booed as Malcolm called for the separation of the "races." One woman told me afterwards, "How can we separate the races in the Caribbean? All the races is in our blood!"

Chapter 6

1. All personal, family, and place names in this chapter are pseudonyms unless otherwise noted.

2. I was highly fortunate that my fieldwork coincided with renewed efforts on the part of the Public Library to bring order to the Government Archives. I would like to express my most sincere thanks to Janice Nibbs Blyden for assisting me in the Government Archives and for locating many documents relevant to my research that I otherwise would never have known existed. I would also like to thank Armina Mohammad Deonarinesing, registrar of the High Court, for giving me access to old court records of land disputes.

3. See Besson 1979 and Besson 1984 for a review of the literature on family land.

4. My thinking on kinship and family in the Caribbean is guided by the work of R. T. Smith, Jack Alexander, and Diane Austin-Broos. See R. Smith 1988; Alexander 1976, 1977, 1984; and Austin 1979, 1983, 1984. My thinking on kinship in this chapter has also been shaped by Delaney (1986, 1991) and Schneider (1984).

5. He labeled the former a "true" kindred and the latter a "nonunilineal descent group." Kindreds were bracketed by Goodenough; the idea did little to illuminate Malayo-Polynesian social structure because by definition they were "ephemeral," lasting only one generation, and therefore could not "function as a land-owning group," which would require some notion of descent in order to pass on rights in land (Goodenough 1955:72).

6. An obvious restriction on a descent group would be for it to be unilinear. But unilineal descent was nowhere to be found in the societies with which Goodenough was concerned. He identified three other restricting mechanisms, mechanisms that permitted nouilinearity but imposed order and discrete groups based on rights in land. One was to tie membership directly to rights in some specified portion of land; a second way was to tie group membership to locality; a third way was to make membership in lineal groups optional depending on the residence choices of an individual. Following the publication of Goodenough's essay, a number of anthropologists reinterpreted data in light of the cognatic model. See the important set of articles by Davenport (1959), Solien (1959), and Ember (1959), which guided subsequent research on the topic, at least in the United States. In England, the Melanesianist critique of Africanist lineal models was in its infancy (Lawrence 1955, Leach 1956).

7. Besson carefully analyzed the work of two previous scholars who had also proposed the existence of nonunlineal descent groups in the Caribbean, but who both sought out restricting mechanisms (Solien 1959, Otterbein 1964). Solien had proposed that for the Black Caribs she studied in Central America, out-migration and nonresidence were the crucial restricting factors. Otterbein concluded that there had been a gradual change in Caribbean descent from unrestricted groups to restricted ones, due primarily to population pressures resulting in scarcity of land. Scarcity in turn necessitated limiting the number of persons entitled to inheritance and thus forced restricting mechanisms to come into operation (Otterbein 1964; see Besson 1979:96–98). Besson strongly criticized the wholesale importation of concepts developed in the study of tribal societies into Caribbean research.

8. Carnegie cites three main ambiguities in family land, all of which are

significant enough, he claims, to question the "institutional" approach to family land. The first has to do with the disposition of lands: Is it through a will, or not? The second concerns nomination of heirs: Are they actively named, or is the system "passive," with land devolving through cognatic descent? The question of fragmentation is closely related: Is the land divided? Are shares given to specific relatives, or do all simply "share" in some unspecified way? Do they share "equally," or in "fractional interests," or are usufruct rights merely haphazardly conceded? Finally, what happens to "illegitimate" children? Are they granted rights to land or not? Or is a better distinction between "home" versus "outside" children (in Jamaica, "home" children are children brought into the father's household, regardless of legitimacy; outside children remain "outside"). The evidence does not follow one neat pattern.

9. Aside from some disagreements (for instance, her lukewarm reception of the possibility of African cultural retentions), Besson (1987b) does not see Carnegie's intersystem approach contradictory to her own. She does wish, however, to define two distinct poles to the continuum, with a customary system basically in opposition to a formal legal one (consistent with her earlier position, esp. Besson 1984). That is because the idea of a resistive response to plantation systems is integral to her analysis of family land. It is also because she finds hard to understand how, for Carnegie, "family land" represents one pole of a continuum and, at the same time, the continuum itself (Besson 1987b:108).

10. There were also *equitable estates*, estates held "to the use of" some other person, that is, an estate of which A holds the fee simple but B is seized of it and enjoys it as s/he would if s/he were the owner of the estate; s/he holds the estate "to the use of" A; s/he has what is called an "equitable interest" in the estate. Equities were created by contract and governed by principles of fairness, not the common law.

11. No other estates or interests can exist within the estate—unlike earlier, the estate is not legally apportionable—except as *equitable* interests. For freeholds, then, entailed interests, life interests, and future interests "can subsist *only in equity, not at law*. Each one must be created behind a trust," effected by the estate owner who creates equitable interests through contract (Cheshire 1982:93, my emphasis).

12. The reference is to *Williams Law of Real Property*, 12th ed., p. 17; see Cheshire 1982:86.

13. And wives seem not to have made use of the Married Women's Property Acts in the British Virgin Islands, as they did in Antigua and elsewhere in the Caribbean (see Lazarus-Black 1994).

14. The contrast between "family" and "genealogy" has also been at work in debates over kinship in anthropology. In Radcliffe-Brown's (1950) vision, society depends upon orderly kinship systems that break the grid up into discrete units—descent groups, or families—which basically haggle among themselves for power and prestige. Society depends upon groups. The creation of families from the grid of kinship makes the groups. In contrast, Melanesianist critiques of the Radcliffe-Brown model hold out the concept of

the cognatic descent group—a descent group that is precisely the genealogical grid. Restricting and limiting mechanisms, which have more to do with land and other resources than with the grid itself, are what produce order in society.

Chapter 7

1. My thinking in this chapter is guided by Horkheimer and Adorno's observation that "[b]ourgeois society is ruled by equivalence. It makes the dissimilar comparable by reducing it to abstract quantities. To the Enlightenment, that which does not reduce to numbers, and ultimately to the one, becomes illusion; modern positivism writes it off as literature" (Horkheimer and Adorno 1944:7).

2. Some identifying details of this case have been changed, and all the names of persons in this chapter are fictitious.

3. These scandals have involved Wickam's Cay, much of the island of Anegada, and Nanny Cay, all of which at one time were leased to developers and then reacquired by the government due to popular protest and in some cases allegations of criminal activities.

Chapter 8

1. This chapter is a revised and expanded version of Maurer 1995b.

2. A tax haven industry specialist claims that more than 50 percent of all money involved in transnational business passes through tax havens (Ginsberg 1991:7; see Roberts 1994).

3. The electorate consisted of white men of property. In 1837, out of a total electorate of 143, only 34 cast votes.

4. Recently, several students of BVI history have attempted to relate the stories of these people (O'Neal 1983, McGlynn 1980).

5. These race terms were elicited from one informant; most people would agree that one member of the first council was "white." Most would avoid classifying the other three with "racial" terms, preferring instead the term "local." The man referred to as "half-white, half-black" referred to himself as "mulatto."

6. The word *sukuya* is itself a "foreign" term for obeah-woman, derived from Caribbean French creole words *soucriante* or *soukwyan(te)* for "vampire" or "witchwoman."

7. Eric Williams (1911–81) was chief minister of Trinidad and Tobago from 1956 to 1959, premier from 1959 to 1962, and prime minister from 1962 to 1981, and was a formidable figure in Caribbean nationalist thought.

8. I do not mean to seem unsympathetic to the concerns of members of LegCo over "nonlocal" laws, nor do I wish to trivialize members' characterizations of nonlocal laws as instances of colonial domination. I do, however, wish to call attention to the discourse with which legislators voice their concerns.

References

Abbreviations Used for References to Archival Materials

LICSO   "Despatches," Leeward Islands Colonial Secretary Office, St. John's, Antigua, numbered sequentially within each year. British Virgin Islands Government Archive, Road Town. Identified in the text by number and date.

Minutes   Minutes of meetings of the Legislative Council of the British Virgin Islands. Archived in the British Virgin Islands Public Library, Caribbean Studies Unit, Road Town, Tortola. Identified in the text by date.

Record   Record of the proceedings of the Legislative Council of the British Virgin Islands. Archived in the British Virgin Islands Public Library, Caribbean Studies Unit, interfiled with Minutes. Identified in the text by date.

VICO   "Despatches," Virgin Islands Commissioner's Office, Road Town, Tortola, numbered sequentially within each year. British Virgin Islands Government Archive, Road Town. Identified in the text by number and date.

Legislation Cited

British Nationality Act, 1981. Gazetted in the BVI in *Government Gazette* No. 32, 1988.

The Revised Laws of the Virgin Islands, 1965. Prepared under the authority of the Revised Edition of the Laws Ordinance, 1959, by P. Cecil Lewis. London: Waterlow and Sons, Ltd. In Six Volumes. Identified in the text by heading ("Cap.") number.

Ordinances and Statutory Rules and Orders and Imperial Legislation of the Virgin Islands. Annual Volumes from 1950 to 1994. Pasea Estate, Road Town: Caribbean Printing Company. Acts and ordinances are identified in the text by number and date. Statutory rules and orders are cited in text as SRO, followed by number and date.

References Cited

Abrahams, Roger
  1968   Public Drama and Common Values in Two Caribbean Islands. *Trans-Action*, July–August, 62–71.
Alexander, Jack
  1976   A Study of the Cultural Domain of "Relatives." *American Ethnologist* 3 (1): 17–38.
  1977   The Culture of Race in Middle-Class Kingston, Jamaica. *American Ethnologist* 4(3): 413–35.
  1984   Love, Race, Slavery, and Sexuality in Jamaican Images of the Family. In *Kinship Ideology and Practice in Latin America*, ed. R. T. Smith. Chapel Hill: University of North Carolina Press, 147–80.
Anderson, Patricia
  1986   Conclusions: Women in the Caribbean. *Social and Economic Studies* (Special Issue: Women in the Caribbean) 35:291–324.
Appadurai, Arjun
  1990   Disjuncture and Difference in the Global Cultural Economy. *Theory, Culture and Society* 7:295–310.
Austin, Diane J.
  1979   History and Symbols in Ideology: A Jamaican Example. *Man*, n.s., 14:497–514.
  1983   Culture and Ideology in the English-Speaking Caribbean: A View From Jamaica. *American Ethnologist* 19(2): 223–40.
  1984   *Urban Life in Kingston, Jamaica: The Culture and Class Ideology of Two Neighborhoods.* New York: Gordon and Breach Science Publishers.
Austin-Broos, Diane
  1988   Class and race in Jamaica. Paper presented at the Conference on the Meaning of Freedom, at the University of Pittsburgh, August.
  1994   Race/Class: Jamaica's Discourse of Heritable Identity. *New West Indian Guide* 68(3, 4): 213–33.
Baber, Willie
  1982   Social Change and the Peasant Community: Horowitz's Morne-Paysan Reinterpreted. *Ethnology* 21(3): 227–41.
Balibar, Etienne
  1991   Is There a 'Neo-racism'? In *Race, Nation, Class: Ambiguous Identities*, ed. E. Balibar and I. Wallerstein. London: Verso.
Barrow, Christine
  1988   Anthropology, the Family, and Women in the Caribbean. In *Gender in Caribbean Development*, ed. Patricia Mohammed and Catherine Shepherd. St. Augustine, Trinidad: Institute for Social and Economic Studies, University of the West Indies.
Basch, Linda, Nina Glick Schiller, and Cristina Szanton Blanc
  1994   *Nations Unbound: Transnational Projects, Postcolonial Predicaments, and Deterritorialized Nation-States.* Langhorne, Penn.: Gordon and Breach Science Publishers.

Baty, T.
 1918–19 The Interconnection of Nationality and Domicile. *Illinois Law
   Review (Northwestern Law Review)* 13:363–74.
Benítez-Rojo, Antonio
 1992 *The Repeating Island: The Caribbean and the Postmodern Perspective.*
   Durham, N.C.: Duke University Press.
Berleant-Schiller, Riva
 1987 Ecology and Politics in Barbudian Land Tenure. In *Land and Devel-
   opment in the Caribbean,* ed. Jean Besson and Janet Momsen. London:
   Macmillan Caribbean.
Berleant-Schiller, Riva, and Bill Maurer
 1993 Women's Place is Everyplace: Merging Domains and Women's Roles
   in Barbuda and Dominica. In *Women and Change in the Caribbean,* ed.
   J. Momsen. Bloomington: Indiana University Press.
Besson, Jean
 1979 Symbolic Aspects of Land in the Caribbean: The Tenure and Transmission of Land Rights among Caribbean Peasantries. In *Peasants,
   Plantations and Rural Communities in the Caribbean,* ed. Malcolm Cross
   and Arnaud Marks. Guildford, England: Department of Sociology,
   University of Surrey; Leiden: Department of Caribbean Studies,
   Royal Institute of Linguistics and Anthropology.
 1984 Family Land and Caribbean Society: Toward an Ethnography of
   Afro-Caribbean Peasantries. In *Perspectives on Caribbean Regional Identity,* ed. Elizabeth Thomas-Hope. Liverpool: Center for Latin American Studies, University of Liverpool.
 1987a A Paradox in Caribbean Attitudes to Land. In *Land and Development
   in the Caribbean,* ed. Jean Besson and Janet Momsen. London:
   Macmillan Caribbean.
 1987b Family Land as a Model for Martha Brae's New History: Culture
   Building in an Afro-Caribbean Village. In *Afro-Caribbean Villages in
   Historical Perspective,* ed. Charles V. Carnegie. Kingston: African-
   Caribbean Institute of Jamaica, ACIJ Research Review No. 2,
   100–132.
 1988 Agrarian Relations and Perceptions of Land in a Jamaican Peasant
   Village. In *Small Farming and Peasant Resources in the Caribbean,* ed.
   John S. Brierley and Hymie Rubenstein. Winnipeg: University of
   Manitoba Department of Geography.
Bhabha, Homi
 1984 Of Mimicry and Man: The Ambivalence of Colonial Discourse. *Octo-
   ber* 28:125–33.
Bolles, A. Lynn
 1985 Economic Crisis and Female Headed Households in Urban Jamaica.
   In *Women and Change in Latin America,* ed. June Nash and Helen I.
   Safa. New York: Bergin and Garvey.
Borah, Woodrow
 1983 *Justice by Insurance: The General Indian Court of Colonial Mexico and*

　　　the Legal Aides of the Half-Real. Berkeley: University of California
　　　Press.
Bourdieu, Pierre
　　1977　*Outline of a Theory of Practice.* Cambridge: Cambridge University
　　　Press.
Braithwaite, Lloyd
　　1975　*Social Stratification in Trinidad.* Mona, Jamaica: Institute of Social and
　　　Economic Research, University of the West Indies.
British Development Division
　　1974　*Regional Cadastral Survey and Registration Project in the Caribbean Report,*
　　　1974. London and St. John's, Antigua: British Development Division
　　　(Caribbean), Ministry of Overseas Development.
British Virgin Islands Boundaries Commission
　　1966　*Report of the British Virgin Islands Boundaries Commission, 1966.* Road
　　　Town: British Virgin Islands Boundaries Commission.
British Virgin Islands Constitutional Conference
　　1966　*Report of the British Virgin Islands Constitutional Conference, 1966.* Road
　　　Town and London: HMSO.
British Virgin Islands Department of Labour
　　1990　*Labour Department Statistics for the Year of 1990.* Road Town: Govern-
　　　ment of the British Virgin Islands, Department of Labour.
British Virgin Islands Development Planning Unit
　　1991　*Population Trends in the British Virgin Islands, 1970 to 1991.* Road
　　　Town: Government of the British Virgin Islands, Development Plan-
　　　ning Unit, Statistics Office.
　　1992　*Population by Country of Birth, 1991 Population Census.* Road Town:
　　　Government of the British Virgin Islands, Development Planning
　　　Unit, Statistics Office.
British Virgin Islands Legislative Council
　　1992　*BVI Recurrent Budget Estimates of Revenue and Expenditure, 1992.* Road
　　　Town: Legislative Council of the British Virgin Islands.
British Virgin Islands United Party
　　1967　*Constitution of the BVI United Party.* Baughers Bay and Road Town:
　　　British Virgin Islands United Party.
Bryan, Patrick
　　1985　The Question of Labor in the Sugar Industry of the Dominican
　　　Republic in the Late Nineteenth and Early Twentieth Centuries. In
　　　Between Slavery and Free Labor: The Spanish-Speaking Caribbean in the
　　　Nineteenth Century, ed. Manuel Moreno Fraginals, Frank Moya Pons,
　　　and Stanley L. Engerman. Baltimore: Johns Hopkins University
　　　Press.
Burton, Jonathan
　　1992　Pleasures of the Caribbean. *Far Eastern Economic Review* 155 (9):
　　　42–43.

Butler, Judith
1993   *Bodies That Matter: On The Discursive Limits of "Sex."* London: Routledge.
Cappelletti, Mauro
1986   Forward to *Integration Through Law: Europe and the American Federal Experience,* by Mauro Cappelletti, Monica Seccombe, and Joseph Weiler, eds. Vol.1, bk. 1. Berlin: Walter de Gruyter.
Carnegie, Charles V.
1987   Is Family Land an Institution? In *Afro-Caribbean Villages in Historical Perspective,* ed. Charles V. Carnegie. Kingston: African-Caribbean Institute of Jamaica, ACIJ Research Review No. 2, 83–99.
Chakrabarty, Dipesh
1992   Postcoloniality and the Artifice of History: Who Speaks for "Indian" Pasts? *Representations* 37:1–26.
Chatterjee, Partha
1988   *Nationalist Thought and the Colonial World: A Derivative Discourse?* London: Zed Books.
1993   *The Nation and Its Fragments: Colonial and Postcolonial Histories.* Princeton: Princeton University Press.
Chavez, Leo
1992   *Shadowed Lives: Undocumented Immigrants in American Society.* Fort Worth, Tex.: Harcourt Brace Jovanovich.
Cheshire, G. C.
1958   *Cheshire's Modern Law of Real Property,* 8th ed. London: Butterworths.
1982   *Cheshire and Burn's Modern Law of Real Property,* 13th ed. London: Butterworths.
Clifford, James
1988   *The Predicament of Culture: Twentieth-Century Ethnography, Literature, and Art.* Cambridge: Harvard University Press.
Cohen, Colleen, and Frances Mascia-Lees
1993   The British Virgin Islands as Nation and Desti-Nation: Representing and Siting Identity in a Post-Colonial Caribbean. *Social Analysis* 33:130–51.
Collier, Jane
1988   *Marriage and Inequality in Classless Societies.* Stanford: Stanford University Press.
1996   From Duty to Desire: Remaking families in a Spanish village. Dept. of Anthropology, Stanford University, Stanford, CA. Photocopy.
Collier, Jane, Bill Maurer, and Liliana Suárez-Navaz
1995   Sanctioned Identities: Legal Constructions of 'Modern' Personhood. *Identities: Global Studies in Culture and Power* 2(1, 2): 1–27.
Comaroff, John L.
1989   Images of Empire, Contests of Conscience: Models of Colonial Domination in South Africa. *American Ethnologist* 16 (4): 661–85.

Coombe, Rosemary J.
  1993   Cultural and Intellectual Properties: Occupying the Colonial
         Imagination. *PoLAR: Political and Legal Anthropology Review* 16(1):
         8–15.
Cooper, Frederick, and Ann Stoler
  1989   Tensions of Empire: Colonial Control and Visions of Rule. *American
         Ethnologist* 16(4): 609–21.
Crichlow, Michaeline
  1994   An Alternative Approach to Family Land Tenure in the Anglophone
         Caribbean: The Case of St. Lucia. *New West Indian Guide/Nieuwe West-
         Indische Gids* 68(1, 2): 77–99.
Danielsen, Dan, and Karen Engle, eds.
  1995   *After Identity: A Reader in Law and Culture.* New York: Routledge.
Davenport, William
  1959   Nonunilinear Descent and Descent Groups. *American Anthropologist*
         61:557–72.
Deere, Carmen Diana
  1979   Rural Women's Subsistence Production in the Capitalist Periphery.
         In *Peasants and Proletarians: The Struggles of Third World Workers,* ed.
         R. Cohen. New York: Monthly Review Press.
Delaney, Carol
  1986   The Meaning of Paternity and the Virgin Birth Debate. *Man,* n.s.,
         21:494– 513.
  1991   *The Seed and the Soil: Gender and Cosmology in Turkish Village Society.*
         Berkeley: University of California Press.
  1995   Father State, Mother Land and the Birth of Turkey. In *Naturalizing
         Power: Essays in Feminist Cultural Analysis,* ed. Sylvia Yanagisako and
         Carol Delaney. London: Routledge.
Dezalay, Yves
  1993   Multinationales de l'expertise et "dépérissement de l'état." *Actes de
         la Recherche en Sciences Sociales* 96/97:3–20, 91.
Dirks, Nicholas B., ed.
  1992   *Colonialism and Culture.* Ann Arbor: University of Michigan Press.
Dirks, Robert
  1975   Ethnic and Ethnic Group Relationships in the British Virgin Islands.
         In *The New Ethnicity: Perspectives from Ethnology,* ed. John Bennett. St.
         Paul: West Publishing Co.
Disraeli, Benjamin
  [1845] *Sybil or the Two Nations.* London: Oxford University Press.
  1964
Dookhan, Isaac
  1975   *A History of the British Virgin Islands, 1672–1970.* Epping, England:
         Caribbean Universities Press/Bowker.
Douglass, Lisa
  1992   *The Power of Sentiment: Love, Hierarchy, and the Jamaican Family Elite.*
         Boulder, Colo.: Westview Press.

Drummond, Lee
  1980   The Cultural Continuum: A Theory of Intersystems. *Man,* n.s., 15:352–74.
Dummet, Ann, and Andrew Nichol
  1990   *Subjects, Citizens, Aliens and Others: Nationality and Immigration Law.* London: Weidenfeld and Nicholson.
Edney, Matthew
  1993   The Patronage of Science and the Creation of Imperial Space: The British Mapping of India, 1799–1843. *Cartographica* 30 (1): 61–67.
Ehrlich, Allen S.
  1976   Race and Ethnic Identity in Rural Jamaica: The East Indian Case. *Caribbean Quarterly* 22(1): 19–27.
Ejercito Zapatista de Liberación Nacional (EZLN)
  1994   *Premier Declaración de la Selva Lacandona.* Courtesy of George A. Collier.
Ember, Melvin
  1959   The Nonunilinear Descent Groups of Samoa. *American Anthropologist* 61:573–77.
Euromoney
  1989   British Virgin Islands: A New Force Emerges (sponsorship statement). *Euromoney* special supplement, May 1989, pp. 47–53.
Evans-Pritchard, E. E.
  1940   *The Nuer: A Description of the Modes of Livelihood and Political Institutions of a Nilotic People.* Oxford: Oxford University Press.
Ferguson, James
  1992   *The Dominican Republic: Beyond the Lighthouse.* London: Latin America Bureau.
Firth, Raymond
  1963   Bilateral Descent Groups: An Operational Viewpoint. In *Studies in Kinship and Marriage,* ed. I. Shapera. London: Royal Anthropological Institute.
Fisher, Lawrence E.
  1976   Dropping Remarks and the Barbadian Audience. *American Ethnologist* 3(2): 227–42.
Fitzpatrick, Peter
  1980   *Law and State in Papua New Guinea.* London: Academic Press, Inc.
  1987   Racism and the Innocence of Law. In *Critical Legal Studies,* ed. Peter Fitzpatrick and Alan Hunt. Oxford: Basil Blackwell.
  1992   *The Mythology of Modern Law.* London: Routledge.
  1993   The Impossibility of Popular Justice. In *The Possibility of Popular Justice,* ed. Sally Merry and Neal Milner. Ann Arbor: University of Michigan Press.
Fortes, Meyer
  1953   The Structure of Unilineal Descent Groups. *American Anthropologist* 55:17–41.

Foucault, Michel
   1975   *The Birth of the Clinic.* New York: Vintage Books.
   1977   *Discipline and Punish: The Birth of the Prison.* New York: Pantheon.
   1979   What is an Author? In *Textual Strategies: Perspectives in Post-Structuralist Criticism,* ed. J. V. Harari. Ithaca: Cornell University Press.
   1980   *The History of Sexuality.* Vol. 1, *Introduction.* New York: Vintage.
Friedland, Jonathan
   1992   How to be Inscrutable: Offshore Financial Institutions Scramble to Manage Asia's Private Wealth. *Far Eastern Economic Review* 155 (9): 29–30.
Gagnier, Regenia
   1991   *Subjectivities: A History of Self-Representation in Britain, 1832–1920.* Oxford: Oxford University Press.
Gallagher, Rodney
   1990   *Report of Mr. Rodney Gallagher of Coopers and Lybrand on the Survey of Offshore Finance Sectors in the Caribbean Dependent Territories.* London: HMSO.
Gilroy, Paul
   1987   *'There Ain't No Black in the Union Jack.'* Chicago: University of Chicago Press.
   1990   One Nation Under a Groove: The Cultural Politics of "Race" and Racism in Britain. In *Anatomy of Racism,* ed. David Theo Goldberg. Minneapolis: University of Minnesota Press.
   1993   *The Black Atlantic: Modernity and Double Consciousness.* Cambridge: Harvard University Press.
Ginsberg, Anthony
   1991   *Tax Havens.* New York: New York Institute of Finance.
Goheen, Mitzi, and Parker Shipton, eds.
   1992   Rights Over Land: Categories and Controversies. *Africa* (Special Issue, 62 [3]).
Goodenough, Ward
   1955   A Problem in Malayo-Polynesian Social Organization. *American Anthropologist* 57(1): 71–83.
Greenfield, Sidney M.
   1960   Land Tenure and Transmission in Rural Barbados. *Anthropological Quarterly* 33(4): 165–76.
   1966   *English Rustics in Black Skin: A Study of Modern Family Forms in a Pre-Industrialized Society.* New Haven: College and University Press.
Greenhouse, Carol
   1986   *Praying For Justice: Faith, Order, and Community in an American Town.* Ithaca. N.Y.: Cornell University Press.
Greenhouse, Carol, Barbara Yngvesson, and David Engel
   1994   *Law and Community in Three American Towns.* Ithaca, N.Y.: Cornell University Press.
Grewal, Inderpal, and Caren Caplan, eds.

1994   *Scattered Hegemonies: Postmodernity and Transnational Feminist Practices.* Minneapolis: University of Minnesota Press.

Guha, Ranajit
1983   *Elementary Aspects of Peasant Insurgency in Colonial India.* Delhi: Oxford University Press.

Gupta, Akhil, and James Ferguson
1992   Beyond 'Culture': Space, Identity, and the Politics of Difference. *Cultural Anthropology* 7 (1): 6–23.

Hall, Stuart
1980   Race, Articulation and Societies Structured in Dominance. In *Sociological Theories: Racism and Colonialism.* Paris: UNESCO.
1995   Fantasy, Identity, Politics. In *Cultural Remix: Theories and Politics of the Popular,* ed. Erica Carter, James Donald, and Judith Squires. London: Lawrence and Wishart.

Handler, Richard
1991   Who Owns the Past? History, Cultural Property, and the Logic of Possessive Individualism. In *The Politics of Culture,* ed. Brett Williams. Washington, D.C.: Smithsonian Institution Press.

Hannerz, Ulf
1990   Cosmopolitans and Locals in World Culture. *Theory, Culture and Society* 7:237–51.
1992   *Cultural Complexity: Studies in the Social Organization of Meaning.* New York: Columbia University Press.

Haraway, Donna
1989   *Primate Visions: Gender, Race and Nature in the World of Modern Science.* New York: Routledge.

Harley, J.
1988   Maps, Knowledge, and Power. In *The Iconography of Landscape,* ed. D. Cosgrove and S. Daniels. Cambridge: Cambridge University Press.

Harrigan, Norwell
1990   Power by Accident: The Making of the Chief Minister. *The Island Sun,* 24 March, p. 15; 31 March, pp. 6, 15; 7 April, p. 15; 14 April, p. 3; 21 April, p. 23.

Harrigan, Norwell, and Pearl Varlack
1975   *The Virgin Islands Story.* Epping, England: Caribbean Universities Press in association with Bowker Publishing Co.

Harvey, David
1989   *The Condition of Postmodernity.* Baltimore: Johns Hopkins University Press.
1993   From Space to Place and Back Again: Reflections on the Condition of Postmodernity. In *Mapping the Futures: Local Cultures, Global Change,* ed. Jon Bird, Barry Curtis, Tim Putnam, George Robertson, and Lisa Tickner. London: Routledge.

Hebdige, Dick
1987   *Cut 'n' Mix: Culture, Identity and Caribbean Music.* London: Routledge.

Hernández-Castillo, R. Aída
  1994   *La Fuerza Extranjera: Mujer.* Courtesy of George A. Collier.
Herskovits, M.
  1937   *Life in a Haitian Valley.* New York: Knopf.
Herskovits, M., and F. Herskovits
  1947   *Trinidad Village.* New York: Knopf.
Hobbes, Thomas
  [1651]   *Leviathan.* Cambridge: Cambridge University Press.
  1994
Horkheimer, Max, and Theodor Adorno
  1944   *Dialectic of Enlightenment.* New York: Continuum, 1991.
Horowitz, Michael
  1967   *Morne Paysan.* New York: Holt, Rinehart and Winston.
International Union for Child Welfare
  1947   *Stateless Children: A Comparative Study of National Legislations and Sug-
          gested Solutions to the Problem of Stateless Children.* Geneva: IUCW.
The Island Sun
  1994a   Chief Minister Criticises UK Decision. 23 July 1994, pp. 1, 4, 25.
  1994b   Findings of the Telephone Poll. 23 July 1994, pp. 2, 3.
Jayawardena, Chandra
  1968   Ideology and Conflict in Lower-Class Communities. *Comparative
          Studies in Society and History* 10:413–46.
Jenkins, Charles F.
  1923   *Tortola: A Quaker Experiment of Long Ago in the Tropics.* London:
          Friends Bookshop.
Jha, J. C.
  1976   The Hindu Festival of Divali in the Caribbean. *Caribbean Quarterly* 22
          (1): 53–61.
Kearney, Michael
  1995   The Local and the Global: Anthropology of Globalization and
          Transnationalism. *Annual Review of Anthropology* 24:547–65.
Keith, Michael, and Steve Pile
  1993   Introduction to *Place and the Politics of Identity,* by Michael Keith and
          Steve Pile, eds. London: Routledge.
Keller, Evelyn Fox
  1993   *Secrets of Life, Secrets of Death.* New York: Routledge.
Kincaid, Jamaica
  1988   *A Small Place.* New York: Plume.
Kinsman, Robert
  1978   *The Robert Kinsman Guide to Tax Havens.* Homewood, Ill.: Dow Jones-
          Irwin.
Koessler, Maximillian
  1946   "Subject," "Citizen," "National," and "Permanent Allegiance." *Yale
          Law Journal* 56:58–76.

Laclau, Ernesto, and Chantal Mouffe
  1985 *Hegemony and Socialist Strategy: Towards a Radical Democratic Politics.*
         London: Verso.
Latour, Bruno
  1993 *We Have Never Been Modern,* trans. Catherine Porter. Cambridge: Har-
         vard University Press.
Lawrence, Peter
  1955 *Land Tenure among the Garia: The Traditional System of a New Guinea
         People.* Canberra: Australian National University.'
Lazarus-Black, Mindie
  1991 Why Women Take Men to Magistrate's Court: Caribbean Kinship
         Ideology and Law. *Ethnology* 30 (2): 119–33.
  1994 *Legitimate Acts and Illegal Encounters: Law and Society in Antigua and
         Barbuda.* Washington, D.C.: Smithsonian Institution Press.
Lazarus-Black, Mindie, and Susan Hirsch, eds.
  1994 *Contested States: Law, Hegemony and Resistance.* New York: Routledge.
Leach, Edmund
  1956 Review of *Land Tenure among the Garia,* by Peter Lawrence. *American
         Anthropologist* 56:32.
Levi-Strauss, Claude
  1961 *Tristes Tropiques,* trans. John Russell. New York: Criterion Books.
Lewis, Arthur
  1977 *Labour in the West Indies: The Birth of a Workers Movement.* London and
         Port of Spain: New Beacon Books. First published by the Fabian
         Society in 1938.
Lewis, Gordon K.
  1972 *The Virgin Islands: A Caribbean Lilliput.* Evanston, Ill.: Northwestern
         University Press.
Lohr, Steve
  1992 Where the Money Washes Up. *New York Times Magazine,* 29 March,
         pp. 27–32, 46, 52.
Macpherson, C. B.
  1962 *The Political Theory of Possessive Individualism: Hobbes To Locke.* Oxford:
         Oxford University Press.
Mahabir, Cynthia
  1985 *Crime and Nation Building in the Caribbean: The Legacy of Legal Barriers.*
         Cambridge, Mass.: Schenckman.
Malinowski, Bronislaw
  [1922] *Argonauts of the Western Pacific.* New York: E. P. Dutton.
  1961
Malkki, Liisa
  1992 National Geographic: The Rooting of Peoples and the Territorial-
         ization of National Identity among Scholars and Refugees. *Cultural
         Anthropology* 7 (1): 24—44.

Marable, Manning
  1987   *African and Caribbean Politics: From Kwame Nkrumah to Maurice Bishop.*
          London: Verso.
Markby, Sir William
  1889   *Elements of Law Considered with Reference to Principles of General Jurispru-
          dence,* 4th ed. Oxford: Clarendon Press.
Martinez-Alier, Verena
  1974   *Marriage, Class and Colour in Nineteenth Century Cuba: A Study of Racial
          Attitudes and Sexual Values in a Slave Society.* Cambridge: Cambridge
          University Press.
Maudsley, Ronald H.
  1979   *The Modern Law of Perpetuities.* London: Butterworths.
Maurer, Bill
  1995a   Orderly Families for the New Economic Order: Belonging and Citi-
          zenship in the British Virgin Islands. *Identities: Global Studies in Cul-
          ture and Power* 2(1, 2): 149–71.
  1995b   Writing Law, Making a "Nation": History, Modernity and Paradoxes
          of Self-Rule in the British Virgin Islands. *Law and Society Review* 29
          (2): 255–86.
  1996   The Land, the Law and Legitimate Children: Thinking Through
          Gender, Kinship and Nation in the British Virgin Islands. In *Gender,
          Kinship, Power: A Comparative and Interdisciplinary History,* ed. M. J.
          Maynes, Ann Waltner, Ulrikke Strasser, and Birgitte Soland. New
          York: Routledge.
McGlynn, Frank
  1980   Marginality and Flux: An Afro-Caribbean Community Through Two
          Centuries. Ph.D. diss., University of Pittsburgh.
Merry, Sally
  1991   Law and Colonialism. *Law and Society Review* 25(4): 889–922.
  1992   Anthropology, Law and Transnational Processes. *Annual Review of
          Anthropology* 21:357–79.
Merry, Sally, and Neal Milner, eds.
  1993   *The Possibility of Popular Justice.* Ann Arbor: University of Michigan
          Press.
Messick, Brinkley
  1993   *The Calligraphic State: Textual Domination and History in a Muslim Soci-
          ety.* Berkeley: University of California Press.
Meyers, Jeffrey A.
  1993a   IBC Numbers Growing Fast. *BVI Beacon,* 8 April, p. 8.
  1993b   Financial Services Driving Economy. *BVI Beacon,* 8 April, pp.1, 8.
  1993c   Stoutt: BVI Still Rejects Board. *BVI Beacon,* 21 January, pp.1, 3, 12.
Miller, Daniel
  1994   *Modernity, An Ethnographic Approach: Dualism and Mass Consumption in
          Trinidad.* Oxford: Berg.
Mintz, Sidney
  1966   The Caribbean as a Socio-Cultural Area. *Cahiers d'Histoire Mondiale*
          9:916–41.

1974   *Caribbean Transformations*. New York: Columbia University Press.

1985   *Sweetness and Power: The Place of Sugar in Modern History*. New York: Penguin.

Mitchell, Timothy

1988   *Colonising Egypt*. Berkeley: University of California Press.

1992   Orientalism and the Exhibitionary Order. In *Colonialism and Culture*, ed. Nicholas B. Dirks. Ann Arbor: University of Michigan Press.

Mittelholzer, Edgar

1950   *A Morning at the Office*. London: Hogarth Press.

Mohammed, Patricia, and Catherine Shepherd, eds.

1988   *Gender in Caribbean Development*. St. Augustine, Trinidad: Institute of Social and Economic Research, University of the West Indies.

Mohanty, Chandra

1991   Introduction to *Third World Women and the Politics of Feminism*, by Chandra Mohanty, Ann Russo, and Lourdes Torres, eds. Bloomington: Indiana University Press.

Momsen, Janet, ed.

1991   *Women and Change in the Caribbean*. Bloomington: Indiana University Press.

Mosse, George

1985   *Nationalism and Sexuality: Respectability and Abnormal Sexuality in Modern Europe*. New York: Howard Fertig.

Murdock, George Peter

1949   *Social Structure*. New York: Macmillan.

Nelson, Diane

1995   *A Finger in the Wound: Ethnicity, Nation and Gender in the Body Politics of Quincentennial Guatemala*. Ph.D. diss., Stanford University.

Olwig, Karen Fog

1993   *Global Culture, Island Identity: Continuity and Change in the Afro-Caribbean Community of Nevis*. Chur, Switzerland: Harwood Academic Publishers.

O'Neal, Michael

1983   British Virgin Islands Transformations: Anthropological Perspectives. Ph.D. diss., Union Graduate School.

O'Neal, Michael, and Bill Maurer

1992   The Socioeconomic Context. In *Challenge and Change: The Awakening of a People, British Virgin Islands*. Office of the Chief Minister, ed. Road Town: Government of the British Virgin Islands.

Otterbein, Keith F.

1964   A Comparison of the Land Tenure Systems of the Bahamas, Jamaica and Barbados. *International Archives of Ethnography* 50(1): 31–42.

Pashukanis, Evgeny

1929   *Law and Marxism: A General Theory*. Worcester: Pluto Press, 1989.

Pateman, Carole

1988   *The Sexual Contract*. Stanford: Stanford University Press.

Penn, Howard R.

1990   *Memoirs of H. R. Penn: A Personal Account of the History and Politics of the*

British Virgin Islands in the Twentieth Century. Road Town: Caribbean
Printing Co.

Penn, Juliette
1986   The System of Land Registration in the British Virgin Islands. Land
Registry, Road Town, Tortola. Photocopy.

Pollack, Sir Frederick, and Frederic William Maitland
1898   *The History of English Law Before the Time of Edward I.* Cambridge: Cambridge University Press.

Proudfoot, Mary
1965   *British Virgin Islands Report of the Constitutional Commissioner—1965.*
London: HMSO.

Radcliffe-Brown, A. R.
1950   Introduction to *African Systems of Kinship and Marriage,* by A. R. Radcliffe-Brown and Daryll Forde, eds. London: Oxford University
Press.

Randall, H. J.
1924   Nationality and Naturalization: A Study in the Relativity of Law. *Law
Quarterly Review* 40:18–30.

Reisman, Karl
1974   Contrapuntal Conversations in an Antiguan Village. In *Explorations
in the Ethnography of Speaking,* ed. Richard Baumann and Joel
Sherzer. London: Cambridge University Press.

Rhymer, Elihu
1986   Talking about the BVI. *BVI Beacon,* 27 March, pp. 5, 13.
1992   Political Development of the British Virgin Islands over the Past 25
Years. In *Challenge and Change: The Awakening of a People, British Virgin
Islands.* Office of the Chief Minister, ed. Road Town: Government of
the British Virgin Islands.

Roberts, Susan
1994   Small Place, Big Money: The Cayman Islands and the International
Financial System. *Economic Geography* 71(3): 237–56.

Robotham, Don
1980   Pluralism as an Ideology. *Social and Economic Studies* 29(1): 69–89.

Romney, Cyril B.
1992   Evolution of the Ministerial System: The Quest for Greater Autonomy. In *Challenge and Change: The Awakening of a People, British Virgin
Islands.* Office of the Chief Minister, ed. Road Town: Government of
the British Virgin Islands.

Rousseau, Jean-Jacques
1967   *The Social Contract and the Discourse on the Origin of Inequality,* ed.
Lester Crocker. New York: Washington Square Press.

Safa, Helen I.
1995   *The Myth of the Male Breadwinner: Women and Industrialization in the
Caribbean.* Boulder, Colo.: Westview Press.

Salmond, John W.
1901   Citizenship and Allegiance, I. *Law Quarterly Review* 17:270–82.

1902   Citizenship and Allegiance, II. *Law Quarterly Review* 18:49–63.

Sandifer, Durward
1935   A Comparative Study of Laws Relating to Nationality at Birth and to Loss of Nationality. *American Journal of International Law* 29:248–79.

Santos, Boaventura de Sousa
1987   Law: A Map of Misreading. Toward a Postmodern Conception of Law. *Journal of Law and Society* 14 (3): 279–302.

Schneider, David
1984   *A Critique of the Study of Kinship.* Ann Arbor: University of Michigan Press.

Segal, Daniel
1993   "Race" and "Colour" in Pre-Independence Trinidad and Tobago. In *Trinidad Ethnicity,* ed. Kevin Yelvington. Knoxville: University of Tennessee Press.

Shapin, Steven, and Steven Schaffer
1984   *Leviathan and the Air Pump.* Cambridge: Harvard University Press.

Shipton, Parker
1992   Debts and Trespasses: Land, Mortgages and the Ancestors in Western Kenya. *Africa* 62 (3): 357–88.

Simpson, A. W. B.
1961   *An Introduction to the History of Land Law.* London: Oxford University Press.

Skinner, Elliot P.
[1955] Social Stratification and Ethnic Identification. In *Peoples and Cul-*
1971   *tures of the Caribbean,* ed. Michael Horowitz. Garden City, N.J.: Natural History Press.

Smith, Carol
1995   Race-Class-Gender Ideology in Guatemala: Modern and Anti-Modern Forms. *Comparative Studies in Society and History* 37:723–49.

Smith, M. G.
1962   *Kinship and Community in Carriacou.* New Haven, Conn.: Yale University Press.
1965   *The Plural Society in the British West Indies.* Berkeley: University of California Press.

Smith, Raymond T.
1970   Social Stratification in the Caribbean. In *Essays in Comparative Social Stratification,* ed. Leonard Plotnicov and Arthur Tuden. Pittsburgh: University of Pittsburgh Press.
1988   *Kinship and Class in the West Indies: A Genealogical Study of Jamaica and Guyana.* Cambridge: Cambridge University Press.
1992   Race, Class, and Gender in the Transition to Freedom. In *The Meaning of Freedom: Economics, Politics, and Culture after Slavery,* ed. Frank McGlynn and Seymour Drescher. Pittsburgh: University of Pittsburgh Press.
1995   "Living in the Gun Mouth": Race, Class, and Political Violence in

Guyana. *New West Indian Guide/Nieuwe West-Indische Gids* 69(3, 4): 223–52.

1996   *The Matrifocal Family: Power, Pluralism, and Politics.* New York: Routledge.

Soja, Edward

1989   *Postmodern Geographies.* London: Verso.

Solien, Nancie

1959   The Nonunilineal Descent Group in the Caribbean and Central America. *American Anthropologist* 61:578–83.

Spivak, Gayatri C.

1988   Can the Subaltern Speak? In *Marxism and the Interpretation of Culture,* ed. Cary Nelson and Lawrence Grossberg. Urbana: University of Illinois Press.

Stolcke, Verena

1989   Introduction to *Marriage, Class and Colour in Nineteenth Century Cuba,* 2d ed. Ann Arbor: University of Michigan Press.

1993   Is Sex to Gender as Race is to Ethnicity? In *Gendered Anthropology,* ed. Teresa del Valle. London: Routledge.

1995   Talking Culture: New Boundaries, New Rhetorics of Exclusion in Europe. *Current Anthropology* 36(1): 1–24.

Strathern, Marilyn

1985   Discovering 'Social Control.' *Journal of Law and Society* 12 (2): 111–34.

1992a   *After Nature: English Kinship in the Late Twentieth Century.* Cambridge: Cambridge University Press.

1992b   *Reproducing the Future: Anthropology, Kinship and the New Reproductive Technologies.* London: Routledge.

Streicker, Joel

1995   Policing Boundaries: Race, Class, and Gender in Cartagena, Colombia. *American Ethnologist* 22:54–74.

Thomas, Nicholas

1994   *Colonialism's Culture: Anthropology, Travel and Government.* Princeton: Princeton University Press.

1996   Cold Fusion. *American Anthropologist* 98:9–16.

Tocqueville, Alexis de

[1835–40] *Democracy in America.* Edited and abridged by Richard D.
1984   Heffner. New York: Mentor Books.

Trouillot, Michel-Rolph

1988   *Peasants and Capital: Dominica in the World Economy.* Baltimore: Johns Hopkins University Press.

Trubek, David, Yves Dezalay, Ruth Buchanan, and John R. Davis

1993   Global Restructuring and the Law: The Internationalization of Legal Fields and the Creation of Transnational Arenas. Working paper no. 1, Global Studies Research Program Working Paper Series on the Political Economy of Legal Change, University of Wisconsin, Madison.

Varlack, Pearl
  1992   Address delivered November 27, at the Recognition Ceremony in Celebration of Twenty-Five Years of Ministerial Government in the (British) Virgin Islands.
Vertovec, Steven
  1992   *Hindu Trinidad: Religion, Ethnicity and Socio-economic Change.* London: Macmillan Caribbean.
Virgin Islands Party (BVI)
  1980   *Programme for the 1980s.* Road Town: Virgin Islands Party.
  1990   *Programme for the 1990s.* Road Town: Virgin Islands Party.
Vogt, Evon
  1990   *The Zinacantecos of Mexico.* Fort Worth, Tex.: Harcourt, Brace, Jovanovich.
Wade, Peter
  1993   "Race," Nature and Culture. *Man,* n.s., 28 (1): 17–34.
White, R. M., and F. J. Hampson
  1981   British Nationality Law—Proposed Changes. *International and Comparative Law Quarterly* 30:247–59.
  1982   "What is my nation? Who talks of my nation?" British Nationality Act 1981. *International and Comparative Law Quarterly* 31: 849–55.
White, R. M., A. C. Evans, and F. J. Hampson
  1981   Unsanguine Observations on the British Nationality Bill. *New Law Journal* 131:328–29, 26 March.
Wiener, Norbert
  1950   *The Human Use of Human Beings: Cybernetics and Society.* Boston: Houghton Mifflin Co.
Williams, Brackette F.
  1991   *Stains on My Name, War in My Veins: Guyana and the Politics of Cultural Struggle.* Durham, N.C.: Duke University Press.
  1993   The Impact of the Precepts of Nationalism on the Concept of Culture: Making Grasshoppers of Naked Apes. *Cultural Critique* 24:143–91.
Wilson, Peter J.
  1969   Reputation and Respectability: A Suggestion for Caribbean Ethnology. *Man,* n.s. 4(1): 70–84.
  1973   *Crab Antics: The Social Anthropology of English-Speaking Negro Societies of the Caribbean.* New Haven, Conn.: Yale University Press.
Wintz, Cary D.
  1988   *Black Culture and the Harlem Renaissance.* Houston: Rice University Press.
Wittig, Monique
  1992   *The Straight Mind and Other Essays.* Boston: Beacon Press.
Yanagisako, Sylvia, and Jane F. Collier
  1987   Toward a Unified Analysis of Gender and Kinship. In *Gender and Kinship: Essays Toward a Unified Analysis,* ed. Jane F. Collier and Sylvia Yanagisako. Stanford, Calif.: Stanford University Press.

Yelvington, Kevin
  1995   *Producing Power: Ethnicity, Gender, and Class in a Caribbean Workplace.*
          Philadelphia: Temple University Press.
Yngvesson, Barbara
  1988   Making Law at the Doorway: The Clerk, The Court, and the Con-
          struction of Community in a New England Town. *Law and Society
          Review* 22(3): 409–48.
  1993   *Virtuous Citizens, Disruptive Subjects: Order and Complaint in a New Eng-
          land Court.* New York: Routledge.
Young, Robert
  1995   *Colonial Desire: Hybridity in Theory, Culture and Race.* London: Rout-
          ledge.

Index